THE HISTORY AND PRESENT STATE OF VIRGINIA

By Robert Beverley

EDITED WITH AN INTRODUCTION BY
LOUIS B. WRIGHT

Published for
THE INSTITUTE OF
EARLY AMERICAN HISTORY AND CULTURE
at Williamsburg, Virginia
By The University of North Carolina Press
CHAPEL HILL, 1947

Copyright, 1947, by
THE UNIVERSITY OF NORTH CAROLINA PRESS

MANUFACTURED IN THE UNITED STATES OF AMERICA

CONTENTS

INTRODUCTION xi

    BOOK I. The History of the First Settlement of VIRGINIA, and the Government thereof, to the present Time 15

    BOOK II. The Natural Productions and Conveniencies of the Country, suited to Trade and Improvement 117

    BOOK III. The Native INDIANS, their Religion, Laws, and Customs, in War and Peace 159

    BOOK IV. The present State of the Country, as to the Polity of the Government, and the Improvements of the Land 237

THE TABLE 321

NOTES 349

PRINCIPAL CHANGES IN THE EDITION OF 1722 .. 356

INDEX 361

LIST OF ILLUSTRATIONS

Original Engraved Title Page 2
PLATE 1. Indians in Canoe 150
PLATE 2. Indians in Summer Dress 160
PLATE 3. Indians in Winter Dress 163
PLATE 4. Priest and Conjuror in Costume 165
PLATE 5. Young Indian Women 167
PLATE 6. Woman and Boy 169
PLATE 7. Indian Mothers and Children 172
PLATE 8. Village Showing Palisades 175
PLATE 9. Methods of Broiling Fish 179
PLATE 10. Man and Wife at Dinner 183
PLATE 11. Idol in Its Tabernacle 199
PLATE 12. Burial Place of Indian Kings 215
PLATE 13. Solemn Festival Dance 223
PLATE 14. Trees Being Felled by Fire and Made Into Canoes 231
PLATE 15. Census List for 1703 253

INTRODUCTION
By LOUIS B. WRIGHT

INTRODUCTION[1]*

NEARLY a century after the earliest settlers went ashore at Jamestown and established themselves as an outpost of English civilization, the first history of the colony by a native Virginian appeared in the bookstalls of London. The book, bearing the date of 1705, was entitled *The History and Present State of Virginia, in Four Parts*. It was printed for Richard Parker, a bookseller who had his shop at the sign of the unicorn under the piazza of the Royal Exchange. The Virginia author, who described himself on the printed title page simply as "a native and inhabitant of the place," was Robert Beverley, brother-in-law of William Byrd of Westover. An engraved title page, which served as a frontispiece, gives a definite suggestion of authorship by announcing that the work was "By R. B. gent."

During the first two decades of colonization in Virginia a number of observers set down their impressions of the venture and published narratives which passed for history. Captain John Smith had dignified his own extensive compilation and personal narrative as *The General History of Virginia, New England, and the Summer Isles* (1624). But after the colony was firmly established, few settlers considered an account of their activi-

---

*Superior Figures refer to notes in the back of the book. Notes on the Introduction begin on page 349.

xi

ties worth the writing. No compulsion existed, as in New England, to justify the ways of God to men. No Anglican parson urged Virginians "to be the Lord's remembrancers or recorders" and to preserve a chronicle of God's infinite mercies and singular favors "that the memory of them may not die and be extinct with the present generation."[2] Those were the injunctions of the Reverend Urian Oakes in 1673 to his brethren of Massachusetts Bay. Tobacco planters on the Chesapeake were less inclined to see the hand of the Almighty in their daily affairs, and they showed little desire to record for posterity either the hardships or the blessings of life in the colony. Virginia therefore can boast no chronicler of the seventeenth century with the earnest zeal of William Bradford or Edward Johnson.

An interest in history, however, was not lacking in Virginians of this period. Indeed, the records of plantation libraries show a predilection for historical reading matter ranging from Herodotus and Thucydides to recent narratives of the Puritan Revolution. From both classical and English history men like William Fitzhugh, Richard Lee, and others of their generation drew precedents of law and government. The ruling class found in the reservoirs of historical wisdom much of the instruction in statecraft which a new country needed. William Fitzhugh himself, in a letter of 1693, noted that he had actually written "a small piece . . . giving a summary account of Virginia and a succinct digest of our laws," but the work never saw print, and if it had, from Fitzhugh's own description, it would have been essentially a promotional tract designed to induce immigrants to settle in Stafford County.[3] In 1697, Henry

Hartwell, James Blair, and Edward Chilton prepared at the request of the Board of Trade a report entitled "The Present State of Virginia, and the College," which gathered dust in the Board's archives until someone in 1727 thought of printing it.

Beverley's *History* of 1705 is the earliest work which attempts a comprehensive description of the colony's past history, its natural environment, the aboriginal inhabitants, and contemporary political and social conditions. More than that, it is a readable book, simple and vigorous in style, with flashes of ironic and satirical humor; not many Americans before 1705 had written with such ease and urbanity. Curiously, few authors have been so completely forgotten by students of American literature. Although Beverley is no unappreciated Gibbon or Macaulay, his *History*, measured by the standards of colonial America, deserves high rank for its simplicity, clarity, and intrinsic interest.

One reason for its neglect by the average literary student and, of course, by the general reader is the rarity of the work. Beverley prepared a revised version of the 1705 edition and brought it out in 1722. This revision was reprinted by Charles Campbell in Richmond, Virginia, in 1855, but both eighteenth century editions and the nineteenth century reprint can be found only in exceptional libraries.[4] The Virginia ruling class in Beverley's own day must have read the *History* with considerable interest, but some of them found it a book which they would willingly let die, for the author was sharply critical of his contemporaries.

Robert Beverley was a stout individualist whose views frequently differed from those held by the ruling faction in the colony. His failure to conform to the normal pattern of the governing class was a legitimate inheritance from an obstreperous father, Major Robert Beverley, who had been one of Governor Berkeley's most loyal supporters at the time of Bacon's Rebellion. Later, however, during the administration of Berkeley's successors, he had been the leader of a people's faction against royal governors and the powerful Council. The future author of the *History* heard from his father much violent talk about the tyranny and misrule of the King's representatives.[5]

Young Robert, born about 1673, had his schooling in England, perhaps at Beverley Grammar School in Yorkshire. On his return to Virginia, he became a volunteer scrivener in the office of the colony's secretary of state, a post which proved a useful apprenticeship in Virginia law and politics. In the last decade of the seventeenth century he held various clerkships in the colonial government, and in the very last year of the century he was elected to represent Jamestown in the House of Burgesses.

Beverley inherited a plantation in Gloucester County and another tract of six thousand acres in the frontier region of King and Queen County. Eventually this latter estate, called Beverley Park, became his permanent home. In 1697 he married Ursula Byrd, the first William Byrd's sixteen-year-old daughter, who had just returned from finishing her education in England. In less than a year the young wife died at the birth of her son William, who lived to become a wealthy landowner, proprietor of the plantation known as "Blandfield." Robert Beverley never remarried.

Like most Virginians of his day, Beverley was land-greedy and litigious. In the furtherance of a law suit over property which he acquired in Elizabeth City, he went to England in June, 1703, to press an appeal to the Privy Council. During his stay in England, he indiscreetly sent back letters attacking Governor Francis Nicholson and Robert Quarry, the surveyor general of customs, for what he believed to be their machinations against the liberties of Virginians. In reports sent to England, these two officials, Beverley charged, had slandered and maligned a dozen or more of the leading planters and had described the House of Burgesses as "a pack of rude, unthinking, willful, obstinate people, without any regard to her Majesty or her interest, and it's laid as a crime to them that they think themselves entitled to the liberties of Englishmen."[6] Beverley also charged that even more dangerous was a scheme of these officials to create a standing army in the American colonies to overawe too much independence of spirit. These accusations naturally aroused the ire of Governor Nicholson, who dismissed Beverley from the office of clerk for King and Queen County; but the House of Burgesses, sympathetic to the charges against Quarry, sent an address to the crown complaining against him. The home government quickly vindicated Quarry and rebuked the House. Beverley returned to Virginia to find himself politically ruined and contented himself thereafter, except for brief intervals, with sardonic aloofness from political activity.

Although personal prejudice and self-interest undoubtedly played some part in the vivid and sarcastic attacks against Nicholson and Quarry, there was also in them a significant note of defiance aimed at rulers who flout inherited liberties and the right of citizens to govern themselves by legislative assemblies. In these letters, as later in the *History*, Beverley demonstrated a spirit of forthright independence and a pride in being a Virginian. While William Byrd eagerly curried favor with titled Englishmen, his brother-in-law took pride in a simple life and boasted that he was above all else a native American.

Life at Beverley Park gave an opportunity for study in both books and nature. As the *History* indicates, Beverley was a careful and accurate observer, possessed of considerable scientific curiosity. He was also greatly concerned with the improvement of agriculture and dreamed of developing a wine industry from grapes which he believed Virginia could grow as successfully as France.

In his later years, Beverley devoted his efforts to a compilation of the laws of Virginia, which he published in London in the year of his death, 1722. The volume was entitled *An Abridgement of the Public Laws of Virginia* and was dedicated to Alexander Spotswood, one of the few royal governors who found favor in his sight.

Beverley may have been the author of another work concerned with the problem of colonial government and the relation of the English crown to possessions overseas. The same bookseller, Richard Parker, who brought out the *History* in 1705, was responsible in 1701 for the publication of *An Essay upon the Government of the English Plantations on the Continent of America . . . By an American*. This pamphlet, avowedly by a Virginian, shows similarities in style and ideas to Beverley's *History*. It is not impossible that the elder William Byrd had some part in it. Clearly the little book is the handiwork of someone in the Beverley-Byrd group.[7]

Beverley's sojourn in England in 1703, so disastrous to his political fortunes, was responsible for the *History* which has given him a permanent place in the annals of colonial literature. Like many a history before and since, Beverley's book had its inception in profound irritation over the errors and misinterpretations in another's work. He himself recounts the circumstances of its composition in the preface to the edition of 1722. The bookseller Parker brought him a manuscript relating to Virginia and requested him to correct it. The copy was intended for a section of John Oldmixon's *The British Empire in America*, finally published in 1708. When Beverley tried to revise it, he found that it was "too faulty and too imperfect to be mended," a patchwork "only of some accounts that had been printed 60 or 70 years ago in which also he had chosen the most strange and untrue parts and left out the more sincere and faithful." Instead of trying to rewrite Oldmixon's garbled manuscript, Beverley reported to Parker that he had some notes on Virginia and would put together a description of the colony. "And this I should the rather undertake in justice to so fine a country," he added, "because it has been so misrepresented to the common people of England as to make them believe that the servants in Virginia are made to draw in cart and plow, as horses and oxen do in England, and that the country turns all people black who go to live there, with other such prodigious phantasms."

If Beverley knew that Oldmixon's account, which he damned so completely, was based on a manuscript supplied by his brother-in-law William Byrd, he gave no indication. But perhaps he did know and took a sardonic pleasure in pointing out its superficiality, for he despised Byrd's social climbing and regarded him as a somewhat flashy fellow. Byrd was in London at this time, and Beverley may have learned of his relations with Oldmixon.

When Oldmixon's two-volume work appeared, the preface asserted that the portion on Virginia was "written with a great deal of spirit and judgment by a gentleman of the province, to whom this historian confesses he is very much indebted," though he had departed from the Virginian's manuscript in places. By the assistance of this gentleman, Oldmixon maintained, "the account of Virginia is one of the most perfect of these histories of our plantations." In the preface to the second edition of 1741, Oldmixon specifically states that his allusion to aid from a "gentleman of the province" "refers to the History of Virginia which was written by Col. Bird, whom the author knew when he was of the Temple; and the performance answered the just opinion he had of that gentleman's ability and exactness."

Since Beverley's *History* appeared in 1705, three years before Oldmixon's, the latter had an opportunity of pillaging material from his rival. Although Oldmixon in several places speaks disparagingly of Beverley's work, he nevertheless borrowed extensively and quoted him verbatim, particularly in the description of the Indians.[8]

When Beverley revised his own *History*, he spoke his mind about Oldmixon's ungenerous allusions and included in the preface to the 1722 edition four pages of errors discovered in Oldmixon's work. Since Beverley had not alluded openly to Oldmixon in 1705, that historian was aggrieved only because the Virginian had anticipated him in publication. "And this I take to be the only reason of that gentleman's so severely reflecting upon me in his book," Beverley asserts, "for I never saw him in my life that I know of. But concerning that work of his, I may with great truth say that (notwithstanding his boast of having the assistance of many original papers and memorials that I had not the opportunity of), he nowhere varies from the account that I gave, nor advances anything new of his own but he commits so many errors and imposes so many falsities upon the world."

Oldmixon, however, had the last word, and in his preface of 1741, after the passage giving credit to William Byrd for help, remarks: "What he [Oldmixon] said of other helps has relation to another *History of Virginia*, written by one R. B., which he made as much use of as he thought necessary for the improvement of his work; but happening to take no notice of some particulars which would not at all have improved it, the writer, for his neglecting them, has been very free with the character of this author's *History*, and not spared even some of the passages which he took from himself."

In addition to a laudable desire to correct errors in a superficial account of Virginia, Beverley may have had a utilitarian purpose in publishing an appealing description of the natural goodness of the country. Owners of large tracts of land in Virginia in this period were eager to attract French Huguenots and other foreign immigrants. As Fitzhugh designed a promotional work in the guise of history, so Beverley may have planned his book to advertise the desirability of homesteads across the Atlantic. At any rate the book served that purpose. In addition to the two eighteenth century editions in English, the *History* had four printings in French on the Continent. In 1707, the stationer Thomas Lombrail of Amsterdam brought out the first French version, a fairly literal translation of the original.[9] In the same year, Pierre Ribou, a bookseller of Paris, had printed at Orleans what appears from internal evidence to be a pirated edition of Lombrail's version. For example, Lombrail had carefully followed the original text in a passage describing a frog so large that it would furnish a meal for six Frenchmen: "Je suis persuadé que six François en auroient pu faire un bon repas." Ribou, evidently feeling that the passage reflected upon his countrymen, changed it to read "six personnes."[10] A little later two other Amsterdam booksellers reissued the Lombrail edition: Claude Jordan in 1712, and J. F. Bernard in 1718.

Whether Beverley had a hand in the Continental publications of his *History*, surviving evidence does not reveal, but he cannot have been displeased at its wide circulation. Four printings in French gave the book greater value as propaganda than Beverley probably had hoped to achieve. That such publicity was not despised by Virginia landowners is indicated by the efforts of William Byrd II; in 1736 he supplied notes to a Swiss promoter for a natural history of Virginia, in German, which was intended to lure Swiss colonists overseas.[11]

Beverley's *History* is significant in the development of American ideas because it is one of the earliest literary works that is self-consciously American. The New England historians, it is true, had written of their godly commonwealths as realms of a peculiar people, set apart and watched over by the Protestant Jehovah, but the distinction they made from other men was religious. Beverley, on the contrary, was thoroughly secular and thoroughly realistic. Though Virginia had been settled by Englishmen, their sons were Virginians before they were Englishmen, with the independence and freedom that a new country, detached from the Old World, made possible. A fierce loyalty to the new soil burned in Beverley's breast, and he did not hesitate to rebuke his fellow Virginians for depending too much, economically and socially, upon the mother country. Political independence he did not envision, but he lashed with a whip of ridicule and sarcasm English governors who encroached upon the liberties of his countrymen. Beverley never forgot his loyalty to the British throne, but he insisted that the English government remember its responsibility to the colony.

Deliberately, Beverley adopted a plain style as best suited to the expression of historical truth, which he determined to write without circumlocution or adornment. Though he was a man of broad reading and sometimes cites both classical and modern authors, his work never smells of the lamp. Pedantic affectations he could not tolerate. "I am an Indian," he informs the reader in the preface of 1705, "and don't pretend to be exact in my language. But I hope the plainness of my dress will give him the kinder impressions of my honesty, which is what I pretend to. Truth desires only to be understood and never affects the reputation of being finely equipped. It depends upon its own intrinsic value, and, like beauty, is rather concealed than set off by ornament." Unlike some writers, Beverley lived up to the standard which he advocated. Simplicity and plainness were almost an obsession with him—a taste which he exemplified, not merely in his literary style, but in his private life. Although other Virginians imported finery from England and hung their walls with fancy portraits, he furnished his own house with wooden stools and furniture made on the plantation.

Beverley divided his book into four sections described on the title page as "I. The History of the First Settlement of Virginia, and the Government thereof, to the present Time. II. The Natural Productions and Conveniencies of the Country, suited to Trade and Improvement. III. The Native Indians, their Religion, Laws, and Customs, in War and Peace. IV. The present State of the Country, as to the Polity of the Government, and the Improvements of the Land."

As history the book's chief value lies in the author's first-hand observations. His descriptions of the country and his comments on the state of society in his day are invaluable to the social historian. The section on the Indians has been long used by anthropologists as a fundamental document on the Southern Indians. His observations upon his contemporaries are sometimes prejudiced, but he never disguises his prejudice, and his very animosity leads him to reveal facts that friendlier and more discreet writers might have omitted.

The weakest portion of the history is the first part,

the annals of the early period, which are sketchy and inaccurate. Thomas Jefferson, after commenting upon William Stith's tedious prolixity, complains that Beverley had "run into the other extreme" and had condensed his narrative into "the hundredth part of the space which Stith employs for the fourth part of the period.[12] In describing the first years of colonial settlement, Beverley leaned heavily upon Captain John Smith's *General History of Virginia*, but he did not accept all of this narrative at face value. Although modern scholarship heavily discounts Smith's egotism and prejudice, his account has more value than some historians have realized, and Beverley's instinct in choosing apt quotations from Smith was sound, at least from a literary point of view.

As literature the rare 1705 edition in most respects is superior to Beverley's revised version of 1722 in which he softened his acidulous but often amusing comments upon his contemporaries. Because Charles Campbell, with a Victorian feeling for decorum, chose the less colorful version for reprinting in 1855, readers of Beverley have often missed some of his more vivid observations.

Beverley's own reasons for modifying his work are obscure. Apparently, with the increase of years, he softened and became more tolerant of his fellowmen. Even though he still remembered the shortcomings of those who had earned his ill will, he preferred to purge his *History* of personal acerbities. "In this edition," he wrote in the preface of 1722, "I have also retrenched some particulars as related only to private transactions and characters in the historical past as being too diminutive to be transmitted to posterity, and set down the succession of the governors with the more general incidents of their government without reflection upon the private conduct of any person." A considerable number of additions and changes were made in 1722 to bring the account up-to-date.

Some of the revisions of 1722 were corrections of fact or changes which the author believed to be an improvement in style or tone. In several instances, Beverley's own opinions had changed with the years, and he modified his statements accordingly. In a few cases, his amplifications add information acquired since the first edition. In the natural history portion, for example, the author added new observations and made a few corrections. In 1705 he drily remarked that Virginia cattle might be improved by crossing with buffaloes if the inhabitants could catch enough buffalo calves—an opinion which he deleted as unscientific and frivolous, and in 1722 he no longer maintained that Virginia pork, bacon, and all manner of fowls were superior to any in England. But in seventeen years he had seen some notable snakes, and he could not forego a long amplification of his discussion of rattlers. Curiously, in 1722 he deleted an account of eating a rattlesnake which he had earlier pronounced "dainty food." In place of the description of the bullfrog so monstrous that it would provide a comfortable meal for six Frenchmen, he substituted in 1722 the colorless remark that "if any be good to eat, these must be the kind." With the exception of the passage on rattlesnakes, scarcely any of Beverley's changes were a literary improvement. In nearly every case he weakened his original idiom.

Beverley in 1705 showed no desire to appease the prejudices of his fellow Virginians. On the contrary, he went out of his way to shock them. Some of his remarks about the Indians, for instance, must have been made deliberately to annoy certain of his fellow-planters, already becoming a little stuffy in their family pride. The example set by John Rolfe in marrying Pocahontas, he observes, might well have been followed by other settlers to the vast improvement of the country.[13] Other passages described the beauty and chastity of the Indian women. Concerning a report of Indian girls selling their honor for wampum, he declares the story to be "an aspersion cast on those innocent creatures by reason of the freedom they take in conversation, which uncharitable Christians interpret as criminal upon no other ground than the guilt of their own consciences." Warming to the subject of Indian beauty and virtue, he adds that the native damsels are full of mirth, spirit, and good humor—qualities which churlish white men have misunderstood, for Englishmen "are not very nice in distinguishing betwixt guilt and harmless freedom."[14] These and other comments on the virtues of the Indians, the author later omitted or changed, but even in the modified version his account of the Indians remained sympathetic, and often his comparisons with the settlers display the red men in the more favorable light. The author's brethren on the frontier could scarcely have been pleased at this.

In later years, Beverley evidently felt that he had been a little too romantic in his description of the nobility of the Indians. To a paragraph relating King James's irritation over John Rolfe's marriage to the princess Pocahontas, the daughter of an Indian king, without asking the English sovereign's permission, the historian added a sardonic sentence in 1722: "But had their [the Indians'] true condition here been known, that pother had been saved."[15]

With the exception of a tendency to over-enthusiasm about the beauty and good qualities of Indian men and women, Beverley wrote a realistic report on the Indians as he had observed them. Ironically, he criticizes the descriptions of romantic writers like Lahontan or pious authors like Father Hennepin. In his opinion the Indians are neither noble savages nor sons of the devil, but human beings possessing some of the virtues and vices common to mankind.

In a description of the Indian's religion, Beverley expresses his own distaste for priestcraft and ironically compares Indian conjurers with Christian clerics. "I don't pretend to have dived into all the mysteries of the Indian religion," he remarks, "nor have I had such opportunities of learning them as Father Hennepin and Baron Lahontan had, by living much among the Indians in their towns. And because my rule is to say nothing but the naked truth, I intend to be very brief upon this head."[16] Actually he writes nearly twenty-two pages on the subject and reveals that he had made careful investigations, on one occasion exploring, at the risk of his life, an Indian shrine. With the scientific spirit of a rationalist, on another occasion he plied an Indian with hard cider until he overcame his reticence and then cross-examined him on religion. As he suspected, the Indian admitted that his people were in bondage to the priests.[17]

As elsewhere in his book, Beverley reveals an ironic

skepticism in a passage describing the religious rites of "huskanawing"—the ceremonial which young men underwent before being admitted to adult status in the tribe. At one stage the youths were given a narcotic brew to make them forget all of their previous life, and if they betrayed any memory of the past, they were dosed again until they forgot. "I confess," he observes, "I judged it at first sight to be only an invention of the seniors to engross the young men's riches to themselves, for, after suffering this operation, they never pretended to call to mind anything of their former property; but their goods were either shared among the old men, or brought to some public use, and so these younkers were obliged to begin the world again."[18] These passages on Indian religion Beverley left unchanged in the second edition.

The omission in 1722 of pungent criticism of royal governors whom Beverley had known may have been evidence of a fine Christian charity, but the alterations did not improve the style or even the historical value of the work. Some of the unfavorable commentary, even that prompted by personal malice, suggests a point of view useful in correcting the tendency to whitewash or romanticize the past. Beverley's opinions of Nathaniel Bacon and his rebellion are at variance, for example, with the commonly accepted view of that worthy as a patriotic leader against tyranny. Beverley, whose father had been one of Governor Berkeley's stoutest adherents, was admittedly prejudiced against Bacon, but clearly he is not all wrong in interpreting the rebellion, and some of the clues he gives to Bacon's character and the motives behind the outbreak require careful appraisal in writing about that episode in Virginia history.

Many of Beverley's incidental remarks, omitted in the later edition as too trivial or too ill-natured, contain shrewd observations that say a great deal. For example, he remarks concerning Culpeper's success in persuading the House of Burgesses to enact certain laws: "In these he had the art of mixing the good of the country with his own particular interest, which was a sure means of getting them passed."[19] In reference to the same governor's part in drafting the act of pardon and oblivion in favor of Bacon's rebels, he comments:

But he put a sting into the tail of this law that justifies oppression whenever the people happen to fall into the hands of an ill governor. I mean the clause that imposes a penalty of five hundred pounds and a year's imprisonment upon any man that shall presume to speak disrespectfully of the governor. This is such a safeguard to tyranny that, let a governor commit never so many abuses, no person while he is there dare say a word against him; nor so much as go about to represent it to the throne of England for redress for fear of incurring a severe penalty.[20]

In a long passage he condemned Culpeper's highhanded methods as liable to destroy the liberties of Virginians, "for, at this rate of proceeding, people looked upon their Acts of Assembly to be of no more force than the laws of an Ottoman province which are liable to be suspended or repealed at the pleasure of the Bashaw."[21]

If Beverley looked with a jaundiced eye upon Culpeper, he could likewise see little good in the next titled Englishman, Francis, Lord Howard of Effingham, who came to preside over the colony. "This noble lord," he remarks, "had as great an affection for money as his predecessor, and made it his business to equip himself with as much of it as he could without respect either to the laws of the plantation or the dignity of his office." Lest the smaller grafters be spared from his indictment, the historian adds: "His lordship condescended to share with his clerk the meaner profits of ministerial office. And to serve this turn the more effectually, he imposed the charge of a license under seal on all schoolmasters for teaching of children, and on all practitioners at the bar for pleading." Of Philip Ludwell's appeal to the King against this governor's acts, Beverley observes, "And though Col. Ludwell had not the good fortune to get his Lordship turned out, yet his indefatigable application in that affair deserves an honourable commemoration."[22]

Against Governor Francis Nicholson, Beverley had a particular grudge. He blamed the governor for the removal of the capital from Jamestown to Middle Plantation, or Williamsburg—a change which he himself stoutly disapproved. Perhaps the historian's three-acre lot at Jamestown colored his views. At any rate, Nicholson found small favor in his eyes, and Beverley impugned the motives even of his philanthropies. Of Nicholson's zeal for the church, he comments that "his practice was not of a piece with his pious pretensions. . . . He likewise gave himself airs of encouraging the college. But he used this pretext for so many by-ends that at last the promoters of that good work grew weary of the mockery."[23]

All of these passages, and others like them, Beverley carefully deleted or replaced with colorless substitutes. That is not to say that he purged his later version of criticism or pungent commentary, but he softened the tone and spoke with more tolerance. Too vigorous

xxix

partisanship, he evidently decided, might well be omitted from a work labelled history.

Not only did Beverley soften his comments on personalities, but he made an effort in the revision to restrain a naturally satirical vein. For instance, in a paragraph concerning the diseases of the country, he could not forbear to remark in 1705 that Virginians

> have the happiness to have very few doctors, and those such as make use only of simple remedies, of which their woods afford great plenty. And indeed, their distempers are not many, and their cures are so generally known that there is not mystery enough to make a trade of physic there, as the learned do in other countries to the great oppression of mankind.[24]

In deference to doctors, this passage did not find its way into the edition of 1722.

When Beverley was composing his history in 1703, he inserted one passage that would both flatter his father-in-law, William Byrd I, and appeal to prospective Huguenot immigrants. In describing the ease with which foreigners, particularly Frenchmen, adapt themselves to the new country, he added several paragraphs praising the generosity of Colonel Byrd toward the distressed Huguenots. These immigrants had found him a charitable friend and protector. He made them "the object of his particular care, employing all his skill and all his friends to advance their interest. . . . His mills have been at their service to grind their corn toll-free, and his people are ordered upon all occasions to assist them." In the Assembly, he labored to see that they received proper titles to their holdings "lest the land which they have improved by their industry from the wild woods should hereafter unjustly be taken away from their children."[25] In a lyrical description of Virginia gardens a few pages further on, Beverley again mentions his father-in-law, who had a particular pride in the shrubs and flowers at Westover.[26]

The elder William Byrd died the year before the *History* appeared in print, and Beverley deleted the passages in the second edition. He apparently did not intend that anyone should think that his flattering allusions referred to his brother-in-law.

Some of the most charming parts of Beverley's *History* are the passages describing the natural beauty of the country—the land in a state of nature before ambitious planters had spoiled it. Rare in the eighteenth century, and rarer still on the frontier, was the appreciation of external nature displayed by this Virginian. With the acute attention of a Thoreau, he had observed God's creation and liked it.

Almost wistfully he envied the Indians their simplicity of life, their closeness to nature, and the freedom which they enjoyed "without the curse of industry, their diversion alone and not their labor, supplying their necessities." And he adds, in concluding his remarks on the Indians:

Thus I have given a succinct account of the Indians, happy, I think, in their simple state of nature, and in their enjoyment of plenty without the curse of labor. They have on several accounts reason to lament the arrival of the Europeans, by whose means they seem to have lost their felicity, as well as their innocence. The English have taken away [a] great part of their country, and consequently made every thing less plenty amongst them. They have introduced drunkenness and luxury amongst them, which have multiplied their wants and put them upon desiring a thousand things they never dreamt of before. I have been the most concise in my account of this harmless people because I have inserted several figures, which I hope have both supplied the defect of words and rendered the descriptions more clear. I shall in the next place proceed to treat of Virginia as it is now improved (I should say, rather, altered) by the English, and of its present constitution and settlement.[27]

Thus Beverley contemplated primitive man's conquest by civilization and, like others after him, he deemed it a tragedy.

In natural beauty, fertility, and benevolence of climate, Virginia was like unto Canaan. "As Judea was full of rivers, and branches of rivers, so is Virginia," he boasts.[28] The weather of Virginia could scarcely be improved. Even the thunderstorm in summer is so beneficial by "cooling and refining of the air that it is oftener wished for than feared," and he is pleased that the land is not afflicted with earthquakes "which the Caribbee Islands are so much troubled with." Heat is very seldom troublesome, and cold is never a problem. The "spring and fall afford as pleasant weather as Mahomet promised in his Paradise."[29]

Beverley was too honest to pretend that the country was entirely free of pests, and he warned against mosquitoes and chiggers (which he calls "red worms"). But these and other vermin were a negligible annoyance, and the land, as he looked upon it, was remarkably benign.

Although he viewed with sympathetic appreciation the natural goodness of a country untouched by man, he was not unmindful of the human helps to nature. "Have you pleasure in a garden?" he asks. "All things thrive in it most surprisingly. You can't walk by a bed of flowers but besides the entertainment of their beauty your eyes will be saluted with the charming colors of the humming bird . . . a glorious shining mixture of scarlet, green, and gold."[30] In a region where gardens could be made with such ease and success, he thought his countrymen had been negligent of their opportunities, for there were not "many gardens in the country fit to bear the name."[31]

So beneficent was nature that Beverley found it hard to understand why Virginians had not made better use of their opportunities. Already he observed that the one crop system would be their ruin. Without stint, therefore, he criticized them for their shiftlessness and indolence:

> Thus they depend altogether upon the liberality of nature without endeavoring to improve its gifts by art or industry. They sponge upon the blessings of a warm sun and a fruitful soil, and almost grutch the pains of gathering in the bounties of the earth. I should be ashamed to publish this slothful indolence of my countrymen, but that I hope it will rouse them out of their lethargy and excite them to make the most of all those happy advantages which nature has given them. And if it does this, I am sure they will have the goodness to forgive me.[32]

In this fashion, Beverley ends *The History and Present State of Virginia*. The concluding paragraph is characteristic of the work, for throughout the book the author has the interest of Virginia at heart. When he is critical—and he misses few opportunities to point out shortcomings—his motives are usually constructive. Except in the expression of his personal animosities, he did not criticize without suggesting methods of improvement. In Virginia he foresaw a great commonwealth of free and independent citizens. He did not intend for his countrymen, in their complacence, to sleep over their birthright. Although Beverley did not endear himself to his contemporaries, he wrote a wise book which may still be read with profit.

A Note on the Text and the Illustrations

THE TEXT of Beverley's *History* reproduced here is based on the Huntington Library copy, which came from the collection of Americana brought together by E. D. Church.

An effort has been made to reprint the original text faithfully. The original spelling, capitalization, and most punctuation have been preserved, but broken letters and a few obvious misprints have been silently corrected. The errors noted by Beverley in his own "Errata" have been corrected in the text. To prevent misreading, the editor has altered a few of the original marks of punctuation. In the original edition, the Preface and the "Table" are set in italics with occasional words in Roman type. The designers of the present edition have reversed this usage in the interest of greater legibility. Elsewhere, with a few exceptions, this edition follows the use of italics and Roman type in the original.

In the preparation of the text, the editor has had the help of Mrs. Marion Tinling of the Huntington Library staff, and of the staff of the Department of Research of Colonial Williamsburg, Incorporated. He is especially indebted to the late Hunter Dickinson Farish and to Mr. Lester J. Cappon.

The illustrations in Beverley's *History* consist of fourteen engravings, signed by Simon Gribelin, which are adapted from the engravings used to illustrate Theodore DeBry's edition in 1590 of Thomas Hariot's *Virginia*. As everyone knows, DeBry's engravings were made from the water colors painted by John White, who went out with Raleigh's colonists to Roanoke in 1585.[33]

Simon Gribelin was a minor French artist, born in Blois in 1661, who came to England in 1680 and made a career as an engraver. He died in London in 1733. His best work, in the opinion of present-day historians of art, consisted of conventional designs for jewelers, printers, and similar craftsmen. He published three small volumes of his designs. One of these, *A Book of Ornaments Useful to Jewelers, Watchmakers, and All Other Artists* (1697), has recently been reproduced from a second edition of the work brought out in London in 1704. The engraved title page of Beverley's *History* of 1705 illustrates the quality of Gribelin's designs.[34]

The HISTORY *and*
Present State
of Virginia

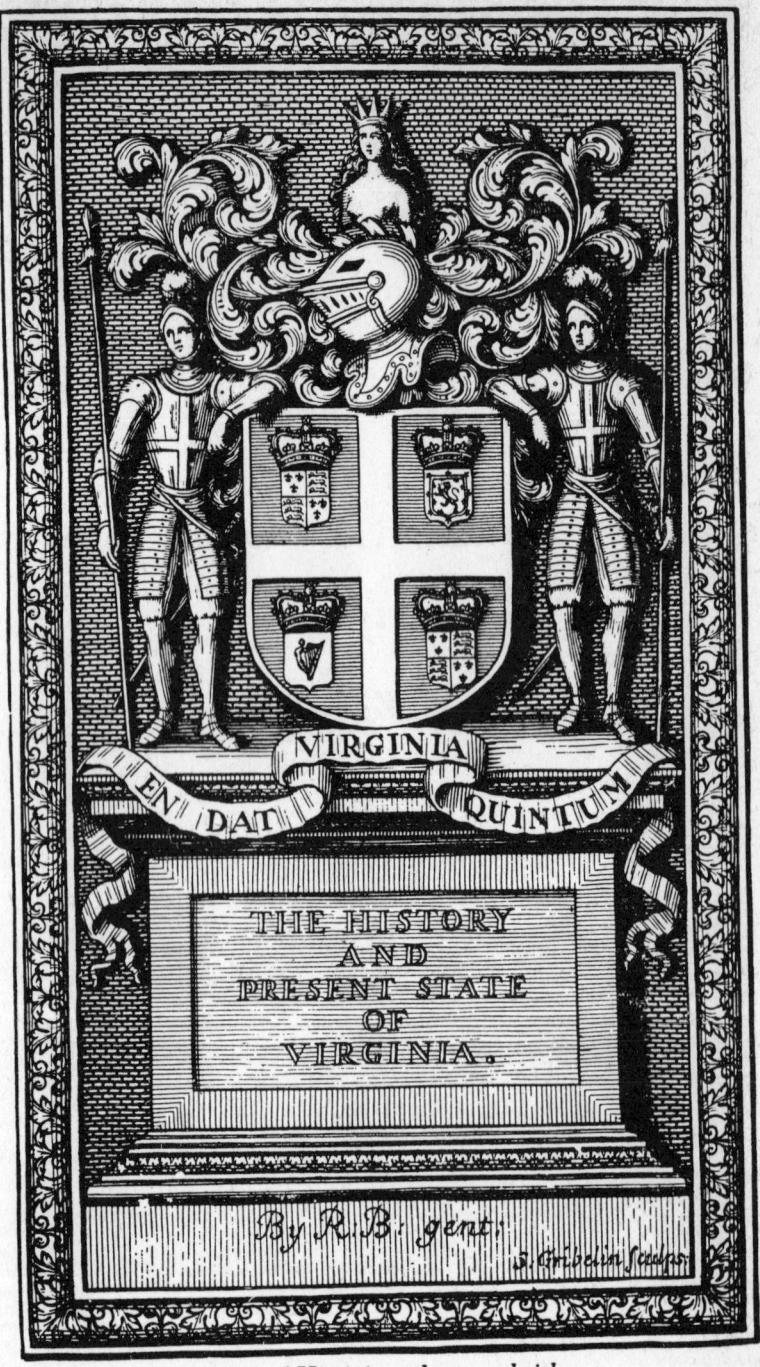

Arms of Virginia and engraved title

THE
HISTORY
AND
Present STATE
OF
VIRGINIA,

In Four PARTS.

I. The HISTORY of the First Settlement of *Virginia*, and the Government thereof, to the present Time.

II. The Natural Productions and Conveniencies of the Country, suited to Trade and Improvement.

III. The Native *Indians*, their Religion, Laws, and Customs, in War and Peace.

IV. The present State of the Country, as to the Polity of the Government, and the Improvements of the Land.

By *a* Native *and* Inhabitant *of the* PLACE.

LONDON:
Printed for *R. Parker*, at the *Unicorn*, under the *Piazza's* of the *Royal-Exchange*. MDCCV.

TO THE

Right HONOURABLE,

*R*OBERT *HARLEY,* Esq;

Speaker of the *H. of Commons,*

AND

One of Her Majesty's Principal

Secretaries of State.[1]*

I Flatter my self, that I am not without Reason, for imploring Your Protection of the following Discourse. It is an honest Account of the ancientest, as well as most profitable Colony, depending on the Crown of *England;* and therefore ought naturally to address it self to the Patron of the *Plantations.*

No Body is better instructed in the true Interest of *England*, than Your Self; No Body is more convinced, how much the *Plantations* advance that Interest; and consequently, no Body knows how to set a juster Value

*Superior figures refer to notes in the back of the book. Notes on the text of the History begin on page 351.

upon them. While some People, upon very mistaken Principles of Policy, are for loading those Countries with heavy Impositions, and oppressing them with Rapacious, and Arbitrary Governours; You, *Sir*, who are a better Judge of their Importance, are for milder Methods, and for extending the Blessings of Justice, and Property, to all the *English* Dominions.

How happy therefore ought we of the *Plantations* to think our selves, in the Favour of a Gentleman, whose Thoughts are directed by unbiass'd Reason, and the real Advantages of *England?* Those are the Measures we wish to be govern'd by; and ask no other Treatment, than what is due to a loyal People, whose Lives are devoted to the Benefit of their Mother-Country. And sure we can never despair of this Common Justice, in the Reign of a Gracious Queen, who wishes the Happiness of all Her Subjects. *England* is infinitely to be envy'd, for lying under the immediate Influences of Her Goodness: While the *Plantations*, which are farther remov'd from Her Royal Presence, have those kindly Beams more weakly reflected on them. Their Distance makes 'em liable to be ill used by Men, that over-act Her Sacred Authority, and under-act Her Vertues. But we please our selves with the Hopes, that these Misfortunes will be made lighter to us, by the Justice of the present Administration.

I must not presume to celebrate Your bright Qualities, because, next to having a great deal of Merit, the hardest Thing in the World, is to give it a just Commendation. You have by Your Publick Services, taken Care to convince Mankind of Your Worth. You alone have Abilities not only to fill, but to adorn, at the same time, Two of the most important Posts of the Nation. You, *Sir*, have reconcil'd the long Difference there has been betwixt the Patriot and the Publick Minister. And 'tis a plain Demonstration, that the QUEEN has no other View, than the Happiness of Her People, when Her Majesty is pleased to employ such Persons in Her Service, as have all along signaliz'd a constant Love to their Country.

I am,

SIR,

Your most Faithful Servant.

THE
PREFACE.

'TIS agreed, that Travellers are of all Men, the most suspected of Insincerity. This does not only hold, in their private Conversations; but likewise in the *Grand Tours*, and Travels, with which they pester the Publick, and break the Bookseller. There are no Books, (the Legends of Saints always excepted,) so stuff'd with Poetical Stories, as Voyages; and the more distant the Countries lie, which they pretend to describe, the greater License those priviledg'd Authors take, in imposing upon the World. The *French* Travels are commonly more infamous on this Account, than any other, which must be imputed to the strong Genius of that Nation to *Hyperbole*, and *Romance*. They are fond of dressing up every thing in their gay Fashion, from a happy Opinion, that their own *Fopperies* make any Subject more entertaining. The *English*, it must be granted, invent more within the Compass of Probability, and are contented to be less Ornamental, while they are more Sincere.

I make no Question, but the following Account will come in for its Share of this Imputation. I shall be reputed as arrant a Traveller as the rest, and my Credit, (like that of Women,) will be condemn'd for the Sins of my Company. However, I intreat the gentle Reader to be so just, as not to convict me upon bare Suspicion;

let the Evidence be plain, or at least amount to a violent Presumption, and then I don't fear being acquitted. If an honest Author might be believ'd in his own Case, I wou'd solemnly declare, that I have not knowingly asserted any untrue Thing in the whole Book. On the contrary, I fear, I shall rather be accused of saying too much Truth, than too little. If I have had the Misfortune to have err'd in any Particular this Way, which yet I have used all imaginable Care to avoid, I hope the World, with all its Uncharitableness, will vouchsafe to forgive my Understanding.

If I might be so happy, as to settle my Credit with the Reader, the next Favour I wou'd ask of him, shou'd be, not to Criticize too unmercifully upon my Stile. I am an *Indian*, and don't pretend to be exact in my Language: But I hope the Plainness of my Dress, will give him the kinder Impressions of my Honesty, which is what I pretend to. Truth desires only to be understood, and never affects the Reputation of being finely equipp'd. It depends upon its own intrinsick Value, and, like Beauty, is rather conceal'd, than set off, by Ornament.

I wonder no Body has ever presented the World, with a tolerable Account of our *Plantations*. Nothing of that kind has yet appear'd, except some few General Descriptions, that have been calculated more for the Benefit of the Bookseller, than for the Information of Mankind. If I may judge of the rest, by what has been publish'd concerning *Virginia*, I will take the Liberty to say, that there's none of 'em either true, or so much as well invented. Such Accounts are as impertinent as ill Pictures, that resemble any Body, as much as the Persons they are drawn for. For my part, I have endeavour'd to hit the *Likeness;* though, perhaps, my *Colouring* may not have all the Life and Beauty I cou'd wish.

The Method I have taken in this Performance, is as follows. I have divided the Whole into Four distinct Parts. The first contains, a Chronological History, of the most remarkable Things that have happen'd in *Virginia*, ever since it was first seated by the *English*. It shows all the Wars with the *Indians*, and their Causes, all the Massacres, and other Disasters, occasion'd by the Resentment of the Natives. It likewise gives a faithful Account, of all the successive Governours of that Country, and their Administration, together with the principal Laws, that have been enacted in the Time of Each. In the doing of which, I have been careful to mention nothing, but what I can make good by very Authentique Testimony. So that if I have taken the Freedom, to represent the Mismanagements of several Gentlemen, it is their Fault, that acted such Irregularities, and not mine, that report them to the World. If Men will please to be unjust, run counter to the *Royal Instructions*, oppress the People, and offer Violence to all the *Laws* of a Country, they ought to be known, and abhorr'd by Mankind.

The Second Part treats of the Spontaneous Productions of that Country, and the Original State, wherein the *English* found it at their first Arrival. This is a very copious Subject, but I have handled it with more Brevity than it deserves, because I am conscious of my want of Skill in the *Works of Nature*. However I flatter my self, that what I have said, will be sufficient, to give a Handle to a more compleat Undertaking. The World had some Years ago an unhappy Loss, by the Death of Mr. *Banister*,[2] who was making curious Collections for a *Natural History of* Virginia: But the sudden Death of that Gentleman, put an End to that excellent Design. He had great Talents that Way, and if he had liv'd a few Years longer, he wou'd have done Justice to so fine a Country, by describing it in all its Native Perfections.

The Third Part gives a true Account of the *Indians*, together with their Religion, Customs, and Government. There I have added Fourteen Copper Plates, to illustrate the Dress, and Way of Living of the Natives, the Draughts of which were taken exactly from the Life. Herein, as well as throughout the whole Book, I have been very scrupulous, not to insert any thing, but what I can justifie, either by my own Knowledge, or by credible Information.

In the Fourth Part, I have represented the *English* Form of Government in that Country, with all the Publick Officers, their Business, and Salary. There I have mention'd many of their most material Laws, and Methods of proceeding. I have likewise shown the small Improvements, that the *English* have made, since they have been in Possession, and pointed at several great Advantages, which they might secure to themselves, by a due Spirit of Industry, and Management. I have every-where made it my chief Business, to avoid *Partiality;* and therefore have fairly expos'd the Inconveniencies, as well as proclaim'd the Excellencies of my Country.

This is the *Bill of Fare*, of what the Reader may expect to meet with in the following Discourse; and I shou'd be very happy, if he wou'd have the Goodness, to think it a tolerable Entertainment.

THE HISTORY AND Present STATE OF VIRGINIA.

BOOK I.[3]

CHAP. I.

Shewing what happen'd in the first Attempts to settle Virginia, *before the Discovery of* Chesapeak *Bay.*

¶.1. THE Learned and Valiant Sir *Walter Raleigh* having entertain'd some deeper and more serious Considerations upon the State of the Earth, than most other Men of his Time, as may sufficiently appear by his incomparable Book, *The History of the World:* And having laid together the many Stories then in *Europe* concerning *America;* the Native Beauty, Riches, and Value of this Part of the World; and the immense Profits the *Spaniards* drew from a small Settlement or two thereon made; resolv'd upon an Adventure for further Discoveries.

According to this Purpose, in the Year of our Lord, 1583, He got several Men of great Value and Estate to join with him in an Expedition of this Nature: And for their Incouragement obtain'd Letters Patents from Queen *Elizabeth*, bearing date the 25th of *March*, 1584, for turning their Discoveries to their own Advantage.

¶.2. In *April* following they set out Two small Vessels under the Command of Capt. *Philip Amidas*, and Capt. *Arthur Barlow;* who, after a prosperous Voyage, anchor'd at the Inlet by *Roenoke*, at present under the Government of North *Carolina*. They made good Profit of the *Indian* Truck, which they bought for Things of much inferior Value, and return'd. Being over-pleased with their Profits, and finding all Things there entirely new, and surprizing; they gave a very advantageous Account of Matters; by representing the Country so delightful, and desirable; so pleasant, and plentiful; the Climate, and Air, so temperate, sweet, and wholsome; the Woods, and Soil, so charming, and fruitful; and all other Things so agreeable, that Paradice it self seem'd to be there, in its first Native Lustre.

They gave particular Accounts of the Variety of good Fruits, and some whereof they had never seen the Like before; but above all, that there were Grapes in such abundance, as was never known in the World: Stately tall large Oaks, and other Timber; Red Cedar, Cypress, Pines, and other Evergreens, and Sweetwoods; for tallness and largeness exceeding all they had ever heard of: Wild Fowl, Fish, Deer, and other Game in such Plenty, and Variety; that no Epicure could desire more than this New World did seem naturally to afford.

And, to make it yet more desirable, they reported the Native *Indians* (which were then the only Inhabitants) so affable, kind, and good-natur'd; so uncultivated in Learning, Trades, and Fashions; so innocent, and ignorant of all manner of Politicks, Tricks, and Cunning; and so desirous of the Company of the *English:* That they seem'd rather to be like soft Wax, ready to take any Impression, than any ways likely to oppose the Settling of the *English* near them: They represented it as a Scene laid open for the good and gracious Q. *Elizabeth*, to propagate the Gospel in, and extend her Dominions over: As if purposely reserv'd for her Majesty, by a peculiar Direction of Providence, that had brought all former Adventures in this Affair to nothing: And to give a further Taste of their Discovery, they took with them, in their Return for *England*, Two Men of the Native *Indians*, named *Wanchese* and *Manteo*.

☾.3. Her Majesty accordingly took the Hint, and espoused the Project, as far as her present Engagements in War with *Spain* would let her; being so well pleased with the Account given, that as the greatest Mark of

Honour she could do the Discovery, she call'd the Country by the Name of *Virginia;* as well, for that it was first discover'd in her Reign, a Virgin Queen; as that it did still seem to retain the Virgin Purity and Plenty of the first Creation, and the People their Primitive Innocence: For they seem'd not debauch'd nor corrupted with those Pomps and Vanities, which had depraved and inslaved the Rest of Mankind; neither were their Hands harden'd by Labour, nor their Minds corrupted by the Desire of hoarding up Treasure: They were without Boundaries to their Land; and without Property in Cattle; and seem'd to have escaped, or rather not to have been concern'd in the first Curse, *Of getting their Bread by the Sweat of their Brows:* For, by their Pleasure alone, they supplied all their Necessities; namely, by Fishing, Fowling and Hunting; Skins being their only Cloathing; and these too, Five Sixths of the Year thrown by: Living without Labour, and only gathering the Fruits of the Earth when ripe, or fit for use: Neither fearing present Want, nor solicitous for the Future, but daily finding sufficient afresh for their Subsistance.

¶.4. This Report was back'd, nay much advanc'd, by the vast Riches and Treasure mention'd in several Merchants Letters from *Mexico* and *Peru,* to their Correspondents in *Spain;* which Letters were taken with their Ships and Treasure, by some of ours in her Majesty's Service, in Prosecution of the *Spanish* Wars: This was Incouragement enough for a new Adventure, and set Peoples Invention at work, till they had satisfied themselves, and made sufficient Essays for the further Discovery of the Country. Pursuant whereunto Sir *Richard Greenvile,* the Chief of Sir *Walter Raleigh*'s Associates, having obtain'd Seven Sail of Ships, well laden with Provision, Arms, Ammunition, and spare Men to make a Settlement, set out in Person with them early in the Spring of the succeeding Year, to make further Discoveries, taking back the Two *Indians* with him; and according to his Wish, in the latter End of *May*, arriv'd at the same Place, where the *English* had been the Year before; there he made a Settlement, sow'd Beans and Peas, which he saw come up and grow to Admiration while he staid, which was about Two Months; and having made some little Discoveries more in the *Sound* to the Southward, and got some Treasure in Skins, Furs, Pearl, and other Rarities of the Country, for Things of inconsiderable Value, he return'd for *England*, leaving One Hundred and Eight Men upon *Roenoke* Island, under the Command of Mr. *Ralph Lane*, to keep Possession.

¶.5. As soon as Sir *Richard Greenvile* was gone, they, according to Order and their own Inclination, set themselves earnestly about discovering the Country, and ranged about a little too indiscreetly up the Rivers, and into the Land backward from the Rivers, which gave the *Indians* a Jealousie of their Meaning: For they cut off several Straglers of them, and had laid Designs to destroy the rest, but were happily prevented. This put the *English* upon the Precaution of keeping more within Bounds, and not venturing themselves too defenceless Abroad, who till then had depended too much upon the Natives Simplicity and Innocence.

After the *Indians* had done this Mischief, they never observ'd any real Faith towards those *English:* For being naturally suspicious and revengeful themselves, they never thought the *English* could forgive them; and so by this Jealousie, caus'd by the Cowardize of their Nature, they were continually doing Mischief.

The *English*, notwithstanding all this, continued their Discoveries, but more carefully than they had done before, and kept the *Indians* in some Awe, by threatening them with the Return of their Companions again with a greater Supply of Men and Goods: And, before the Cold of the Winter became uneasie, they had extended their Discoveries near an Hundred Miles along the Sea-Coast to the Northward; but not reaching the Southern Cape of *Chesapeak* Bay in *Virginia*, they had as yet found no good Harbour.

¶.6. In this Condition they maintain'd their Settlement all the Winter, and till *August* following; but were much distress'd for Want of Provisions, not having learn'd to gather Food, as the *Indians* did, nor having Conveniencies like them of taking Fish and Fowl: Besides, being now fallen out with the *Indians*, they fear'd to expose themselves to their Contempt and Cruelty; because they had not received the Supply they talk'd of, and which had been expected in the Spring.

All they could do under these Distresses, and the Despair of the Recruits promised them this Year, was only to keep a good looking out to Seaward, if, perchance, they might find any Means of Escape, or Recruit. And, to their great Joy and Satisfaction, in *August* aforesaid, they happen'd to espy, and make themselves be seen to Sir *Francis Drake*'s Fleet, consisting of Twenty Three Sail, who being sent by her Majesty upon the Coast of *America*, in Search of the *Spanish* Treasures, had Orders from her Majesty to take a View of this Plantation, and see what Assistance or Encouragement it wanted: Their first Petition to him was to grant them a fresh Supply of Men and Provisions, with a small Vessel, and Boats to attend them; that so if they should be put to Distress for want of Relief, they might imbark for *England*. This was as readily granted by Sir *Francis Drake* as ask'd by them; and a Ship was appointed them, which Ship they began immediately to fit up, and supply plentifully with all manner of Stores for a long Stay; but while they were a doing this, a great Storm arose, and drove that very Ship (with some others) from her Anchor to Sea, and so she was lost for that Occasion.

Sir *Francis* would have given them another Ship, but

this Accident coming on the Back of so many Hardships which they had undergone, daunted them, and put them upon imagining that Providence was averse to their Designs: And now having given over, for that Year, the Expectation of their promised Supply from *England*, they consulted together, and agreed to desire Sir *Francis Drake* to take them along with him, which he did.

Thus their first Intention of Settlement fell, after discovering many Things of the natural Growth of the Country, useful for the Life of Man, and beneficial to Trade, they having observ'd a vast Variety of Fish, Fowl and Beasts; Fruits, Seeds, Plants, Roots, Timber-Trees, Sweet-Woods and Gums: They had likewise attain'd some little Knowledge in the Language of the *Indians*, their Religion, Manners, and Ways of Correspondence one with another; and been made sensible of their Cunning and Treachery towards themselves.

¶.7. While these Things were thus acting in *America*, the Adventurers in *England* were providing, tho' too tediously, to send them Recruits. And tho' it was late before they could dispatch them (for they met with several Disappointments, and had many Squabbles among themselves.) However, at last they provided Four good Ships, with all manner of Recruits suitable for the Colony, and Sir *Walter Raleigh* designed to go in Person with them.

Sir *Walter* got his Ship ready first, and fearing the ill Consequence of a Delay, and the Discouragement it might be to those that were left to make a Settlement, he set Sail by himself. And a Fortnight after him Sir *Richard Greenvile* sail'd with the Three other Ships.

Sir *Walter* fell in with the Land at Cape *Hattoras*, a little to the Southward of the Place, where the 108 Men had been settled, and after Search not finding them, he return'd: However, Sir *Richard*, with his Ships, found the Place where he had left the Men, but entirely deserted, which was at first a great Disheartening to him, thinking them all destroy'd, because he knew not that Sir *Francis Drake* had been there, and taken them off; but he was a little better satisfied by *Manteo*'s Report, that they were not cut off by the *Indians*, tho' he could give no good Account what was become of them. However, notwithstanding this seeming Discouragement, he again left Fifty Men in the same Island of *Roenoke*, built them Houses necessary, gave them Two Years Provision, and return'd.

¶.8. The next Summer, being *Anno* 1587. Three Ships more were sent, under the Command of Mr. *John White*, who himself was to settle there as Governour with more Men, and some Women, carrying also plentiful Recruits of Provisions.

In the latter End of *July* they arrived at *Roenoke* aforesaid, where they again encounter'd the uncomfortable News of the Loss of these Men also; who (as they were inform'd by *Manteo*) were secretly set upon by the *Indians*, some cut off, and the others fled, and not to be heard of, and their Place of Habitation now all grown up with Weeds. However, they repair'd the Houses on *Roenoke*, and sate down there again.

The 13th of *August* they christen'd *Manteo*, and stiled him Lord of *Dassamonpeak*, an *Indian* Nation so call'd, in Reward of the Fidelity he had shown to the *English* from the Beginning; who being the first *Indian* that was made a Christian in that Part of the World, I thought it not amiss to remember him.

On the same Occasion also may be mention'd the first Child there born of Christian Parentage, *viz.* a Daughter of Mr. *Ananias Dare*. She was born the 18th of the same *August* upon *Roenoke*, and, after the Name of the Country, was christen'd *Virginia*.

This seem'd to be a Settlement prosperously made,

being carry'd on with much Zeal and Unanimity among themselves. The Form of Government consisted of a Governour and Twelve Councellors, incorporated by the Name of the Governour and Assistants of the City of *Raleigh* in *Virginia.*

Many Nations of the *Indians* renew'd their Peace, and made firm Leagues with the Corporation: The chief Men of the *English* also were so far from being dishearten'd at the former Disappointments, that they disputed for the Liberty of remaining on the Spot; and by meer Constraint compell'd Mr. *White*, their Governour, to return for *England*, to negociate the Business of their Recruits and Supply, as a Man the most capable to manage that Affair, leaving at his Departure One Hundred and Fifteen in the Corporation.

¶.9. It was above Two Years before Mr. *White* could obtain any Grant of Supplies; and then, in the latter End of the Year 1589. he set out from *Plimouth* with Three Ships, and sail'd round by the *Western* and *Carribbee* Islands, they having hitherto not found any nearer Way: For tho' they were skill'd in Navigation, and understood the Use of the Globes, yet did Example so much prevail upon them, that they chose to sail a Thousand Leagues about, rather than attempt a more direct Passage.

Towards the Middle of *August,* 1590. they arriv'd upon the Coast, at Cape *Hattoras*, and went to search upon *Roenoke* for the People; but found, by Letters on the Trees, that they were remov'd to *Croatan*, one of the Islands forming the *Sound*, and Southward of *Roenoke* about Twenty Leagues, but no Sign of Distress. Thither they design'd to sail to them in their Ships; but a Storm arising in the mean while, lay so hard upon them, that their Cables broke; they lost Three of their Anchors, were forced to Sea; and so return'd Home, without ever going near those poor People again for Sixteen Years following: And it is supposed, that the *Indians* seeing them forsaken by their Country, and unfurnish'd of their expected Supplies, cut them off: For to this Day they were never more heard of.

Thus, after all this vast Expence and Trouble, and the Hazard and Loss of so many Lives, Sir *Walter Raleigh*, the great Projector and Furtherer of these Discoveries and Settlements, being under Trouble, all Thoughts of further prosecuting these Designs, lay dead for about Twelve Years following.

℄.10. And then, in the Year 1602 Capt. *Gosnell*[4] who had made one in the former Adventures, furnish'd out a small Bark from *Dartmouth*, and set Sail in her himself, with Thirty odd Men; designing a more direct Course, and not to stand so far to the Southward, nor pass by the *Carribbee* Islands, as all former Adventurers had done. He attain'd his Ends in that; but touch'd upon the Coast of *America* much to the Northward of any of the Places where the former Adventurers had landed: For he fell first among the Islands, forming the Northern Side of *Massachusett*'s Bay in *New-England*; but not finding the Conveniencies that Harbour affords, set Sail again Southward, and, as he thought, clear of Land into the Sea; but fell upon the Byte of Cape *Codd*.

Upon this Coast, and a little to the Southward, he spent some time in Trade with the *Indians;* and gave Names to the Islands of *Martha*'s *Vineyard*, and *Elizabeth*'s *Isle*, which retain the same to this Day. Upon *Elizabeth*'s *Isle* he made an Experiment of *English* Grain, and found it spring up and grow to Admiration, as it had done at *Roenoke*: Here also his Men built Huts to shelter them in the Nights, and bad Weather; and made good Profit by their *Indian* Traffick of Furs, Skins, &c. And, as their Pleasure invited them, would visit the Main; set Receivers, and save the Gums, and Juices distilling from Sweet-Woods; and try and examine the lesser Vegetables.

After a Month's Stay here, they return'd for *England*, as well pleased with the natural Beauty and Richness of the Place they had view'd, as they were with the Treasure they had gather'd in it: Neither had they a Head, nor a Finger that ach'd among them all the time.

¶.11. The Noise of this short, and most profitable of all the former Voyages, set the *Bristol* Merchants to Work also; who early in the Year 1603. sent Two Vessels in Search of the same Place and Trade; which Vessels fell luckily in with the same Land. They follow'd the same Methods Capt. *Gosnell* had done, and having got a rich Lading, they return'd.

¶.12. In the Year 1605, a Voyage was made from *London* in a single Ship, with which they design'd to fall in with the Land about the Latitude 39°; but the Winds put her a little further Northward, and she fell upon the Eastern Parts of *Long-Island* (as it is now call'd, but all went then under the Name of *Virginia*.) Here they traffick'd with the *Indians*, as the others had done before them; made short Trials of the Soil by *English* Grain, and found the *Indians*, as in all other Places, very fair and courteous at first, till they got more Knowledge of the *English*, and perhaps thought themselves over-reach'd, because one bought better Pennyworths than another; upon which afterwards they never fail'd to take Revenge as they found their Opportunity or Advantage. So this Company also return'd with the Ship, having ranged Forty Miles up *Connecticut* River, and call'd the Harbour where they rid *Penticost* Harbour because of their Arrival there on *Whitsunday*.

In all these latter Voyages, they never so much as endeavour'd to come near the Place where the first Settlement was attempted at Cape *Hattoras;* neither had they any Pity on those poor Hundred and Fifteen Souls settled there in 1587 of whom there had never since been any Account, no Relief sent to them, nor so much as any Enquiry made after them, whether they were dead or alive, till about Three Years after this, when *Chesapeak* Bay in *Virginia* was settled, which hitherto had never been seen by any *English* Man. So strong was the Desire of Riches, and so eager the Pursuit of a rich Trade, that all Concern for the Lives of their fellow Christians, Kindred, Neighbours and Country-men, weigh'd nothing in the Comparison; tho' an Enquiry might have been easily made, when they were so near them.

CHAP. II.

Containing an Account of the first Settlement of Chesapeak *Bay, in* Virginia, *by the Corporation of* London *Adventurers, and their Proceedings during their Government by a President and Council Elective.*

§.13. THE Merchants of *London, Bristol, Exeter* and *Plimouth,* soon perceived what great Gains might be made of a Trade this Way, if it were well managed, and Colonies could be rightly settled; which was sufficiently evinced by the great Profits some Ships had made, which had not met with ill Accidents. Encouraged by this Prospect, they join'd together in a Petition to King *James* the First; shewing forth, That it would be too much for any single Person to attempt the Settling of Colonies, and to carry on so considerable a Trade: They therefore pray'd his Majesty to incorporate them, and enable them to raise a joint Stock for that Purpose, and to countenance their Undertaking.

His Majesty did accordingly grant their Petition, and by Letters Patents bearing Date the 10th of *April,* 1606, did in one Patent incorporate them into Two distinct Companies to make Two separate Colonies, *viz.* "Sir *Tho. Gates,* Sir *George Summers,* Knights; Mr. *Richard Hackluit,* Clerk Prebend of *Westminster,* and *Edward-Maria Wingfield,* Esq; Adventurers of the City of *London,* and such others as should be join'd unto them of that Colony, which should be call'd, *The First Colony;* with Liberty to begin their first Plantation and Seat, at any Place upon the Coast of *Virginia,* where they should think fit and conve[ni]ent between the Degrees of 34 and 41 of Northern Latitude: And that they should extend their Bounds from the said first Seat of their Plantation and Habitation, Fifty *English* Miles along the Sea-Coast each Way; and include all the Lands within an Hundred Miles directly over-against the same Sea-Coast, and also back into the Main-Land One Hundred Miles from the Sea-Coast: And that no other should be permitted or suffer'd to plant or inhabit behind, or on the Back of them towards the Main-Land, without the express License of the Council of that Colony thereunto in Writing first had and obtain'd. And for the Second Colony, To *Tho. Hanham, Rawleigh Gilbert, William Parker,* and *George Popham,* Esqs; of the Town of *Plimouth,* and all others who should be join'd to them of that Colony; with Liberty to begin their first Plantation and Seat at any Place upon the Coast of *Virginia,* where they should think fit, between the Degrees of 38 and 45 of Northern Latitude, with the like Liberties and Bounds as the First Colony: Provided they did not seat within an Hundred Miles of them."

₡.14. By Virtue of this Patent, Capt. *John Smith* was sent by the *London* Company in *December,* 1606, on his Voyage with Three small Ships; and a Commission was given to him, and to several other Gentlemen, to establish a Colony, and to govern by a President, to be chosen Annually, and Council, who should be invested with sufficient Authorities and Powers. And now all Things seem'd to promise a Plantation in good Earnest. Providence seem'd likewise very favourable to them: For tho' they designed only for that Part of *Virginia* where the Hundred and Fifteen were left, and where there is no Security of Harbour: Yet, after a tedious Voyage of passing the old Way again, between the *Carribbee* Islands and the Main, he, with Two of his Vessels, luckily fell in with *Virginia* it self, that Part of the Continent now so call'd, anchoring in the Mouth of the Bay of *Chesapeak:* And the first Place they landed upon, was the Southern Cape of that Bay, which they named Cape *Henry*, and the Northern Cape *Charles*, in Honour of the King's Two eldest Sons; and the first great River they search'd, whose *Indian* Name was *Powhatan*, they call'd *James* River, after the King's own Name.

€.15. Before they would make any Settlement here, they made a full Search of *James* River; and then by an unanimous Consent pitched upon a *Peninsula* about Fifty Miles up the River; which, besides the Goodness of the Soil, was esteem'd as most fit, and capable to be made a Place both of Trade and Security, Two Thirds thereof being environ'd by the main River, which affords good Anchorage all along; and the other Third by a small narrow River, capable of receiving many Vessels of an Hundred Tun, quite up as high as till it meets within Thirty Yards of the main River again, and where generally in Spring-Tides it overflows into the main River: By which Means the Land they chose to pitch their Town upon, has obtain'd the Name of an Island. In this back River Ships and small Vessels may ride lashed to one another, and moor'd a Shore secure from all Wind and Weather whatsoever.

The Town, as well as the River, had the Honour to be called by King *James*'s Name. The whole Island thus enclosed contains about Two Thousand Acres of high Land, and several Thousands of very good and firm Marsh, and is an extraordinary good Pasture as any in that Country.

By Means of the narrow Passage, this Place was of great Security to them from the *Indian* Enemy: And if they had then known of the Biting of the Worm in the Salts, they would have valued this Place upon that Account also, as being free from that Mischief.[5]

€.16. They were no sooner settled in all this Happiness

and Security, but they fell into Jars and Dissentions among themselves, by a greedy Grasping at the *Indian* Treasures, envying and overreaching one another in that Trade.

After Five Weeks Stay before this Town, the Ships return'd Home again, leaving One Hundred and Eight Men settled in the Form of Government before spoken of.

After the Ships were gone, the same sort of Feuds and Disorders happen'd continually among them, to the unspeakable Damage of the Plantation.

The *Indians* were the same there as in all other Places; at first very fair and friendly, tho' afterwards they gave great Proofs of their Deceitfulness. However, by the Help of the *Indian* Provisions, the *English* chiefly subsisted till the Return of the Ships the next Year; when Two Vessels were sent thither full freighted with Men and Provisions for Supply of the Plantation, one of which only arriv'd directly, and the other being beat off to the *Carribbee* Islands, did not arrive till the former was sail'd hence again.

C. 17. In the Interval of these Ships returning from *England*, the *English* had a very advantageous Trade with the *Indians;* and might have made much greater Gains of it, and managed it both to the greater Satisfaction of the *Indians*, and the greater Ease and Security of themselves; if they had been under any Rule, or subject to any Method in Trade, and not left at Liberty to outvie or outbid one another; by which they not only cut short their own Profit, but created Jealousies and Disturbances among the *Indians*, by letting one have a better Bargain than another: For they being unaccustom'd to barter, such of them as had been hardest dealt by in their Commodities, thought themselves cheated and abused; and so conceiv'd a Grudge against the *English* in general, making it a National Quarrel: And this seems to be the original Cause of most of their subsequent Misfortunes by the *Indians*.

What also gave a greater Interruption to this Trade, was an Object that drew all their Eyes and Thoughts aside, even from taking the necessary Care for their Preservation, and for the Support of their Lives; which was this; They found in a Neck of Land, on the Back of *James-Town-Island*, a fresh Stream of Water springing out of a small Bank, which wash'd down with it a yellow sort of Dust-Isinglass, which being cleansed by the fresh streaming of the Water, lay shining in the Bottom of that limpid Element, and stirr'd up in them an unseasonable and inordinate Desire after Riches: For they, taking all to be Gold that glister'd, run into the utmost Distraction, neglecting both the necessary Defence of their Lives from the *Indians*, and the Support of their Bodies by securing of Provisions; absolutely relying, like *Midas*, upon the Almighty Power of Gold, thinking, that where this was in plenty nothing could be wanting: But they soon grew sensible of their Error; and found that if this gilded Dirt had been real Gold, it could have been of no Advantage to them. For, by their Negligence, they were reduced to an exceeding Scarcity of Provisions, and that little they had, was lost by the Burning of their Town, while all Hands were employ'd upon this imaginary Golden Treasure; so that they were forced to live for sometime upon the wild Fruits of the Earth, and upon Crabs, Muscles, and such like, not having a Day's Provision before-hand; as some of the laziest *Indians*, who have no Pleasure in Exercise, and won't be at the Pains to fish and hunt: And, indeed, not so well as they neither; For by this careless neglecting of their Defence against the *Indians*, many of 'em were destroy'd by that cruel People; and the Rest durst not venture abroad, but were forced to be content with what fell just into their Mouths.

¶.18. In this Condition they were, when the first Ship of the Two before-mention'd came to their Assistance, but their Golden Dreams overcame all Difficulties: They spoke not, nor thought of any thing but Gold, and that was all the Lading that most of them were willing to take Care for; accordingly they put into this Ship all the yellow Dirt they had gathered, and what Skins and Furs they had trucked for; and filling her up with Cedar, sent her away.

After she was gone, the other Ship arrived, which they stow'd likewise with this supposed Gold-Dust, designing never to be poor again; filling her up with Cedar and Clap-board.

Those Two Ships being thus dispatched, they made several Discoveries in *James* River, and up *Chesapeak* Bay, by the Undertaking and Management of Capt. *John Smith:* And the Year 1608 was the first Year in which they gather'd *Indian* Corn of their own planting.

While these Discoveries were making by Capt. *Smith*, Matters run again into Confusion in *James* Town; and several uneasie People, taking Advantage of his Absence, attempted to desert the Settlement, and run away with the small Vessel that was left to attend upon it; for Capt. *Smith* was the only Man among them that could manage the Discoveries with Success, and he was the only Man too that could keep the Settlement in Order. Thus the *English* continued to give themselves as much Perplexity by their own Distraction, as the *Indians* did by their Watchfulness and Resentments.

¶.19. Anno 1609, *John Laydon* and *Anna Burrows* were marry'd together, the first Christian Marriage in that Part of the World: and the Year following the Plantation was increased to near Five Hundred Men.

This Year *James-Town* sent out People, and made Two other Settlements; One at *Nansamond* in *James-River*, above Thirty Miles below *James-Town*, and the Other at *Powhatan*, Six Miles below the Falls of *James-River*, (which last was bought of *Powhatan* for a certain Quantity of Copper), each Settlement consisting of about a Hundred and Twenty Men. Some small Time after another was made at *Kiquotan* by the Mouth of *James-River*.

CHAP. III.

Shewing what happen'd after the Alteration of the Government from an Elective President to a Commissionated Governour, until the Dissolution of the Company.

¶.20. IN the mean while the Treasurer, Council, and Company of *Virginia* Adventurers in *London*, not finding that Return and Profit from the Adventures they expected; and rightly judging that this Disappointment, as well as the idle Quarrels in the Colony, proceeded from a Mismanage of the Government; petition'd his Majesty, and got a new Patent with Leave to appoint a Governour.

Upon this new Grant they sent out Nine Ships, and plentiful Supplies of Men and Provisions; and made Three Joint Commissioners or Governours in equal Power, *viz.* Sir *Thomas Gates*, Sir *George Summers*, and Capt. *Newport*. They agreed to go all together in one Ship.

This Ship, on Board of which the Three Governours had embarqued, being separated from the Rest, was put to great Distress in a severe Storm; and after Three Days and Nights constant Baling and Pumping, was at last cast Ashore at *Bermudas*, and there staved, but by good Providence the Company was preserved.

Notwithstanding this Shipwreck, and Extremity they were put to, yet could not this common Misfortune make them agree. The Best of it was, they found Plenty of Provisions in that Island, and no *Indians* to annoy them: But still they quarrell'd amongst themselves, and none more than the Two Knights; who made their Parties, built each of them a Cedar Vessel, one call'd the *Patience*, the other the *Deliverance*, and used what they gather'd of the Furniture of the old Ship for Rigging, and Fish-Oil, and Hogs-Grease mix'd with Lime and Ashes instead of Pitch and Tar: For they found great Plenty of *Spanish* Hogs in this Island, which are supposed to have swam ashore from some Wrecks, and there afterwards increased.

¶.21. While these Things were acting in *Bermudas*, Capt. *Smith* being very much burnt by the accidental Firing of some Gun-Powder, as he was upon a Discovery in his Boat, was forced for his Cure sake, and the Benefit of a Surgeon, to take his Passage for *England* in a Ship that was then upon the Point of Sailing.

Several of the Nine Ships that came out with the Three Governours arrived, with many of the Passengers; some of which in their Humours wou'd not submit to the Government there, pretending the New Commission destroy'd the Old one; that Governours were appointed instead of a President, and that they themselves were to be of the Council; and so wou'd assume an independent Power, inspiring the People with Disobedience; by which Means they became frequently exposed in great Parties to the Cruelty of the *Indians;* all sorts of Discipline was laid aside, and their necessary Defence neglected; so that the *Indians* taking Advantage of those Divisions, form'd a Stratagem to destroy them Root and Branch, and indeed they did cut many of 'em off, by massacring whole Companies at a time; so that all the Out-Settlements were deserted, and the People that were not destroy'd took Refuge in *James-Town*, except the small Settlement at *Kiquotan*, where they had built themselves a little Fort, and call'd it *Algernoon* Fort: And yet, for all this, they continued their Disorders, wasting their old Provisions, and neglecting to gather others; so that they who remain'd alive were all near famish'd, having brought themselves to that Pass, that they durst not stir from their own Doors to gather the Fruits of the Earth, or the Crabs and Mussels from the Water-side: Much less to hunt or catch wild Beasts, Fish or Fowl, which were found in great Abundance there. They continued in these scanty Circumstances till they were at last reduced to such Extremity, as to eat the very Hides of their Horses, and the Bodies of the *Indians* they had killed; and sometimes also upon a Pinch they wou'd not disdain to dig them up again to make a homely Meal of after they had been buried. And that Time is to this Day remember'd by the Name of the *Starving Time*.

Thus a few Months indiscreet Management brought such an Infamy upon the Country, that to this Day it cannot be wiped away: And the Sicknesses occasion'd by this bad Diet, or rather want of Diet are unjustly remember'd to the Disadvantage of the Country, as a Fault in the Climate; which was only the Foolishness and Indiscretion of those who assumed the Power of Governing. I call it assumed because the New Commission mention'd, by which they pretended to be of the Council, was not in all this time arrived, but remain'd in *Bermudas* with the new Governours.

Here I can't but admire the Care, Labour, Courage and Understanding that Capt. *John Smith* show'd in the Time of his Administration; who not only founded, but also preserved all these Settlements in good Order, while he was amongst them. And without him, they had certainly all been destroy'd, either by Famine, or the Enemy long before; tho' the Country naturally afforded Subsistance enough, even without any other Labour than that of Gathering and Preserving its Spontaneous Provisions.

For the first Three Years that Capt. *Smith* was with them, they never had in that whole Time above Six Months *English* Provisions. But as soon as he had left 'em to themselves, all went to Ruine; for the *Indians* had no longer any Fear for themselves, or Friendship for the *English*. And Six Months after this Gentleman's Departure, the 500 Men that he left were reduced to Threescore; and they too must of Necessity have starved, if their Relief had been with-held a Week longer.

⟨.22. In the mean time, the Three Governours put to Sea from *Bermudas* in their Two small Vessels, with their Company, to the Number of One Hundred and Fifty, and in Fourteen Days, *viz*. the 25th of *May*, 1610. they arrived both together in *Virginia;* and went with their Vessels up to *James-Town*, where they found the small Remainder of the Five Hundred Men, in that melancholy Way I just now hinted.

⟨.23. Sir *Thomas Gates*, Sir *George Summers*, and Capt. *Newport*, the Governours, were very compassionate of their Condition; and call'd a Council, wherein they inform'd them, that they had but Sixteen Days Provision Aboard; and therefore desired to know their Opinion, whether they would venture to Sea under such a Scarcity: Or if they resolved to continue in the Settlement, and take their Fortunes; they would stay likewise, and share the Provisions among them; but desired that their Determination might be speedy. They soon came to the Conclusion of returning for *England:* But because their Provisions were short, they resolved to go by the Banks of *Newfoundland*, in Hopes of meeting with some of the Fishermen, (this being now the Season) and dividing themselves among their Ships for the greater Certainty of Provision, and for their better Accommodation.

According to this Resolution, they all went aboard, and fell down to *Hog-Island* the 9th of *June* at Night, and the next Morning to *Mulberry-Island* Point, which is Eighteen Miles below *James-Town*, and Thirty above.the Mouth of the River; and there they spied a Long-Boat, which the Lord *Delawar* (who was just arrived with Three Ships) had sent before him up the River sounding the Channel. His Lordship was made sole Governour, and was accompanied by several Gentlemen of Condition. He caused all the Men to return again to *James-Town;* resettled them with Satisfaction, and staid with them till *March* following; and then being very sick, he return'd for *England*, leaving about Two Hundred in the Colony.

¶.24. On the 10th of *May*, 1611, Sir *Thomas Dale* being then made Governour, arriv'd with Three Ships, which brought Supplies of Men, Cattle and Hogs. He found them growing again into the like Disorders as before, taking no Care to plant Corn, and wholly relying upon their Store, which then had but Three Months Provision in it. He therefore set them to work about Corn, and tho' it was the Middle of *May* before they began to prepare the Ground, yet they had an indifferent good Crop.

¶.25. In *August* the same Year Sir *Thomas Gates* arriv'd at *James-Town* with Six Ships more, and with a plentiful Supply of Hogs, Cattle, Fowls, *&c.* with a good Quantity of Ammunition, and all other Things necessary for a new Colony, and besides this a Reinforcement of Three Hundred and Fifty chosen Men. In the Beginning of *September* he settled a new Town at *Arrahattuck*, about Fifty Miles above *James-Town*, Paling in the Neck above Two Miles from the Point, from one Reach of the River to the other. Here he built Forts and Centry-Boxes, and in Honour of *Henry* Prince of *Wales*, call'd it *Henrico*. And also run a Palissado on the other Side of the River at *Coxendale*, to secure their Hogs.

¶.26. *Anno* 1612, Two Ships more arriv'd with Supplies: And Capt. *Argall*,[6] who commanded one of them, being sent in her to *Patowmeck* to buy Corn, he there met with *Pocahontas*, the Excellent Daughter of *Powhatan*; and having prevail'd with her to come Aboard to a Treat, he detain'd her Prisoner, and carried her to *James-Town*, designing to make Peace with her Father by her Release: But on the Contrary, that Prince resented the Affront very highly; and although he loved his Daughter with all imaginable Tenderness, yet he would not be brought to Terms by that unhandsome Treachery; till about Two Years after a Marriage being proposed between Mr. *John Rolfe*, an *English* Gentleman, and this Lady; which *Powhatan* taking to be a sincere Token of Friendship, he vouchsafed to consent to it, and to conclude a Peace.

Intermarriage had been indeed the Method proposed very often by the *Indians* in the Beginning, urging it frequently as a certain Rule, that the *English* were not their Friends, if they refused it. And I can't but think it wou'd have been happy for that Country, had they embraced this Proposal: For, the Jealousie of the *Indians*, which I take to be the Cause of most of the Rapines and Murders they committed, wou'd by this Means have been altogether prevented, and consequently the Abundance of Blood that was shed on both sides wou'd have been saved; the great Extremities they were so often reduced to, by which so many died, wou'd not have happen'd; the Colony, instead of all these Losses of Men on both Sides, wou'd have been encreasing in Children to its Advantage; the Country wou'd have escaped the *Odium* which undeservedly fell upon it, by the Errors and Convulsions in the first Management; and, in all Likelihood, many, if not most, of the *Indians* would have been converted to Christianity by this kind Method; the Country would have been full of People, by the Preservation of the many *Christians* and *Indians* that fell in the Wars between them. Besides, there would have been a Continuance of all those Nations of *Indians* that are now dwindled away to nothing by their frequent Removals, or are fled to other Parts; not to mention the Invitation that so much Success and Prosperity would have been for others to have gone over and settled there, instead of the Frights and Terrors that were produced by all those Misfortunes that happen'd.

¶.27. *Pocahontas* being thus married in the Year 1613, a firm Peace was concluded with her Father, tho' he would not trust himself at her Wedding. Both the *English* and *Indians* thought themselves intirely secure and quiet. This brought in the *Chickahomony Indians* also, tho' not out of any Kindness or Respect to the *English*, but out of Fear of being, by their Assistance, brought under *Powhatan's* absolute Subjection, who used now and then to threaten and tyrannize over them.

¶.28. Sir *Thomas Dale* returning for *England Anno* 1616. took with him Mr. *Rolf* and his Wife *Pocahontas*, who upon the Marriage, was Christen'd, and call'd *Rebecka*. He left Capt. *George Yardly* Deputy-Governour during his Absence, the Country being then intirely at Peace; and arriv'd at *Plimouth* the 12th of *June*.

Capt. *John Smith* was at that Time in *England*, and hearing of the Arrival of *Pocahontas* at *Portsmouth*, used all the Means he could to express his Gratitude to her, as having formerly preserv'd his Life by the Hazard of her own: For, when by the Command of her Father, Capt. *Smith's* Head was upon the Block to have his Brains knock'd out, she saved his Head by laying her's close upon it. He was at that Time suddenly to imbark for *New-England*, and fearing he should sail before she got to *London*, he made an humble Petition to the Queen in her Behalf, which I here choose to give you in his own Words, because it will save me the Story at large.

¶.29.   *Capt.* Smith*'s* PETITION *to Her* Majesty, *in Behalf of* Pocahontas, *Daughter to the* Indian *Emperor* Powhatan.

To the most High and Vertuous Princess, Queen ANNE, of *Great Britain.*

Most Admir'd Madam,

THE Love I bear my God, my King and Country, hath so often embolden'd me in the worst of extream Dangers, that now Honesty doth constrain me to presume thus far beyond my self, to present your Majesty this short Discourse. If Ingratitude be a deadly Poison to all honest Vertues, I must be guilty of that Crime, if I should omit any Means to be thankful.

So it was,

That about Ten Years ago, being in *Virginia,* and taken Prisoner by the Power of *Powhatan,* their chief King, I receiv'd from this great Savage exceeding great Courtesie, especially from his Son *Nantaquaus;* the manliest, comliest, boldest Spirit I ever saw in a Savage; and his Sister *Pocahontas,* the King's most dear and well beloved Daughter, being but a Child of Twelve or Thirteen Years of Age, whose compassionate pitiful Heart of my desperate Estate gave me much Cause to respect her. I being the first *Christian* this proud King and his grim Attendants ever saw, and thus inthrall'd in their barbarous Power; I cannot say I felt the least Occasion of Want, that was in the Power of those my mortal Foes to prevent, notwithstanding all their Threats. After some Six Weeks Fatting amongst those Savage Courtiers, at the Minute of my Execution she hazarded the Beating out of her own Brains to save mine, and not only that, but so prevail'd with her Father, that I was safely conducted to *James-Town,* where I found about Eight and Thirty miserable, poor and sick Creatures to keep Possession for all those large

Territories of *Virginia*. Such was the Weakness of this poor Commonwealth, as had not the Savages fed us, we directly had starv'd.

And this Relief, *most Gracious Queen*, was commonly brought us by this Lady *Pocahontas*, notwithstanding all these Passages, when unconstant Fortune turn'd our Peace to War, this tender Virgin would still not spare to dare to visit us; and by her our Jars have been oft appeased, and our Wants still supplied. Were it the Policy of her Father thus to employ her, or the Ordinance of God thus to make her His Instrument, or her extraordinary Affection to our Nation, I know not: But of this I am sure, when her Father, with the utmost of his Policy and Power, sought to surprize me, having but Eighteen with me, the dark Night could not affright her from coming through the irksome Woods, and, with water'd Eyes, give me Intelligence, with her best Advice to escape his Fury; which had he known, he had surely slain her.

James-Town, with her wild Train, she as freely frequented as her Father's Habitation; and during the time of Two or Three Years, she, next under God, was still the Instrument to preserve this Colony from Death, Famine, and utter Confusion, which if, in those Times, had once been dissolv'd, *Virginia* might have lain, as it was at our first Arrival, till this Day. Since then, this Business having been turn'd and varied by many Accidents from what I left it, it is most certain, after a long and troublesome War, since my Departure, betwixt her Father and our Colony, all which Time she was not heard of, about Two Years after she herself was taken Prisoner, being so detain'd near Two Years longer, the Colony by that Means was reliev'd, Peace concluded, and at last, rejecting her barbarous Condition, she was married to an *English* Gentleman, with whom at this Present she is in *England*. The first *Christian* ever of that Nation: The first *Virginian* ever spake *English*, or had a

Child in Marriage by an *English* Man. A Matter surely, if my Meaning be truly consider'd and well understood, worthy a Prince's Information.

Thus, *most Gracious Lady*, I have related to your Majesty what at your best Leisure our approv'd Histories will recount to you at large, as done in the Time of your Majesty's Life: And, however this might be presented you from a more worthy Pen, it cannot from a more honest Heart.

As yet I never begg'd any thing of the State, or any; and it is my want of Ability, and her exceeding Desert; your Birth, Means and Authority; her Birth, Vertue, Want and Simplicity, doth make me thus bold, humbly to beseech your Majesty to take this Knowledge of her, tho' it be from one so unworthy to be the Reporter as my self: Her Husband's Estate not being able to make her fit to attend your Majesty.

The most and least I can do, is to tell you this, and the rather because of her being of so great a Spirit, however her Stature. If she should not be well receiv'd, seeing this Kingdom may rightly have a Kingdom by her Means; her present Love to us, and Christianity, might turn to such Scorn and Fury, as to divert all this Good to the worst of Evil: Where finding that so Great a Queen should do her more Honour than she can imagine, for having been kind to her Subjects and Servants, 'twou'd so ravish her with Content, as to endear her dearest Blood to effect that your Majesty and all the King's honest Subjects most earnestly desire. And so I humbly kiss your gracious Hands, *&c.*

(Sign'd)

Dated June, *1616.*   *John Smith.*

¶.30. This Account was presented to her Majesty, and graciously received: But before Captain *Smith* sail'd for *New-England*, the *Indian* Princess arrived at *London*, and her Husband took Lodgings for her at *Branford*, to be a little out of the Smoak of the City, whither Capt. *Smith*, with some of her Friends, went to see her, and congratulate her Arrival, letting her know the Address he had made to the Queen in her Favour.

Till this Lady arrived in *England*, she had all along been inform'd that Capt. *Smith* was dead, because he had been diverted from that Colony by making Settlements in the Second Plantation, now call'd *New-England:* For which Reason, when she see him, she seem'd to think herself much affronted, for that they had dared to impose so gross an Untruth upon her, and at first Sight of him turn'd away. It cost him a great deal of Intreaty, and some Hours Attendance, before she would do him the Honour to speak to him: But at last she was reconcil'd, and talk'd freely to him. She put him in mind of her former Kindnesses, and then upbraided him for his Forgetfulness of her, shewing by her Reproaches, that even a State of Nature teaches to abhor Ingratitude.

She had in her Retinue a Great Man of her own Nation, whose Name was *Uttamaccomack:* This Man had Orders from *Powhatan*, to count the People in *England*, and give him an Account of their Number. Now the *Indians* having no Letters among them, he at his going ashore provided a Stick, in which he was to make a Notch for every Man he see; but this Accomptant soon grew weary of that tedious Exercise, and threw his Stick away: And at his return, being asked by his King, *How many People there were;* He desired him to count the Stars in the Sky, the Leaves upon the Trees, and the Sand on the Seashore, for so many People (he said) were in England.

⁋.31. *Pocahontas* had many Honours done her by the Queen upon Account of Capt. *Smith's* Story; and being introduced by the Lady *Delawarr*, she was frequently admitted to wait on her Majesty, and was publickly treated as a Prince's Daughter; she was carried to many Plays, Balls, and other publick Entertainments, and very respectfully receiv'd by all the Ladies about the Court. Upon all which Occasions she behaved her self with so much Decency, and show'd so much Grandure in her Deportment, that she made good the brightest Part of the Character Capt. *Smith* had given of her. In the mean while she gain'd the good Opinion of every Body, so much that the poor Gentleman her Husband had like to have been call'd to an Account for presuming to marry a Princess Royal without the King's Consent; because it had been suggested that he had taken Advantage of her being a Prisoner, and forc'd her to marry him. But upon a more perfect Representation of the Matter, his Majesty was pleased at last to declare himself satisfied.

Every Body paid this young Lady all imaginable Respect; and it is supposed, she wou'd have sufficiently acknowledged those Favours, had she lived to return to her own Country, by bringing the *Indians* to have a kinder Disposition towards the *English*. But upon her Return she was unfortunately taken ill at *Gravesend*, and died in a few Days after, giving great Testimony all the Time she lay sick, of her being a very good Christian. She left Issue one Son, nam'd *Thomas Rolfe*, whose Posterity is at this Day in good Repute in *Virginia*.

₡.32. Captain *Yardly* made but a very ill Governour, he let the Buildings and Forts go to Ruine; not regarding the Security of the People against the *Indians*, neglecting the Corn, and applying all Hands to plant Tobacco, which promised the most immediate Gain. In this Condition they were when Capt. *Samuel Argall* was sent thither Governour, *Anno* 1617. who found the Number of People reduc'd to something more than Four Hundred, of which not above Half were fit for Labour. In the mean while the *Indians* mixing among 'em, got Experience daily in Fire-Arms, and some of 'em were instructed therein by the *English* themselves, and em-

ploy'd to hunt and kill wild Fowl for them. So great
was their Security upon this Marriage: But Governour
Argall not liking those Methods, regulated them on his
Arrival, and Capt. *Yardly* return'd to *England*.

℄.33. Governour *Argall* made the Colony flourish and
increase wonderfully, and kept them in great Plenty
and Quiet. The next Year, *viz.* Anno 1618, the Lord
Delawarr was sent over again with Two Hundred Men
more for the Settlement, with other Necessaries suitable: But Sailing by the Western Islands, they met with
contrary Winds, and great Sickness; so that about Thirty
of them died, among which the Lord *Delawarr* was one.
By which Means the Government there still continued
in the Hands of Capt. *Argall*.

℄.34. *Powhatan* died in *April* the same Year, leaving his
Second Brother *Itopatin* in Possession of his Empire, a
Prince far short of the Parts of *Oppechancanough*, who by
some was said to be his Elder Brother, and then King of
Chickahomony; but he having debauch'd them from the
Allegiance of *Powhatan*, was disinherited by him. This
Oppechancanough was a cunning and a brave Prince, who
soon grasp'd all the Empire to himself: But at first they
jointly renew'd the Peace with the *English*, upon the
Accession of *Itopatin* to the Crown.

℄.35. Governour *Argall* flourishing thus under the
Blessings of Peace and Plenty, and having no Occasion
of Fear or Disturbance from the *Indians*, sought new
Occasions of incouraging the Plantation. To that End
he intended a Coasting Voyage to the Northward, to
view the Places where the *English* Ships had so often
laded; and if he miss'd them, to reach the Fisheries on
the Banks of *Newfoundland*, and so settle a Trade and
Correspondence either with the One or the Other. In Ac-
complishing whereof, as he touch'd at Cape *Codd*, he

was inform'd by the *Indians*, That some White People like him were come to inhabit to the Northward of them, upon the Coast of their Neighbouring Nations. Capt. *Argall* not having heard of any *English* Plantation that Way, was jealous that it might be (as it proved) the People of some other Nation. And being very zealous for the Honour and Benefit of *England*, he resolved to make Search according to the Information he had receiv'd, and see who they were. Accordingly he found the Settlement, and a Ship riding before it. This belong'd to some *French* Men, who had fortified themselves upon a small Mount in the North of *New-England*.

☾.36. His unexpected Arrival so confounded the *French*, that they cou'd make no Preparation for Resistance on Board their Ship; which Captain *Argall* drew so close to, that with his small Arms he beat all the Men from the Deck, so that they cou'd not use their Guns, their Ship having only a single Deck. Among others, there were Two Jesuits on Board, one of which being more bold than wise, with all that Disadvantage, endeavor'd to fire one of their Cannon, and was shot dead for his Pains.

Capt. *Argall* having taken the Ship, landed and went before the Fort, summoning it to surrender. The Garrison ask'd Time to advise: But that being denied them, they stole privately away, and fled into the Woods. Upon this Capt. *Argall* enter'd the Fort, and lodged there that Night; and the next Day the *French* came to him, and surrender'd themselves. It seems the King of *France* had granted them a Patent for this Settlement, but they gave it up to Capt. *Argall* to be cancell'd. He used them very well, and suffer'd such as had a Mind to return to *France*, to seek their Passage among the Ships of the Fishery: But obliged them to desert this Settlement. And those that were willing to go to *Virginia*, he took with him.

¶.37. These People were under the Conduct of Two Jesuits, who upon taking a Pique against their Governour in *Acadia*, named *Biencourt*, had lately separated from a *French* Settlement at *Port-Royal*, lying in the Bay, upon the South-West Part of *Acadia*.

¶.38. As Governour *Argall* was about to return to *Virginia*, Father *Biard*, the surviving Jesuit (out of Malice to *Biencourt*) told him of this *French* Settlement at *Port-Royal*, and offer'd to Pilot him to it; which Governour *Argall* readily accepted of. With the same Ease he took that Settlement also; where the *French* had sow'd and reap'd, built Barns, Mills, and other Conveniencies, which Capt. *Argall* did no Damage to: But unsettled them, and obliged them to make a Desertion from thence. He gave these the same Leave he had done the Others to dispose of themselves; some whereof return'd to *France*, and others went to settle up the River of *Canada*. After this Governour *Argall* return'd satisfied with the Provision and Plunder he had got in those Two Settlements.

¶.39. The Report of these Exploits soon reach'd *England*; and whether they were approved or no, being acted without particular Direction, I have not learn'd: But certain it is, that in *April* following there arrived a small Vessel, which did not stay for any Thing, but took on Board Governour *Argall*, and return'd for *England*. He left Captain *Nathaniel Powell* Deputy: And soon after Captain *Yardly* being Knighted, was sent Governour thither again.

¶.40. Very great Supplies of Cattle and other Provisions were sent there that Year, and likewise 1000 or 1200 Men. They resettled all their old Plantations that had been deserted, made Additions to the Number of the Council, and call'd an Assembly of Burgesses from all

Parts of the Country, which were to be elected by the People in their several Plantations.

These Burgesses met the Governour and Council at *James-Town* in *May*, 1620,[7] and sate in Consultation in the same House with them, as the Method of the *Scots* Parliament is, debating Matters for the Improvement and good Government of the Country.

This was the First General Assembly that ever was held there. I heartily wish, tho' they did not unite their Houses again, they wou'd however unite their Endeavours and Affections for the Good of the Country.

⁋.41. In *August* following a *Dutch* Man of War landed Twenty *Negroes* for Sale;[8] which were the First of that kind that were carried into the Country.

⁋.42. This Year they bounded the Corporations, (as they call'd them:) But there does not remain among the Records any one Grant of these Cor[po]rations. There is enter'd a Testimony of Governour *Argall*, concerning the Bounds of the Corporation of *James* City, declaring his Knowledge thereof; and this is in one of the New transcribed Books of Records: But there is not to be found one Word of the Charter or Patent it self of this Corporation.

Then also they apportion'd and laid out Lands in several Allotments, *viz.* to the Company in several Places, to the Governour, to a College, to *Glebes*, and to several particular Persons; many new Settlements were made in *James* and *York* Rivers. The People now knew their own Property, and having the Encouragement of Working for their own Advantage, many became very industrious, and began to vie one with another, in Planting, Building, and other Improvements. Two Gentlemen went over as Deputies to the Company, for the Management of their Lands, and those of the College. All Thoughts of Danger from the *Indians* were laid aside. Several great

Gifts were made to the Church and College, and for the Bringing up Young *Indians* at School. Forms were made, and Rules appointed for granting Patents for Land, upon the Condition of importing Goods and Persons to supply and increase the Colony. And all there then began to think themselves the happiest People in the World.

¶.43. Thus *Virginia* continued to flourish and increase, great Supplies continually arriving, and new Settlements being made all over the Country. A Salt-Work was set up at Cape *Charles*, on the Eastern Shore; and an Iron-Work at *Falling-Creek*, in *James* River, where they made Proof of good Iron Oar, and brought the whole Work so near Perfection, that they writ Word to the Company in *London*, that they did not doubt but to finish the Work, and have plentiful Provision of Iron for them by the next *Easter*. At that time the Fame of the Plenty and Riches in which the *English* lived there, was very great: and Sir *George Yardly* now had all the Appearance of making Amends for the Errors of his former Government. Nevertheless he let them run into the same Sleepyness and Security as before, neglecting all Thoughts of a necessary Defence, which laid the Foundation of the following Calamities.

¶.44. But the Time of his Government being near expired, Sir *Francis Wyat*, then a young Man, had a Commission to succeed him. The People began to grow numerous, Thirteen Hundred settling there that Year; which was the Occasion of making so much Tobacco, as to overstock the Market. Wherefore his Majesty, out of Pity to the Country, sent his Commands, That they should not suffer their Planters to make above One Hundred Pounds of Tobacco *per* Man; for the Market was so low, that he cou'd not afford to give 'em above Three Shillings the Pound for it. He advised them rather to turn their spare Time towards providing Corn and Stock, and towards the Making of Potash, or other Manufactures.

It was, *October*, 1621, that Sir *Francis Wyat* arrived Governour, and in *November* Capt. *Newport* arrived with Fifty Men imported at his own Charge, besides Passengers; and made a Plantation on *Newport's News*, naming it after himself. The Governour made a Review of all the Settlements, and suffer'd new Ones to be made even as far [as] *Patowmeck* River. This ought to be observed of the Eastern Shore *Indians*, that they never gave the *English* any Trouble, but courted and befriended them from first to last. Perhaps the *English*, by the Time they came to settle those Parts, had consider'd how to rectifie their former Mismanagement, and learn'd better Methods of regulating their Trade with the *Indians*, and of treating them more kindly than at first.

ℭ.45. *Anno*, 1622, Inferior Courts were first appointed by the General Assembly, under the Name of *County Courts*, for Tryal of Minute Causes; the Governour and Council still remaining Judges of the Supream Court of the Colony. In the mean time, by the great Increase of People, and the long Quiet they had enjoy'd among the *Indians*, since the Marriage of *Pocahontas*, and the Accession of *Oppechancanough* to the Imperial Crown; all Men were lull'd into a fatal Security, and became every where familiar with the *Indians*, Eating, Drinking and Sleeping amongst them; by which Means they became perfectly acquainted with all our *English* Strength, and the Use of our Arms: Knowing at all Times, when and where to find our People; whether at Home, or in the Woods; in Bodies, or disperst; in Condition of Defence, or indefencible. This Exposing of their Weekness gave them Occasion to think more contemptibly of them, than otherwise, perhaps, they would have done; for which Reason they became more peevish, and more hardy to attempt any thing against them.

€.46. Thus upon the Loss of one of their leading Men, (a War Captain, as they call him,) who was likewise supposed to be justly kill'd, *Oppechancanough* took Affront, and in Revenge laid the Plot of a general Massacre of the *English*, to be executed on the 22d of *March*, 1622, a little before Noon, at a Time when our Men were all at Work abroad in their Plantations, disperst and unarm'd. This Hellish Contrivance was to take Effect upon all the several Settlements at one and the same Instant, except on the Eastern Shore, whither this Plot did not reach. The *Indians* had been made so familiar with the *English*, as to borrow their Boats and Canoes to cross the Rivers in, when they went to consult with their Neighbouring *Indians* upon this execrable Conspiracy. And, to colour their Design the better, they brought Presents of Deer, Turkies, Fish and Fruits to the *English* the Evening before. The very Morning of the Massacre, they came freely and unarm'd among them, eating with them, and behaving themselves with the same Freedom and Friendship as formerly, till the very Minute they were to put their Plot in Execution. Then they fell to Work all at once every where, knocking the *English* unawares on the Head, some with their Hatchets, which they call *Tommahauks*, others with the Hows and Axes of the *English* themselves, shooting at those who escap'd the Reach of their Hands; sparing neither Age nor Sex, but destroying Man, Woman and Child, according to their cruel Way of leaving none behind to bear Resentment. But whatever was not done by Surprize that Day, was left undone, and many that made early Resistance escaped.

By the Account taken of the *Christians* murder'd that Morning, they were found to be Three Hundred Forty Seven, most of them falling by their own Instruments, and Working-Tools.

€.47. The Massacre had been much more general, had

not this Plot been providentially discover'd to the *English* some Hours before the Execution. It happen'd thus:

Two *Indians* that used to be employ'd by the *English* to hunt for them, happen'd to lie together, the Night before the Massacre, in an *English* Man's House, where one of them was employ'd. The *Indian* that was the Guest fell to perswading the other to rise and kill his Master, telling him, that he would do the same by his own the next Day. Whereupon he discover'd the whole Plot that was design'd to be executed on the Morrow. But the other, instead of entering into the Plot, and murdering his Master, got up (under Pretence of going to execute his Comrade's Advice) went into his Master's Chamber, and reveal'd to him the whole Story that he had been told. The Master hereupon arose, secur'd his own House, and before Day got to *James-Town*, which, together with such Plantations as cou'd receive Notice time enough, was saved by this Means; the rest, as they happen'd to be watchful in their Defence, also escaped: But such as were surpriz'd, were massacred. Captain *Croshaw* in his Vessel at *Patowmeck*, had Notice also given him by a young *Indian*, by which means he came off untouch'd.

¶.48. The Occasion upon which *Oppechancanough* took Affront was this. The War Captain mention'd before to have been kill'd, was called *Nemattanow*. He was an active *Indian*, a great Warriour, and in much Esteem among them; so much, that they believed him to be invulnerable, and immortal, because he had been in very many Conflicts, and escaped untouch'd from them all. He was also a very cunning Fellow, and took great Pride in preserving and increasing this their Superstition concerning him, affecting every thing that was odd and prodigious to work upon their Admiration. For which Purpose he wou'd often dress himself up with Feathers after a fantastick Manner, and by much Use of that Ornament, obtain'd among the *English* the Nickname of *Jack of the Feather*.

This *Nemattanow* coming to a private Settlement of one *Morgan*, who had several Toys which he had a mind to, perswaded him to go to *Pamunky* to dispose of them. He gave him Hopes what mighty Bargains he might meet with there, and kindly offer'd him his Assistance. At last *Morgan* yielded to his Perswasion: But was no more heard of; and it is believ'd, that *Nemattanow* kill'd him by the Way, and took away his Treasure. For within a few Days, this *Nemattanow* return'd to the same House with *Morgan's* Cap upon his Head; where he found Two sturdy Boys, who ask'd for their Master. He very frankly told them, he was dead. But they, knowing the Cap again, suspected the Villain had kill'd their Master, and wou'd have had him before a Justice of Peace: But he refused to go, and very insolently abused them. Whereupon they shot him down, and as they were carrying him to the Governour, he died.

As he was dying, he earnestly press'd the Boys to promise him Two Things; First, That they wou'd not tell how he was kill'd; and, Secondly, That they wou'd bury him among the *English*. So great was the Pride of this vain Heathen, that he had no other Thoughts at his Death, but the Ambition of being esteem'd after he was dead, as he had endeavour'd to make them believe of him while he was alive, *viz*. That he was Invulnerable and Immortal; tho' his increasing Faintness convinc'd himself of the Falsity of both. He imagined that being buried among the *English*, perhaps, might conceal his Death from his own Nation, who might think him translated to some happier Country. Thus he pleased himself to the last Gasp with the Boys Promises to carry on the Delusion. This was reckon'd all the Provocation given to that haughty and revengeful Man *Oppechancanough*, to act this bloody Tragedy, and to take indefatigable Pains to engage in so horrid Villany all the Kings and Nations bordering upon the *English* Settlements, on the Western Shore of *Chesepeak*.

❡.49. This gave the *English* a fair Pretence of endeavouring the total Extirpation of the *Indians*, but more-especially of *Oppec[h]ancanough*, and his Nation. Accordingly they set themselves about it, making use of the *Roman* Maxim, (*Faith is not to be kept with Hereticks*) to obtain their Ends. For, after some Months fruitless Pursuit of them, who cou'd too dexterously hide themselves in the Woods, the *English* pretended Articles of Peace, giving them all manner of fair Words and Promises of Oblivion. They design'd thereby (as their own Letters now on Record, and their own Actions thereupon, prove) to draw the *Indians* back, and intice them to plant their Corn on their Habitations nearest adjoining to the *English;* and then to cut it up when the Summer should be too far spent to leave them Hopes of another Crop that Year; by which Means they proposed to bring them to want Necessaries, and starve. And the *English* did so far accomplish their Ends, as to bring the *Indians* to plant their Corn at their usual Habitations, whereby they gain'd an Opportunity of repaying them some part of the Debt in their own Coin; for they fell suddenly upon them, cut to Pieces such of them as could not make their Escape, and afterwards totally destroy'd their Corn.

❡.50. Another Effect of the Massacre of the *English*, was the Reducing all their Settlements again to Six or Seven in Number, for their better Defence. Besides, it was such a Disheartening to some good Projects, then just advancing, that to this Day they have never been put in Execution, namely, the Glass-Houses in *James-Town*, and the Iron-Work at *Falling-Creek*, which has been already mention'd. The Massacre fell so hard upon this last Place, that no Soul was saved, but a Boy and a Girl, who, with great Difficulty, hid themselves.

The Superintendent of this Iron-Work had also discover'd a Vein of Lead Oar, which he kept private, and made use of it to furnish all the Neighbours with Bullets and Shot. But he being cut off with the rest, and the Secret not having been communicated, this Lead Mine could never after be found; till Colonel *Byrd*,[9] some few Years ago, prevail'd with an *Indian*, under Pretence of Hunting, to give him a Sign, by dropping his *Tomahawk* at the Place, (he not daring publickly to discover it, for fear of being murder'd.) The Sign was accordingly given, and the Company at that Time found several Pieces of good Lead Oar upon the Surface of the Ground, and mark'd the Trees thereabouts: Notwithstanding which, I know not by what Witchcraft it happens, but no Mortal to this Day could ever find that Place again, tho' it be upon part of the Colonel's own Possessions. And so it rests, till Time and thicker Settlements discover it.

¶.51. Thus the Company of Adventurers having, by those frequent Acts of Mismanagement, met with vast Losses and Misfortunes; Many grew sick of it, and parted with their Shares; and others came into their Places, and promoted the sending in fresh Recruits of Men and Goods. But the chief Design of all Parties concern'd was to fetch away the Treasure from thence, aiming more at sudden Gain, than to form any regular Colony, or establish a Settlement in such a Manner, as to make it a lasting Happiness to the Country.

Several Gentlemen went over upon their particular Stocks, separate from that of the Company, with their own Servants and Goods, each designing to obtain Land from the Government, as Capt. *Newport* had done; or, at least, to obtain Patents according to the Regulation for granting Lands to Adventurers. Others sought their Grants of the Company in *London*, and obtain'd Authorities and Jurisdictions, as well as Land, distinct from the Authority of the Government, which was the Foundation of great Disorder, and the Occasion of their following Misfortunes. Among others, one Capt. *Martin*, having made very considerable Preparations towards a Settlement, obtain'd a suitable Grant of Land, and was made of the Council there. But he grasping still at more, hanker'd after Dominion, as well as Possession, and caused so many Differences, that at last he put all Things into Distraction; insomuch, that the *Indians*, still seeking Revenge, took Advantage of these Dissentions, and fell foul again of the *English*, gratifying their Vengence with new Blood-shed.

¶.52. The fatal Consequences of the Company's Male-Administration cried so loud, that King *Charles* the First, coming to the Crown of *England*, had a tender Concern for the poor People that had been betray'd thither, and lost. Upon which Consideration he dissolv'd the Company in the Year 1626,[10] reducing the Country and Government into his own immediate Direction, appointing the Governor and Council himself, and ordering all Patents and Process to issue in his own Name; reserving only to himself an easie Quit-Rent of Two Shillings for every Hundred Acres of Land, and so *pro rato*.

CHAP. IV.

Containing the History of the Goverment from the Dissolution of the Company, to the year 1704.

§.53. THE Country being thus taken into the King's Hands, his Majesty was pleased to establish the Constitution to be by a Governour, Council and Assembly, and to confirm the former Methods and Jurisdictions of the several Courts, as they had been appointed in the Year 1620, and placed the last Resort in the Assembly. He likewise confirm'd the Rules and Orders made by the first Assembly for apportioning the Land, and granting Patents to particular Adventurers.

§.54. This was a Constitution according to their Hearts Desire, and Things seem'd now to go on in a happy Course for Encouragement of the Colony. People flock'd over thither apace; every one took up Land by Patent to his Liking; and, not minding any thing but to be Masters of great Tracts of Land, they planted themselves separately on their several Plantations. Nor did they fear the *Indians*, but kept them at a greater Distance than formerly: And they for their Parts, seeing the *English* so sensibly increase in Number, were glad to keep their Distance, and be peaceable.

This Liberty of taking up Land, and the Ambition each Man had of being Lord of a vast, tho' unimprov'd Territory, together with the Advantage of the many Rivers, which afforded a commodious Road for Shipping at every Man's Door, has made the Country fall into such an unhappy Settlement and Course of Trade; that to this Day they have not any one Place of Cohabitation among them, that may reasonably bear the Name of a Town.

€.55. The Constitution being thus firmly established, and continuing its Course regularly for some time, People began to lay aside all Fears of any future Misfortune. Several Gentlemen of Condition went over with their whole Families; some for bettering their Estates; others for· Religion, and other Reasons best known to themselves. Among those, that Noble *Cæcilius Calvert*, Lord *Baltemore*, a Roman Catholick, thought for the more quiet Exercise of his Religion to retire, with his Family, into that new World. For this Purpose he went to *Virginia*, to try how he liked the Place: But the People there look'd upon him with an evil Eye, on Account of his Religion, for which alone he sought this Retreat; and by their ill Treatment, discouraged him from settling in that Country.

€.56. Upon that Provocation, his Lordship resolv'd upon a further Adventure. And finding Land enough up the Bay of *Chesapeak*, which was likewise bless'd with many brave Rivers, and as yet altogether uninhabited by the *English;* he began to think of making a new Plantation of his own. And for his more certain Direction in obtaining a Grant of it, he undertook a Journey Northward, to discover the Land up the Bay, and observe what might most conveniently square with his Intent.

His Lordship finding all Things in this Discovery according to his Wish, return'd to *England*. And because the *Virginia* Settlements at that Time reached no further than the South Side of *Patowmeck* River, his Lordship got a Grant of the Propriety of *Maryland*, bounding it to the South by *Patowmeck* River, on the Western Shore, and by an East Line from Point *Look-out*, on the

Eastern Shore: But died himself before he could embark for the promised Land.

Maryland had the Honour to receive its Name from Queen *Mary*, Royal Consort to King *Charles* the First.

¶.57. The old Lord *Baltemore* being thus taken off, and leaving his Designs unfinish'd, his Son and Heir, in the Year 1633, obtain'd a Confirmation of the Patent to himself, and went over in Person to plant his new Colony.

By this unhappy Accident, a Country which Nature had so well contriv'd for one, became Two seperate Governments. This produced a most unhappy Inconvenience to both; for, these Two being the only Countries under the Dominion of *England*, that plant Tobacco in any Quantity, the Consequence of that Division is, that when one Colony goes about to prohibit the Trash of that Commodity, to help the Market; then the other, to take Advantage of that Market, pours into *England* all they can make, both good and bad, without Distinction. This is very injurious to the other Colony, which had voluntarily suffer'd so great a Diminution in the Quantity to mend the Quality.

¶.58. Neither was this all the Mischief that happen'd to poor *Virginia* upon this Grant; for the Example of it had dreadful Consequences, and was in the End one of the Occasions of another Massacre by the *Indians*. For this Precedent of my Lord *Baltemore's* Grant, which intrench'd upon the Charters and Bounds of *Virginia*, was Hint enough for other Courtiers, (who never intended a Settlement, as my Lord did) to find out something of the same kind to make Money of. This was the Occasion of several very large Defalcations from *Virginia* within a few Years afterwards; which were forwarded and assisted by the Contrivance of the Governour Sir *John Harvey*. Insomuch, that not only the Land it self, Quit-Rents and all: But the Authorities and Jurisdictions that belonged to that Colony, were given away; nay, sometimes in those unjust Grants he included the very Settlements that had been before made; countenancing them with the usual Pretence of his Majesty's Instructions.

€.59. As this Gentleman was irregular in this, so he was very unjust and arbitrary in his other Methods of Government. He improved the Fines and Penalties, which the unwary Assemblies of those Times had given chiefly to himself. He was so haughty and furious to the Council, and to the best Gentlemen of the Country, that his Tyranny grew at last unsupportable; so that in the Year 1639, the Council sent him a Prisoner to *London*, and with him Two of their Number to maintain the Articles against him. This News being brought to King *Charles* the First, his Majesty was very much displeased; and, without hearing any thing, caused him to return Governour again: But by the next Shipping he was graciously pleased to change him; and so made Amends for this Man's Male-Administration, by sending in the good and just Sir *William Berkeley* to succeed him.[11]

€.60. While these Things were transacting, there was so general a Dissatisfaction, occasion'd by the Oppressions of Sir *John Harvey*, and the Difficulties in getting him out; that the whole Colony was in Confusion. The subtle *Indians*, who took all Advantages, resented the Incroachments upon them by his Grants. They see the *English* uneasie and disunited among themselves, and by the Direction of *Oppecancanough* their King, laid the Ground-work of another Massacre; wherein by Surprize they cut off near Five Hundred Christians more. But this Execution did not take so general Effect as formerly; because the *Indians* were not so frequently suffer'd to come among the inner Habitations of the *English*. And therefore the Massacre fell severest on the South-side of *James* River, and on the Heads of the other Rivers; but chiefly of *York* River, where the Emperor *Oppechancanough* kept the Seat of his Government.

¶.61. This *Oppechancanough* was a Man of large Stature, noble Presence, and extraordinary Parts. Tho' he had no Advantage of Literature, (that being no where to be found among the *Indians*,) yet he was perfectly skill'd in the Art of Governing his rude Country-men. He caused all the *Indians* far and near to dread his Name, and had them all entirely in Subjection.

This King in *Smith's* History is call'd Brother to *Powhatan*, but by the *Indians* he was not so esteem'd. For they say he was a Prince of a Foreign Nation, and came to them a great Way from the South-West: And by their Accounts, we suppose him to have come from the *Spanish Indians*, some-where near *Mexico*, or the Mines of St. *Barbe:* But, be that Matter how it will, from that Time till his Captivity, there never was the least Truce between them and the *English*.

¶.62. Sir *William Berkeley*, upon his Arrival, show'd such an Opposition to the unjust Grants made by Sir *John Harvey*, that very few of them took Effect; and such as did, were subjected to the settled Conditions of the other Parts of the Government, and made liable to the Payment of the full Quit-Rents. He encouraged the Country in several Essays of Pot-Ash, Soap, Salt, Flax, Hemp, Silk and Cotton. But the *Indian* War ensuing upon *Oppechancanough's* Massacre, was a great Obstruction to these good Designs, by requiring all the spare Men to be employ'd in Defence of the Country.

¶.63. *Oppechancanough*, by his great Age, and the Fatigues of War, (in which Sir *William Berkeley* follow'd him close) was now grown so decrepit, that he was not able to walk alone; but was carried about by his Men, where-ever he had a Mind to move. His Flesh was all macerated, his Sinews slacken'd, and his Eye-lids became so heavy, that he could not see, but as they were lifted up by his Servants. In this low Condition he was, when Sir *William Berkeley* hearing that he was at some Distance from his usual Habitation, resolved at all Adventures to seize his Person, which he happily effected. For, with a Party of Horse he made a speedy March, surprized him in his Quarters, and brought him Prisoner to *James-Town;* where, by the Governour's Command, he was treated with all the Respect and Tenderness imaginable. Sir *William* had a mind to send him to *England*, hoping to get Reputation, by presenting his Majesty with a Royal Captive; who at his Pleasure, could call into the Field Ten times more *Indians* than Sir *William Berkeley* had *English* in his whole Government. Besides, he thought this ancient Prince wou'd be an Instance of the Healthiness and long Life of the Natives of that Country. However, he could not preserve his Life above a Fortnight; For one of the Soldiers, resenting the Calamities the Colony had suffer'd by this Prince's Means, basely shot him thro' the Back, after he was made Prisoner; of which Wound he died.

He continued brave to the last Moment of his Life, and show'd not the least Dejection at his Captivity. He heard one Day a great Noise of the Treading of People about him; upon which he caused his Eye-lids to be lifted up; and finding that a Crowd of People were let in to see him, he call'd in high Indignation for the Governour; who being come, *Oppechancanough* scornfully told him, That had it been his Fortune to take Sir *William Berkeley* Prisoner, he should not meanly have exposed him as a Show to the People.

¶.64. After this, Sir *William Berkeley* made a new Peace with the *Indians*, which continued for a long time unviolated; insomuch, that all the Thoughts of future Injury from them were laid aside. But he himself did not long enjoy the Benefit of this profound Peace: For, the unhappy Troubles of King *Charles* the First encreasing in *England*, proved a great Disturbance to him and to all the People. They, to prevent the Infection from reaching that Country, made severe Laws against the *Puritans*, tho' there were as yet none among them. But all Correspondence with *England* was interrupted, the Supplies lessen'd, and Trade obstructed. In a Word, all People were impatient to know what would be the Event of so much Confusion.

¶.65. At last the King was traiterously beheaded in *England*, and *Oliver* install'd Protector. However, his Authority was not acknowledged in *Virginia* for several Years after, till they were forced to it by the last Necessity. For in the Year 1651, by *Cromwell*'s Command, Capt. *Dennis*,[12] with a Squadron of Men of War, arriv'd there from the *Carribbee* Islands, where they had been subduing *Bar[ba]dos*. The Country at first held out vigorously against him; and Sir *William Berkeley*, by the Assistance of such *Dutch* Vessels as were then there, made a brave Resistance. But at last *Dennis* contriv'd a Stratagem, which betray'd the Country. He had got a considerable Parcel of Goods aboard, which belong'd to Two of the Council; and found a Method of informing them of it. By this means they were reduced to the *Dilemma* either of submitting, or losing their Goods. This occasion'd Factions among them; so that at last, after the Surrender of all the other *English* Plantations, Sir *William* was forced to submit to the Usurper on the Terms of a general Pardon. However, it ought to be remember'd, to his Praise, and to the immortal Honour of that Colony, that it was the last of all the King's Dominions that submitted to the Usurpation, and afterwards the first that cast it off.

¶.66. *Oliver* had no sooner subdued the Plantations; but he began to contrive how to keep them under, that so they might never be able for the Time to come to give him further Trouble. To this End he thought it necessary to break off their Correspondence with all other Nations; thereby to prevent their being furnish'd with Arms, Ammunition, and other Warlike Provisions. According to this Design, he contrived a severe Act of Parliament, whereby he prohibited the Plantations from receiving or exporting any *European* Commodities, but what should be carried to them by *English* Men, and in *English* built Ships. They were absolutely forbid corresponding with any Nation or Colony, not subject to the Crown of *England*. Neither was any Alien suffer'd to manage a Trade or Factory in any of them. In all which Things the Plantations had been till then indulged, for their Encouragement.

¶.67. Notwithstanding this Act of Navigation, the Protector never thought the Plantations enough secured; but frequently changed their Governours, to prevent their intriguing with the People. So that during the small time of his Protectorship, they had no less than Three Governours there, namely, *Diggs*, *Bennet* and *Mathews*.[13]

¶.68. The strange Arbitrary Curbs he put upon the Plantations, exceedingly afflicted the People. He had the Inhumanity to forbid them all manner of Trade and Correspondence with other Nations, at a Time when *England* it self was in Distraction; and could neither take off their Commodities, nor supply them sufficiently with its own. Neither had they ever been used to supply them with half the Commodities they expended, or to take off above half the Tobacco they made. Such violent Proceedings made the People desperate, and inspired them with a Desire to use the last Remedy, to relieve themselves from his Lawless Usurpation. In a short time afterwards a fair Opportunity happen'd: For Governour *Mathews* died, and no Person was substituted to succeed him in the Government. Whereupon the People apply'd themselves to Sir *William Berkeley*, (who had continued all this time upon his own Plantation in a private Capacity) and unanimously chose him their Governour again.

C.69. Sir *William Berkeley* had all along retain'd an unshaken Loyalty for the Royal Family; and therefore generously told the People, That he could not approve of the Protector's Oppression; and was resolved never to serve any Body, but the lawful Heir to the Crown; and that if he accepted the Government, it should be upon their solemn Promise, after his Example to venture their Lives and Fortunes for the King, who was then in *France*.

This was their dearest Wish, and therefore with an unanimous Voice they told him, That they were ready to hazard all for the King. Now, this was actually before the King's Return for *England*, and proceeded from a brave Principle of Loyalty, for which they had no Example. Sir *William Berkeley* embraced their Choice, and forthwith proclaim'd *Charles* the Second King of *England*, *Scotland*, *France*, *Ireland* and *Virginia*, and caused all Process to be issued in his Name. Thus his Majesty was actually King in *Virginia*, before he was so in *England*. But it pleased God to restore him soon after to the Throne of his Ancestors; and so that Country escaped being chastised for throwing off the Usurpation.

C.70. Upon the King's Restoration, he sent Sir *William*

Berkeley a new Commission, with Leave to return to *England*, and Power to appoint a Deputy in his Absence. For his Majesty in his Exile had received Intelligence of this Gentleman's Loyalty, and during that Time had renew'd his Commission.

¶.71. Upon this, Sir *William Berkeley* appointed Colonel *Francis Morrison* Deputy-Governour, and went for *England* to wait on his Majesty, by whom he was kindly receiv'd. At his Return he carried his Majesty's pressing Instructions for encouraging the People in Husbandry and Manufactures; but more especially to promote Silk and Vineyards. There is a Tradition, that the King, in Compliment to that Colony, wore at his Coronation a Robe made of the Silk, that was sent from thence. But this was all the Reward the Country had for their Loyalty; for the Parliament was pleased to renew the Act contrived by the Usurper for discouraging the Plantations, with severer Restraints and Prohibitions by Bonds, Securities, *&c.*

¶.72. During the Time of Sir *William Berkeley's* Absence, Colonel *Morrison* had, according to his Directions, revised the Laws, and compiled them into one Body, ready to be confirm'd by the Assembly at his Return. By these Laws, the Church of *England* was confirm'd the established Religion, the Charge of the Government sustain'd, Trade and Manufactures were encouraged, a Town projected, and all the *Indian* Affairs settled.

¶.73. The Parishes were likewise regulated, competent Allowances were made to the Ministers to the Value of about Fourscore Pounds a Year, besides Glebes and Perquisites, and the Method of their Preferment was settled. Convenient Churches and Glebes were provided, and all necessary Parish-Officers instituted. Some Steps were made also towards a Free-School, and College, and all the Poor effectually provided for.

₡.74. For Support of the Government the Duty of Two Shillings *per* Hogshead on all Tobacco's, and that of One Shilling *per* Tun Fort Duty on Shipping, were made perpetual; and the Collectors were obliged to account for the same to the General Assembly.

₡.75. For Encouragement of Manufactures, Prices were appointed for the Makers of the best Pieces of Linnen and Woollen Cloth, and a Reward of Fifty Pounds of Tobacco was given for each Pound of Silk. All Persons were enjoin'd to plant Mulberry-Trees, for the Food of the Silk-Worm, according to the Number of Acres of Land they held. Tan-houses were set up in each County, at the County Charge; and publick Encouragement was given to a Salt-work on the Eastern Shore. A Reward was appointed in Proportion to the Tonnage of all Sea-Vessels built there, and an Exemption allow'd from all Fees and Duties payable by such Shipping.

₡.76. The King had commanded, that all Ships trading to *Virginia*, should go to *James-Town*, and there enter before they broke Bulk: But the Assembly, from the Impracticableness of that Command, excused all, except the *James-River* Ships, from that Order. They did not oblige them to any certain Station, in the Rivers they were bound to, but suffer'd them to ride dispers'd, as the Commanders pleased; by whose Example the *James-River* Ships were no sooner enter'd with the Officer at *James-Town*, but they also dispers'd themselves to unload, and trade all over the River. By this Means the Design of Towns was totally baulk'd, and this Order prov'd only an Ease to the Officer of *James-River*, and a Means of creating a good Place to him.

¶.77. Peace and Commerce with the *Indians* was settled by Law, and their Boundaries prescribed. Several other good Acts were made suiting the Necessity of the Government; so that nothing then seem'd to remain, but the Improvement of the Country, and Encouragement of those Manu[fa]ctures the King had been pleased to recommend, together with such others as should be found beneficial.

¶.78. Sir *William Berkeley* being then again in full Possession of his Government, and at perfect Peace with the *Indians*, set all Hands industriously to Work in making Country Improvements. He pass'd a new Act for Encouragement of *James-Town*, whereby several Houses were built therein, at the Charge of several Counties. However, the main Ingredient for the Advancement of Towns was still wanting, namely, the Confinement of all Shipping and Trade to them only; by Defect of which all the other Expedients avail'd nothing; for most of the Buildings were soon converted into Houses of Entertainment.

¶.79. *Anno* 1663, divers Sectaries in Religion beginning to spread themselves there; by a mistaken Zeal great Restraints were laid upon them under severe Penalties, to prevent their Encrease.

This made many of them flie to other Colonies, and prevented abundance of others from going over to seat themselves among 'em. And as the former ill Treatment of my Lord *Baltemore* kept many People away, and drove others to *Maryland;* so the present Severities towards the Non-conformists, robb'd them of many more, who went to the Neighbouring Colonies; and might otherwise have contributed vastly to the Improvement of that.

¶.80. The rigorous Circumscription of their Trade, the Persecution of their Sectaries, and the little Demand of

Tobacco, had like to have had very fatal Consequences. For, the poor People becoming thereby very uneasie, their Murmurings were watch'd and fed, by several mutinous and rebellious *Oliverian* Soldiers, that were sent thither as Servants. These depending upon the discontented People of all sorts, form'd a villanous Plot to destroy their Masters, and afterwards to set up for themselves.

This Plot was brought so near to Perfection, that it was the very Night before the design'd Execution, e're it was discover'd; and then it came out by the Relenting of one of their Accomplices, whose Name was *Birkenhead*. This Man was Servant to Mr. *Smith* of *Purton*, in *Gloucester* County, near which Place, *viz.* at *Poplar-Spring*, the Miscreants were to meet the Night following, and put in Execution their horrid Conspiracy.

¶.81. Upon this Discovery by *Birkenhead*, Notice was immediately sent to the Governour at *Green-Spring*. And the Method he took to prevent it was by private Orders, that some of the Militia should meet before the Time, at the Place where the Conspirators were to rendezvous, and seize them as they came singly up to it. Which Orders being happily executed, their devilish Plot was defeated. However, there were but a few taken; because several of them making their Escape, turn'd back such of their Fellows as they met on the Road, and prevented most of them from coming up, or from being discover'd.

Four of these Rogues were hanged: But *Birkenhead* was gratified with his Freedom, and a Reward of Two Hundred Pounds Sterling.

¶.82. For the Discovery and happy Disappointment of this Plot, an Anniversary Thanksgiving was appointed on the 13th of *September*, the Day it was to have been put in Execution. And it is great pity some other Days are not commemorated, as well as that.

¶.83. The News of this Plot being transmitted to King *Charles* the Second, his Majesty sent his Royal Commands to build a Fort at *James-Town*, for Security of the Governour, and to be a Curb upon all such Traiterous Attempts for the future. But the Country, thinking the Danger over, only raised a Battery of some small Pieces of Cannon.

¶.84. Another Misfortune happen'd to the Plantation this Year, which was a new Act of Parliament in *England*, laying a severer Restraint upon their Supplies than formerly. By this Act they could have no Foreign Goods, which were not first landed in *England*, and carried directly from thence to the Plantations; the former Restraint of importing them only by *English* Men, in *English* built Shipping, not being thought sufficient.

This was a Misfortune that cut with a double Edge; For, First, it reduced their Staple Tobacco to a very low Price; and, Secondly, it raised the Value of *European* Goods, to what the Merchants pleased to put upon them.

¶.85. For this their Assembly could think of no Remedy, but to be even with the Merchants, and make their Tobacco scarce, by prohibiting the Planting of it for one Year; and during that idle Year to invite the People to enter upon Manufactures. But, *Maryland* not concurring in this Project, they were obliged in their own Defence to repeal the Act of Assembly again, and return to their old Drudgery of planting Tobacco.

¶.86. The Country thus miss'd of their Remedy in the Stint of Tobacco; which on the contrary multiplied exceedingly by the great Increase of Servants. This, together with the above-mention'd Curbs on Trade, exasperated the People, because now they found themselves under a Necessity, of exchanging their Commodities with the Merchants of *England* at their own Terms. The Assembly therefore again attempted the Stint of Tobacco, and past another Act against planting it for One Year: And *Carolina* and *Maryland* both agreed to it. But some Accident hindering the Agent of *Carolina* from giving Notice thereof to *Maryland* by the Day appointed, the Governour of that Province proclaim'd the Act void. Altho' every Body there knew, that *Carolina* had fully agreed to all Things required of them. But he took Advantage of this nice Punctilio; because of the Loss such a Diminution would have been to his Annual Income; and so all People relaps'd again into the Disease of planting Tobacco.

Virginia was more nettled at this ill Usage from *Maryland*, than at her former absolute Denial. But being conscious of their own low Condition, they were resolved to take all patiently, and by fair Means get Relief, if they could. They therefore appointed Agents to reassume the Treaty, and submitted so low, as to send them to St. *Mary*'s, then the Residence of the Governour of *Maryland*, and the Place where the Assemblies met. Yet all this Condescention could not hold them to their Bargain. The Governour said, He had observ'd his Part of the Agreement, and would not call an Assembly any more upon that Subject.

¶.87. In this manner Two whole Years were spent, and nothing could be accomplish'd for their Relief. In the mean while, *England* was studious to prevent their receiving Supplies from any other Country. To do that more effectually, it was thought expedient to confine the Trade of that Colony to one Place. But that not being found practicable, because of the many great Rivers that divide their Habitations, and the extraordinary Conveniencies of each; His Majesty sent Directions to build Forts in the several Rivers, and enjoin'd all the Ships to ride under those Forts; and further order'd, that those Places only should be the Ports of Trade.

¶.88. This Instruction was punctually observed for a Year, and Preparations were made for Ports, by casting up Breast-works, in such Places as the Assembly appointed; and the Shipping did for that time ride at those Places. But the great Fire and Plague happening in *London* immediately upon it, made their Supplies that Year very uncertain; and the Terror the People were in, lest the Plague should be brought over with the Goods from *London*, prevented them from residing at those Ports, for fear of being all swept away at once. And so every Body was left at Liberty again.

¶.89. Still no Favour could be obtain'd for the Tobacco Trade; and the *English* Merchants afforded a bare Sufficiency of Cloathing for their Crops. The Assembly were full enough of Resentment, but overlook'd their right Way of Redress. All they cou'd do was to cause Looms and Work-Houses to be set up in the several Counties at the County Charge. They renew'd the Rewards of Silk, and put great Penalties upon every Neglect of making Flax and Hemp. About this Time they sustain'd some Damage by the *Dutch* War; for which Reason they ordered the Forts to be rebuilt of Brick: But having yet no true Notion of the Advantage of Towns, they did not oblige the Ships to ride under them. Which Thing alone well executed, would have answer'd all their Desires.

¶.90. Sir *William Berkeley*, who was always contriving and industrious for the Good of the Country, was not contented to set a useful Example at home, by the Essays he made of Pot-Ash, Flax, Hemp, Silk, *&c.* But was also resolv'd to make new Discoveries abroad amongst the *Indians*.

For this End he employ'd a small Company of about Fourteen *English*, and as many *Indians*, under the Command of Captain *Henry Batt*,[14] to go upon such an Adventure. They set out together from *Appamattox*, and in Seven Days March reach'd the Foot of the Mountains. The Mountains they first arriv'd at, were not extraordinary high or steep: But, after they had pass'd the first Ridge, they encounter'd others, that seem'd to reach the Clouds, and were so perpendicular and full of Precipices, that sometimes in a whole Day's March, they could not travel Three Miles in a direct Line. In other Places they found large level Plains, and fine *Savanna's*, Three or Four Miles wide, in which were an infinite Quantity of Turkies, Deer, Elks and Buffaloes, so gentle and undisturbed, that they had no Fear at the Appearance of the Men: But wou'd suffer them to come almost within Reach of their Hands. There they also found Grapes so prodigiously large, that they seem'd more like Bullace than Grapes. When they travers'd these Mountains, they came to a fine level Country again, and discover'd a Rivulet that descended backwards. Down that Stream they travell'd several Days, till they came to old Fields and Cabbins, where the *Indians* had lately been; but were supposed to have fled at the Approach of *Batt* and his Company. However, the Captain follow'd the old Rule of leaving some Toys in their Cabbins, for them to find at their Return, by which they might know they were Friends. Near to these Cabbins were great Marshes; where the *Indians* which Capt. *Batt* had with him, made a Halt, and would positively proceed no further. They said, that not far off from that Place, lived a Nation of *Indians*, that made Salt, and sold it to their Neighbours. That this was a great and powerful People, which never suffer'd any Strangers to return, that had once discover'd their Towns. Capt. *Batt* used all the Arguments he could to get them forward, but in vain. And so, to please those timorous *Indians*, the Hopes of this Discovery were frustrated, and the Detachment was forced to return.

¶.91. Upon Capt. *Batt*'s Report to Sir *William Berkeley*, he resolved to make a Journey himself; that so there might be no Hindrance for want of sufficient Authority, as had been in the aforesaid Expedition. To this End he concerted Matters for it, and had pitch'd upon his Deputy-Governour. The Assembly also made an Act to encourage it. But all these Preparations came to nothing, by the Confusion which happen'd there soon after by *Bacon*'s Rebellion.[15] And since that, there has never been any such Discovery attempted from *Virginia*.

¶.92. The Occasion of this Rebellion is not easie to be discover'd: But 'tis certain there were many Things that concurr'd towards it. For it cannot be imagined, that upon the Instigation of Two or Three Traders only, who aim'd at a Monopoly of the *Indian* Trade, as some pretend to say, the whole Country would have fallen into so much Distraction; in which People did not only hazard their Necks by Rebellion: But endeavor'd to ruine a Governour, whom they all entirely loved, and had unanimously chosen; a Gentleman who had devoted his whole Life and Estate to the Service of the Country; and against whom in Thirty Five Years Experience, there had never been one single Complaint. Neither can it be supposed, that upon so slight Grounds, they would make Choice of a Leader they hardly knew, to oppose a Gentleman, that had been so long, and so deservedly the Darling of the People. So that in all Probability there was something else in the Wind, without which the Body of the Country had never been engaged in that Insurrection.

Four Things may be reckon'd to have been the main Ingredients towards this intestine Commotion, *viz*. First, The extream low Price of Tobacco, and the ill

Usage of the Planters in the Exchange of Goods for it, which the Country, with all their earnest Endeavours, could not remedy. Secondly, The Splitting the Colony into Proprieties, contrary to the original Charters; and the extravagant Taxes they were forced to undergo, to relieve themselves from those Grants. Thirdly, The heavy Restraints and Burdens laid upon their Trade by Act of Parliament in *England*. Fourthly, The Disturbance given by the *Indians*. Of all which I beg Leave to speak in their Order.

¶.93. First, Of the low Price of Tobacco, and the Disappointment of all sort of Remedy, I have spoken sufficiently before. Secondly, Of splitting the Country into Proprieties.

King *Charles* the Second, to gratifie some Nobles about him, made Two great Grants out of that Country. These Grants were not of the uncultivated Wood-Land only, but also of Plantations, which for many Years had been seated and improv'd, under the Encouragement of several Charters granted by his Royal Ancestors to that Colony. Those Grants were distinguished by the Names of the Northern and Southern Grants of *Virginia*, and the same Men were concern'd in both. They were kept dormant some Years after they were made, and in the Year 1674 begun to be put in Execution. As soon as ever the Country came to know this, they remonstrated against them; and the Assembly drew up an humble Address to his Majesty, complaining of the said Grants, as derogatory to the previous Charters and Privileges granted to that Colony, by his Majesty and his Royal Progenitors. They sent to *England* Mr. Secretary *Ludwell* and Colonel *Park*,[16] as their Agents to address the King to vacate those Grants. And the better to defray that Charge, they laid a Tax of Fifty Pounds of Tobacco *per* Poll, for Two Years together, over and above all other Taxes, which was an excessive Burden. They likewise laid Amercements of Seventy, Fifty, and Thirty Pounds of Tobacco on every Cause tried throughout the Country. Besides all this, they applied the Ballance, remaining due upon Account of the Two Shilling *per* Hogshead, and Fort Duties, to this Use. Which Taxes and Amercements fell heaviest on the poor People, the Effect of whose Labour wou'd not cloath their Wives and Children. This made them desperately uneasie, especially when, after a whole Year's Patience under all these Pressures, they had no Encouragement from their Agents in *England*, to hope for Remedy; nor any Certainty when they should be eased of those heavy Impositions.

€.94. Thirdly, Upon the Back of all these Misfortunes came out the Act of 25 *Car. II.* for better securing the Plantation Trade. By this Act several Duties were laid on the Trade from one Plantation to another. This was a new Hardship, and the rather, because the Revenue arising by this Act, was not applied to the Use of the Plantation wherein it was raised: But given clear away; nay, in that Country it seem'd to be of no other Use, but to create a good Income to the Officers; for the Collector had Half, the Comptroller a Quarter, and the remaining Quarter was subdivided into Salaries, till it was lost.

By the same Act also very great Duties were laid on the Fisheries of the Plantations, if manufactured by the *English* Inhabitants there; while the People of *England* were absolutely free from all Customs. Nay, tho' the Oil, Blubber, and Whale-Bone, which were made by the Inhabitants of the Plantations, were carried to *England* by *English* Men, and in *English* built Ships, yet it was held to a considerable Duty.

€.95. These were the Afflictions that Country labour'd

under, when the Fourth Accident happen'd, *viz.* The Disturbance offer'd by the *Indians* to the Frontiers.

This was occasion'd, First, By the *Indians* on the Head of the Bay. Secondly, By the *Indians* on their own Frontiers.

First, The *Indians* at the Head of the Bay drove a constant Trade with the *Dutch* in *Monadas*, now call'd *New-York;* and, to carry on this, they used to come and return every Year by their Frontiers of *Virginia*, to purchase Skins and Furs of the *Indians* to the Southward. This Trade was carried on peaceably while the *Dutch* held *Monadas;* and the *Indians* used to call on the *English*, to whom they would sell part of their Furs, and with the rest go on to *Monadas*. But after the *English* came to possess that Place, and understood the Advantages the *Virginians* made by the Trade of their *Indians*, they inspired them with such a Hatred to the Inhabitants of *Virginia*, that, instead of coming peaceably to trade with them, as they had done for several Years before, they afterwards never came, but only to commit Robberies and Murders upon the People.

Secondly, The *Indians* upon their own Frontiers were likewise inspir'd with ill Thoughts of 'em. For their *Indian* Merchants had lost a considerable Branch of their Trade they knew not how; and apprehended the Consequences of Sir *William Berkeley's* intended Discoveries, which were espoused by the Assembly, might take away the remaining Part of their Profit. This made them very troublesome to the Neighbour *Indians;* who on their part, observing an unusual Uneasiness in the *English*, and being terrified by their rough Usage, immediately suspected some wicked Design against their Lives, and so fled to their remoter Habitations. This confirm'd the *English* in the Belief, that they had been the Murderers, till at last they provoked them to be so in Earnest.

¶.96. This Addition of Mischief to Minds already full of Discontent, made People ready to vent all their Resentment against the poor *Indians*. There was nothing to be got by Tobacco; neither could they turn any other Manufacture to Advantage; so that most of the poorer Sort were willing to quit their unprofitable Employments, and go Voluntiers against the *Indians*.

At first they flock'd together tumultuously, running in Troops from one Plantation to another without a Head; till at last the seditious Humour of Colonel *Nath. Bacon*, led him to be of the Party. This Gentleman had been brought up at one of the Inns of Court in *England*, and had a moderate Fortune. He was young, bold, active, of an inviting Aspect, and powerful Elocution. In a Word, he was every way qualified to head a giddy and unthinking Multitude. Before he had been Three Years in the Country, he was, for his extraordinary Qualifications, made one of the Council, and in great Honour and Esteem among the People. For this Reason he no sooner gave Countenance to this riotous Mob, but they all presently fix'd their Eyes upon him for their General, and accordingly made their Addresses to him. As soon as he found this, he harangued them publickly. He aggravated the *Indian* Mischiefs, complaining, that they were occasion'd for want of a due Regulation of their Trade. He recounted particularly the other Grievances and Pressures they lay under; and pretended, that he accepted of their Command with no other Intention, but to do them and the Country Service, in which he was willing to encounter the greatest Difficulties and Dangers. He farther assured them, he would never lay down his Arms, till he had revenged their Sufferings upon the *Indians*, and redress'd all their other Grievances.

¶.97. By these Insinuations he wrought his Men into so perfect a Unanimity, that they were one and all at his Devotion. He took care to exasperate them to the utmost, by representing all their Misfortunes. After he had begun to muster them, he dispatch'd a Messenger to the Governour, by whom he aggravated the Mischiefs done by the *Indians*, and desired a Commission of General to go out against them. This Gentleman was in so great Esteem at that Time with the Council, that the Governour did not think fit to give him a flat Refusal: But sent him Word, he would consult the Council, and return him a further Answer.

¶.98. In the mean time, *Bacon* was expeditious in his Preparations, and having all Things in Readiness, began his March, depending on the Authority the People had given him. He would not lose so much Time, as to stay for his Commission; but dispatched several Messengers to the Governour to hasten it. On the other Hand, the Governour, instead of a Commission, sent positive Orders to him to disperse his Men, and come down in Person to him, upon Pain of being declared a Rebel.

¶.99. This unexpected Order, was a great Surprize to *Bacon*, and not a little Trouble to his Men. However, he was resolved to prosecute his first Intentions, depending upon his Strength, and Interest with the People. Nevertheless, he intended to wait upon the Governour, but not altogether defenceless. Pursuant to this Resolution, he took about Forty of his Men down with him in a Sloop to *James-Town*, where the Governour was with his Council.

¶.100. Matters did not succeed there to Mr. *Bacon*'s Satisfaction; wherefore he express'd himself a little too freely. For which being suspended from the Council, he went away again in a Huff with his Sloop and Followers. The Governour fill'd a Long-Boat with Men, and pursued the Sloop so close, that Colonel *Bacon* removed into his Boat to make more Haste. But the Governour had sent up by Land to the Ships at *Sandy-Point*, where he was stopp'd, and sent down again. Upon his Return he was kindly received by the Governour, who, knowing he had gone a Step beyond his Instructions in having suspended him, was glad to admit him again of the Council; after which he hoped all Things might be pacified.

₡.101. Notwithstanding this, Col. *Bacon* still insisted upon a Commission to be General of the Volunteers, and to go out against the *Indians;* from which the Governour endeavour'd to disswade him, but to no Purpose, because he had some secret Project in View. He had the Luck to be countenanced in his Importunities, by the News of fresh Murder and Robberies committed by the *Indians*. However, not being able to accomplish his Ends by fair Means, he stole privately out of Town; and having put himself at the Head of Six Hundred Volunteers, marched directly to *James-Town*, where the Assembly was then sitting. He presented himself before the Assembly, and drew up his Men in Battalia before the House wherein they sat. He urged to them his Preparations; and alledged, that if the Commission had not been delay'd so long, the War against the *Indians* might have been finish'd.

₡.102. The Governour resented this insolent Usage worst of all, and now obstinately refused to grant him any thing, offering his naked Breast against the presented Arms of his Followers. But the Assembly, fearing the fatal Consequence of provoking a discontented Multitude ready arm'd, who had the Governour, Council and Assembly entirely in their Power, address'd the Governour to grant *Bacon* his Request. They prepar'd themselves the Commission, constituting him General of the Forces of *Virginia*, and brought it to the Governour to be sign'd.

With much Reluctancy his Excellency sign'd it, and thereby put the Power of War and Peace into *Bacon*'s Hands. Upon this he march'd away immediately, having gain'd his End, which was in effect a Power to secure a Monopoly of the *Indian* Trade to himself and his Friends.

€.103. As soon as General *Bacon* had march'd to such a convenient Distance from *James-Town*, that the Assembly thought they might deliberate with Safety, the Governour, by their Advice, issued a Proclamation of Rebellion against him, commanding his Followers to surrender him, and forthwith disperse themselves. Not contented with this, he likewise gave Orders at the same time, for raising the Militia of the Country against him.

€.104. The People being much exasperated, and General *Bacon* by his Address and Eloquence having gain'd an absolute Dominion over their Hearts, they unanimously resolved, that not a Hair of his Head shou'd fall to the Ground, much less that they shou'd surrender him as a Rebel. Therefore, they kept to their Arms, and instead of proceeding against the *Indians*, they march'd back to *James-Town;* directing their Fury against such of their Friends and Country-men, as should dare to oppose them.

€.105. The Governour seeing this, fled over the Bay to *Accomack*, whither he hoped the Infection of *Bacon*'s Conspiracy had not reach'd. But there, instead of People's receiving him with open Arms, in Remembrance of the former Services he had done them; they began to make Terms with him for Redress of their Grievances, and for the Ease and Liberty of Trade. Thus Sir *William*, who had been almost the Idol of the People, was, by reason of the loyal Part he acted, abandon'd by all; except some few, who went over to him from the Western Shore in Sloops and Boats. So that it was some time before he could make head against *Bacon:* But he left him to range through the Country at Discretion.

⁋.106. General *Bacon* at first held a Convention of such of the chief Gentlemen of the Country, as would come to him, especially of those about *Middle-Plantation*,[17] who were near at Hand. At this Convention they made a Declaration to justifie his unlawful Proceedings; and obliged People to take an Oath of Obedience to him as their General. Then, by their Advice, on Pretence of the Governour's Abdication, he call'd an Assembly, by Writs sign'd by himself, and Four others of the Council. The Oath was Word for Word as follows.

WHereas the Country hath raised an Army against our common Enemy the *Indians*, and the same under the Command of General *Bacon*, being upon the Point to march forth against the said common Enemy, hath been diverted, and necessitated to move to the Suppressing of Forces, by evil disposed Persons raised against the said General *Bacon*, purposely to foment and stir up Civil War among us, to the Ruine of this his Majesty's Country. And, *Whereas* it is notoriously manifest, that Sir *William Berkeley*, Knight, Governour of the Country, assisted, counselled and abetted by those evil disposed Persons aforesaid, hath not only commanded, fomented and stirr'd up the People to the said Civil War; but failing therein, hath withdrawn himself, to the great Astonishment of the People, and the Unsettlement of the Country. And, *Whereas* the said Army, raised by the Country for the Causes aforesaid, remain full of Dissatisfaction in the Middle of the Country, expecting Attempts from the said Governour and the evil Counsellors aforesaid. And since no proper Means have been found out for the Settlement of the Distractions, and preventing the horrid Outrages and Murders daily committed in many Places of the Country by the barbarous Enemy; It hath been thought fit by the said General, to call unto him all such sober and discreet Gentlemen, as the present Circumstances of the Country will admit, to the *Middle-Plantation*, to consult and advise of re-establishing the Peace of the Country. So we the said Gentlemen, being this 3d of *August, 1676,* accordingly met, do advise, resolve, declare and conclude, and for our selves do swear in manner following.

First, That we will at all Times join with the said General *Bacon*, and his Army, against the common Enemy in all Points whatsoever.

Secondly, That whereas certain Persons have lately contrived and design'd the Raising Forces against the said General, and the Army under his Command, thereby to beget a Civil War; We will endeavour the Discovery and Apprehending of all and every of those evil disposed Persons, and them secure, untill further Order from the General.

Thirdly, And whereas it is credibly reported, that the Governour hath inform'd the King's Majesty, that the said General, and the People of the Country in Arms under his Command, their Aiders and Abettors, are Rebellious, and removed from their Allegiance; and that upon such like Information, he the said Governour hath advised and petition'd the King to send Forces to reduce them; We do further declare and believe in our Consciences, That it consists with the Welfare of this Country, and with our Allegiance to his most Sacred Majesty, that we the Inhabitants of *Virginia*, to the utmost of our Power, do oppose and suppress all Forces whatsoever of that Nature, until such time as the King be fully inform'd of the State of the Case, by such Person or Persons, as shall be sent from the said *Nathaniel*

Bacon, in the Behalf of the People; and the Determination thereof be remitted hither. And we do swear, That we will him the said General, and the Army under his Command, aid and assist accordingly.

⁋.108. By this Time the Governor had got together a small Party to side with him. These he furnished with Sloops, Arms and Ammunition, in order to cross the Bay, and oppose the Malecontents. By this Means there happen'd some Skirmishes, in which several were kill'd, and others taken Prisoners. Thus they were going on by a Civil War to destroy one another, and lay waste their Infant Country; when it pleased God, after some Months Confusion, to put an End to their Misfortunes, as well as to *Bacon*'s Designs, by his natural Death.

He died at Dr. *Green*'s,[18] in *Gloucester* County: But where he was bury'd was never yet discover'd; tho' afterward there was great Enquiry made, with Design to expose his Bones to publick Infamy.

⁋.109. In the mean while, those Disorders occasion'd a general Neglect of Husbandry, and a great Destruction of the Stocks; so that People had a dreadful Prospect of Want and Famine. But the Malecontents being thus disunited by the Loss of their General, in whom they all confided, they began to squabble among themselves; and every Man's Business was how to make the best Terms he could for himself.

Lieutenant-General *Ingram*[19] (whose true Name was *Johnson*) and Major-General *Walklate* surrender'd on Condition of Pardon for themselves and their Followers; tho' they were both forced to submit to an Incapacity of bearing Office in that Country for the future.

Peace being thus restored, Sir *William Berkeley* return'd to his former Seat of Government, and every Man to his several Habitation.

¶.110. While this intestine War was fomenting there, the Agents of the Country in *England* could not succeed in their Remonstrance against the Propriety Grants; tho' they were told, that those Grants should be revok'd. But the News of their Civil War reaching *England* about the same time, the King would then proceed no further in that Matter. So the Agents thought it their best way to compound with the Proprietors. Accordingly they agreed with them for Four Hundred Pounds a Man, which was paid; and so all the Clamour against those Grants ended, neither was there any more heard of them there till above a Dozen Years afterwa[r]ds.

¶.111. When this Storm, occasion'd by *Bacon*, was blown over, and all Things quiet again, Sir *William Berkeley* called an Assembly for settling the Affairs of the Country, and for making Reparation to such as had been oppress'd. After which a Regiment of Soldiers arrived from *England*, which were sent to suppress the Insurrection: But they coming after the Business was over, had no Occasion to exercise their Courage. However, they were kept on Foot there about Three Years after, and in the Lord *Colepepper*'s Time paid off, and disbanded.

¶.112. After the Agents had compounded with the Proprietors, they obtain'd a new Charter of the King, by which he confirm'd to that Country their former Constitution, with full Assurance, that they should for ever after remain under the Protection of his Majesty and his Successors, and always hold their Lands immediately from the Crown.

¶.113. The Confusion occasion'd by the Civil War, and the Advantage the *Indians* made of it in butchering the *English* upon all their Frontiers, caused such a Desolation, and put the Country so far back, that to this Day they have seated very little beyond the Boundaries that were then inhabited. At that Time *James-Town* was again burnt down to the Ground by *Richard Lawrence*, one of *Bacon*'s Captains, who, when his own Men, that abhorr'd such Barbarity, refused to obey his Command, he himself became the Executioner, and fired the Houses with his own Hands.

This unhappy Town did never after arrive at the Perfection it then had: And now it is almost deserted by the wild Project of Governour *Nicholson*, who procured that the Assembly and General Court should be removed from thence to *Williamsburgh*, an Inland Place about Seven Miles from it.

€.114. With the Regiment above-mention'd arrived Commissioners, to enquire into the Occasion and Authors of this Rebellion; and Sir *William Berkeley* came to *England*. Where from the Time of his Arrival his Sickness obliged him to keep his Chamber, till he died; so that he had no Opportunity of kissing the King's Hand. But his Majesty declared himself well satisfied with his Conduct in *Virginia*, and was very kind to him during his Sickness; often enquiring after his Health, and commanding him not to hazard it by, too early an Endeavour to come to Court.

€.115. Upon Sir *William Berkeley*'s Voyage to *England*, *Herbert Jeffreys*, Esq; was appointed Governour. He made formal Articles of Peace with the *Indians*, and held an Assembly at *Middle-Plantation*, wherein they settled and allow'd a free Trade with the *Indians;* but restrain'd it to certain Marts, to which the *Indians* should bring their Commodities: And this also to be under such certain Rules as were by that Assembly directed. But this Method was not agreeable to the *Indians*, who had never before been under any Regulation. They thought, that if all former Usages were not restored, the Peace was not perfect; and therefore did not much rely upon it, which made those new Restrictions useless.

Governour *Jeffreys* his Time was very short there, he being taken off by Death the Year following.

(.116. After him Sir *Henry Chicheley* was made Deputy-Governour, in the latter End of the Year 1678. In his Time the Assembly, for the greater Terror of the *Indians*, built Magazines at the Heads of the Four great Rivers, and furnished them with Arms, Ammunition, and Men in constant Service.

This Assembly also prohibited the Importation of Tobacco, which *Carolina*, and sometimes *Maryland*, were wont to send thither, in order to its being shipp'd off for *England*. But in that, I think, *Virginia* mistook her Interest. For, had they permitted this Custom to become habitual, and thus engross'd the Shipping, as wou'd soon have happen'd, they could easily have regulated the Trade of Tobacco at any Time, without the Concurrence of those other Colonies, and without submitting to their perverse Humours, as formerly.

(.117. The Spring following, *Thomas* Lord *Colepepper* arrived there Governour, and carry'd with him some Laws, which had been drawn up in *England*, to be enacted in their Assembly. In these he had the Art of mixing the Good of the Country with his own particular Interest, which was a sure Means of getting them pass'd. And coming with the Advantage of restoring Peace to a troubled Nation, it was not difficult for him to obtain whatever he pleased from the People. His Influence too was the greater; by the Power he had of pardoning those who had a Hand in the Disorders committed in the late Rebellion.

(.118. In his first Assembly he pass'd several Acts very

obliging to the Country, *viz*. First, An Act of Naturalization, whereby the Power of Naturalizing Foreigners was placed in the Governour. Secondly, An Act for Cohabitation, and Encouragement of Trade and Manufactures; whereby a certain Place in each County was appointed for a Town, in which all Goods imported, and exported were to be landed and shipp'd off, bought and sold. Which Act was kindly brought to nothing by the Opposition of the Merchants of *London*. Thirdly, An Act of general Pardon and Oblivion, whereby all the Transgressions and Outrages committed in the Time of the late Rebellion, were entirely remitted; and Reparation allow'd to People that should be evil spoken of on that Account.

But he put a Sting into the Tail of this Law, that justifies Oppression, whenever the People happen to fall into the Hands of an ill Governour. I mean the Clause that imposes a Penalty of Five Hundred Pounds, and a Year's Imprisonment, upon any Man that shall presume to speak disrespectfully of the Governour. This is such a Safeguard to Tyranny, that, let a Governour commit never so many Abuses, no Person, while he is there, dare say a Word against him; nor so much as go about to represent it to the Throne of *England* for Redress, for fear of incurring this severe Penalty.

The same Law also gives One Hundred Pounds, and Three Months Imprisonment, without Bail, for daring to speak or write disrespectfully of any one of the Council, or of any Judge, or other principal Officer in the Country.

Although this Law was at first intended merely to suppress Rebellion, and to pacifie and reconcile the People one towards another; and no Governour hath ever thought fit to put that Clause in Execution: Yet it has of late been trump'd up in Revenge of Personal Injuries, and for Support of the heavy Mismanagements, which the Country now groans under.

¶.119. By passing some Laws that obliged the Country, the Lord *Colepepper* carried one that was very pleasing to himself, *viz.* The Act for raising a publick Revenue for the better Support of the Government. By this he got the Duties contain'd therein to be made perpetual; and that the Money which before used to be accounted for to the Assembly, should be from thenceforth disposed of by his Majesty's sole Direction, for the Support of the Government. When this was done, he obtain'd of the King a Salary of Two Thousand Pounds *per Annum*, instead of One Thousand, which was formerly allow'd. Also One Hundred and Fifty Pounds *per Annum* for House-Rent, besides all the usual Perquisites.

¶.120. In those submissive Times his Lordship reduced the greatest Perquisite of his Place to a Certainty, which before that was only Gratuitous; that is, instead of the Masters of Ships making Presents of Liquors or Provisions towards the Governour's House-keeping, as they were wont to do, he demanded a certain Sum of Money, remitting that Custom. This Rate has ever since been demanded of all Commanders as a Duty; and is Twenty Shillings for each Ship or Vessel, under an Hundred Tuns, and Thirty Shillings for each Ship upwards of that Burden, to be paid every Voyage, or Port-clearing.

¶.121. This Noble Lord was skilful in all the Ways of getting Money, and never let slip any Opportunity of doing it. To this End he seem'd to lament the unhappy State of the Country, in relation to their Coin. He was tenderly concern'd that all their Cash should be drain'd away by the Neighbouring Colonies, which had not set so low an Estimate upon it as *Virginia;* and therefore he proposed the Raising of it.

This was what the Country had formerly desired, and the Assembly was at that time making a Law for it: But his Lordship stopt them, alledging it was the King's

Prerogative, by Virtue of which he wou'd do it by Proclamation. This they did not approve of, well knowing, if that were the Case, his Lordship, and every other Governour, would at any time have the same Prerogative of altering it; and so People shou'd never be at any Certainty, as they quickly after found from his own Practice. For his Drift in all this Proceeding, tho' gilded over with an affected Kindness to the Country, was only to make Advantage of paying the Soldiers; the Money for that Purpose being put into his Lordship's Hands. He had prudently provided light Pieces of Eight, which he with this View had bought at a cheap Rate. When his Contrivance was ripe for Execution, he extended the Royal Prerogatives, and issued forth a Proclamation, for raising the Value of Pieces of Eight from Five to Six Shillings; and as soon as they were admitted current at that Value, he produced an Order for paying and disbanding the Soldiers. Then those poor Fellows, and such as had maintain'd them, were forced to take their Pay, in those light Pieces of Eight, at Six Shillings. But his Lordship soon after himself found the Inconvenience of that Proclamation; for People began to pay their Duties, and their Ship-Money, in Coin of that high Estimate, which was like to cut short both his Lordship's Salary, and Perquisites; and so he was forced to make use of the same Prerogative, to reduce the Money again to its former Standard.

¶.122. According to this Despotick way of Government, this Noble Lord tried another Experiment in the tender Part of their Constitution: But did it so cautiously, that it seem'd to take off all Reflection.

He put out a Proclamation to repeal several Laws, which had been made since *Bacon*'s Rebellion: But all of them related to the Transactions of *Bacon*'s Time, and were virtually, tho' not expresly repeal'd, by the Act of Indemnity and Oblivion.

¶.123. However, this Arbitrary Method of doing Business, had like to have had a very unhappy Effect; insomuch, that if the late Misfortunes of *Bacon*, had not been so fresh in Memory, it might, perhaps, have occasion'd a new Commotion. For, at this rate of proceeding, People look'd upon their Acts of Assembly, to be of no more Force, than the Laws of an *Ottoman* Province, which are liable to be suspended or repeal'd, at the Pleasure of the *Bashaw*. In short, it bred such a Mutiny in the Country, that the succeeding Assembly was forced to make a particular Law, to provide against the ill Consequences of it.

Some few Instances of repealing Acts of Assembly after this absolute manner, were also attempted in the Time of the Lord *Effingham*'s Government. But, notwithstanding his Proclamations, the Laws thereby pretended to be repeal'd, are allow'd to be of as great Force in all Courts of Justice, as they were before those Proclamations; the Law for paying the Quit-Rent only excepted. This Law allowed them to pay Quit-Rents in Tobacco at Two Pence *per* Pound; but Tobacco after that falling low, the Proclamation repeal'd that Law, and demanded the Payment in Money, according to the Tenour of their Patents; or else in Tobacco at One Penny *per* Pound. And this Imposition has been generally submitted to, rather than any Single Man would stand a Law-Suit against a Governour; especially seeing that by the Words of his Patent, the Quit-Rent was reserved in Money.

Afterwards Colonel *Nicholson*, when he was Lieutenant-Governour under the same Lord *Effingham*, among the many Arbitrary Proceedings which he boasts to have learn'd formerly in the Kingdom of *Morocco*, was pleased by his Proclamation officiously to repeal a Law, which had been before repeal'd to his Hand, by another Law. And these are all the Attempts that have been made in that Colony, of the *French* Method of governing by Edicts.

₡.124. In less than a Year the Lord *Colepepper* return'd to *England*, leaving Sir *Henry Chicheley* Deputy-Governour.

The Country being then settled again, made too much Tobacco for the Market; and the Merchants, would hardly allow the Planter any thing for it.

This occasion'd much Uneasiness again, and the People, from former Experience, despairing of succeeding in any Agreement with the Neighbouring Governments, resolved a total Destruction of the Tobacco in that Country, especially of the Sweet-scented; because that was planted no where else. In Pursuance of which Design, they contrived, that all the Plants should be destroy'd, while they were yet in the Beds, and after it was too late to sow more.

Accordingly the Ring-leaders in this Project began with their own first, and then went to cut up the Plants of such of their Neighbours as were not willing to do it themselves. However, they had not Resolution enough to go through with their Work.

This was adjudged Sedition and Felony. Several People were committed upon it, and some condemn'd to be hang'd. And afterwards the Assembly pass'd a Law to make such Proceedings Felony for the future.

₡.125. After this Accident of Plant-cutting, the Lord *Colepepper* return'd, and held his Second Assembly, in which he contrived to gain another great Advantage over the Country. His Lordship in his first Voyage thither, perceiving how easily he could twist and manage the People, conceived new Hopes of retrieving the Propriety of the Northern Neck, as being so small a Part of the Colony. He conceiv'd that while the Remainder escaped free, which was far the greater Part, they would not engage in the Interest of the lesser Number; especially considering the Discouragements they had met with, before in their former Sollicitation: Tho' all this while, and for many Years afterwards, his Lordship did not pretend to lay publick Claim to any Part of the Propriety.

It did not square with this Project that Appeals should be made to the General Assembly, as till then had been the Custom. He fear'd the Burgesses would be too much in the Interest of their Country-men, and adjudge the Inhabitants of the Northern Neck, to have an equal Liberty and Privilege in their Estates, with the rest of *Virginia*, as being settled upon the same Foot. In order therefore to make a better Pennyworth of those poor People, he studied to overturn this odious Method of Appealing, and to fix the last Resort in another Court, that might judge more favourably of his unrighteous Patents.

To bring this Point about, his Lordship contrived to blow up a Difference in the Assembly, between the Council and the Burgesses, privately encouraging the Burgesses, to insist upon the Privilege of determining all Appeals by themselves, exclusive of the Council; because they, having given their Opinions before in the General Court, were for that Reason, unfit Judges in Appeals from themselves to the Assembly. This succeeded according to his Wish, and the Burgesses bit at the Bait, under the Notion of Privilege, never dreaming of the Snake that lay in the Grass, nor considering the Danger of altering an old Constitution so abruptly. Thus that cunning Lord gain'd his End; for he represented that Quarrel with so many Aggravations, that he got an Instruction from the King, to take away all Appeals from the General Court to the Assembly, and cause them to be made to himself in Council.

⟨.126. Of this his Lordship made sufficient Advantage; for in the Confusion that happen'd in the End of King *James* the Second's Reign, *viz.* in *October*, 1688, he got an Assignment from the other Patentees, and gain'd a favourable Report from the King's Council, upon his Patent for the Northern Neck.

When he had succeeded in this, his Lordship's next Step was to engage some noted Inhabitant of the Place to be on his Side. Accordingly he made use of his Cousin Secretary *Spencer*,[20] who liv'd in the said Neck. This Gentleman did but little in his Lordship's Service, and only gain'd some few Strays, that used to be claim'd by the Coroner, in Behalf of the King.

Upon the death of Mr. Secretary *Spencer*, he engaged another noted Gentleman, an old Stander in that Country, Col. *Philip Ludwell*, who was then in *England*. He went over with this Grant in the Year 1690, and set up an Office in the Neck, claiming some Escheats; but he likewise could make nothing of it. After him Col. *George Brent* and Col. *William Fitz-Hugh*, that were likewise Inhabitants of the said Neck, were employ'd in that Affair: But succeeded no better than their Predecessors. The People in the mean while, complain'd frequently to their Assemblies, who at last made another Address to the King; but there being no Agent in *England* to prosecute it, that likewise miscarried. At last Colonel *Richard Lee*, one of the Council, an Inhabitant of the Northern Neck, privately made a Composition with the Proprietors themselves for his own Land. This broke the Ice, and several were induced to follow so great an Example; so that by Degrees, they were generally brought to pay their Quit-Rents into the Hands of the Proprietors Agents. And now at last it is managed for them by Col. *Robert Carter*, another of the Council, and one of the greatest Freeholders of that Propriety.

¶.127. To return to my Lord *Colepepper*'s Government, I cannot omit a useful Thing which his Lordship was pleased to do, with Relation to their Courts of Justice. It seems, Nicety of Pleading, with all the Juggle of

Westminster-Hall, was creeping into their Courts. The Clerks began in some Cases to enter the Reasons with the Judgments, pretending to set Precedents of inviolable Form to be observed in all future Proceedings. This my Lord found fault with, and retrench'd all Dilatory Pleas, as prejudicial to Justice, keeping the Courts close to the Merits of the Cause, in order to bring it to a speedy Determination, according to the Innocence of former Times. He caused the Judgments to be enter'd up short, without the Reasons, alledging, that their Courts were not of so great Experience, as to be able to make Precedents to Posterity; who ought to be left at Liberty to determine, according to the Equity of the Controversie before them.

¶.128. In his Time also were dismantled the Forts built by Sir *Henry Chicheley* at the Heads of the Rivers, and the Forces there were disbanded, as being too great a Charge. The Assembly appointed small Parties of Light Horse in their Stead, to range by Turns upon the Frontiers. These being chosen out of the Neighbouring Inhabitants, might afford to serve at easier Rates, and yet do the Business more effectually.

¶.129. After this, the Lord *Colepepper* return'd again for *England*, his second Stay not being much longer than the first; and Sir *Henry Chicheley* being dead, he irregularly proclaim'd his Kinsman Mr. Secretary *Spencer* President, tho' he was not the eldest Member of the Council.

¶.130. The next Year, being 1684, upon the Lord *Colepepper*'s refusing to return, *Francis* Lord *Howard* of *Effingham* was sent over Governour. This Noble Lord had as great an Affection for Money as his Predecessor, and made it his Business to equip himself with as much of it as he could, without Respect either to the Laws of the Plantation, or the Dignity of his Office. His Lordship condescended to share with his Clerk, the meaner Profits of Ministerial Offices. And to serve this Turn the more effectually, he imposed the Charge of a License under Seal, on all School-masters for teaching of Children, and on all Practitioners at the Bar, for Pleading. He also extorted an excessive Fee for putting the Seal, to all Probates of Wills, and Letters of Administration, even where the Estates of the Deceased were of the meanest Value. Neither could any be favour'd with such Administration, or Probate, without paying that Extortion. If any Body presum'd to remonstrate against it, his Lordship's Behaviour towards that Man was very severe. He kept several Persons in Prison, and under Confinement from Court to Court, without bringing them to Trial. Which Proceedings, and many others, were so oppressive, that Complaints were made thereof to the King, and Col. *Philip Ludwell* was appointed Agent to appear against him in *England:* And tho' Col. *Ludwell* had not the good Fortune to get his Lordship turn'd out; yet his indefatigable Application in that Affair deserves an honourable Commemoration.

℃.131. During the first Session of Assembly in this Noble Lord's Time, the Duty on Liquors imported from the other *English* Plantations, was first imposed. It was then laid on Pretence of lessening the Levy by the Poll, for Payment of publick Taxes; but more especially for rebuilding the State-House, which had not been rebuilt, since *Lawrence* burnt it in *Bacon*'s Time.

This Duty was at first laid on Wine and Rum only, at the Rate of Three Pence *per* Gallon, with an Exemption of all such, as should be imported in the Ships of *Virginia* Owners. But the like Duty has since been laid on other Liquors also, and is raised to Four Pence *per* Gallon on Wine, and Rum, and One Penny *per* Gallon on Beer, Cyder, Lime-Juice, *&c.* and the Privilege of

Virginia Owners is quite taken away, to the great Discouragement of their Shipping, and Home Trade.

¶.132. This Lord, though he pretended to no great Skill in Legal Procceedings, yet he made great Innovations in their Courts, pretending to follow the *English* Forms. Thus he created a new Court of *Chancery*, distinct from the General Court, who had ever before claim'd that Jurisdiction. He erected himself into a Lord Chancellor, taking the Gentlemen of the Council, to sit with him as meer Associates and Advisers, not having any Vote in the Causes before them. And that it might have more the Air of a new Court, he would not so much as sit in the State-House, where all the other publick Business was dispatch'd, but took the Dining-Room of a private House for that Use. He likewise made Arbitrary Tables of Fees, peculiar to this High Court. However, his Lordship not beginning this Project very long before he left the Country, all these Innovations came to an End upon his Removal; and the Jurisdiction return'd to the General Court again, in the Time of Col. *Nath. Bacon*, whom he left President.

¶.133. During that Gentleman's Presidency, which began *Anno* 1689, the Project of a College was first agreed upon. The Contrivers drew up their Scheme, and presented it to the President and Council. This was by them approved, and referr'd to the next Assembly. But Col. *Bacon*'s Administration being very short, and no Assembly call'd all the while, this pious Design cou'd proceed no further.

¶.134. *Anno* 1690. *Francis Nicholson*, Esq; being appointed Lieutenant-Governour under the Lord *Effingham*, arrived there. This Gentleman's Business was to fix himself in my Lord's Place, and recommend himself to the supream Government. For that End, he studied Popularity, discoursing freely of Country Improvements. He made his Court to the People, by instituting Olympick Games, and giving Prizes to all those, that shou'd excel in the Exercises of Riding, Running, Shooting, Wrestling, and Backsword. When the Design of a College was communicated to him, he foresaw what Interest it might create him with the Bishops in *England*, and therefore promised it all imaginable Encouragement. The first Thing desired of him in its Behalf, was the Calling of an Assembly; but this he wou'd by no Means agree to, being under Obligations to the Lord *Effingham*, to stave off Assemblies as long as he could, for fear there might be further Representations sent over against his Lordship, who was conscious to himself, how uneasie the Country had been under his Despotick Administration.

₵.135. When that could not be obtain'd, then they proposed, that a Subscription might pass thro' the Colony, to try the Humour of the People in general, and see what voluntary Contributions they could get towards it. This he granted, and he himself, together with the Council, set a generous Example to the other Gentlemen of the Country; so that the Subscriptions at last amounted to about Two Thousand Five Hundred Pounds, in which Sum is included the generous Benevolences of several Merchants of *London*.

₵.136. *Anno* 1691, an Assembly being called, this Design was moved to them, and they espoused it heartily; and soon after made an Address to King *William* and Queen *Mary* in its Behalf, and sent the Reverend Mr. *James Blair* their Agent to *England*, to sollicite their Majesties Charter for it.

It was proposed, that Three Things should be taught

in this College, *viz*. Languages, Divinity, and Natural Philosophy.

They appointed a certain Number of Professors, and their Salaries.

And they form'd Rules for the Continuation, and good Government thereof to Perpetuity. But of this I shall speak more particularly in the last Part of my Book, wherein the present State will be consider'd.

The Assembly was so fond of Governour *Nicholson* at that Time, that they presented him with the Sum of Three Hundred Pounds, as a Testimony of their good Disposition towards him. But he having an Instruction to receive no Present from the Country, they drew up an Address to their Majesties, praying that he might have Leave to accept it.

This he took an effectual Way to secure, by making a Promise, that if their Majesties would please to permit him to accept it, he would give one Half thereof to the College; and so he secured at once both the Money, and the Character of being a generous Person.

¶.137. Their Majesties were well pleased with that pious Design of the Plantation, and granted a Charter, according to their Desire; in obtaining which, the Address and Assiduity of Mr. *Blair*, their Agent, was highly to be admired.

Their Majesties were graciously pleased, to give near Two Thousand Pounds Sterling, the Ballance due upon the Account of Quit-Rents, towards the Founding the College; and towards the Endowing of it, they allow'd Twenty Thousand Acres of choice Land, together with the Revenue arising by the Penny *per* Pound, on Tobacco exported from *Virginia* and *Maryland* to the other Plantations.

It was a great Satisfaction to the Archbishops and Bishops to see such a Nursery of Religion founded in that new World; especially for that it was begun in an Episcopal Way, and carried on wholly by zealous Conformists to the Ch. of *England*.

⁋.138. In this first Assembly, Lieutenent-Governour *Nicholson* pass'd Acts for Encouragement of the Linnen Manufacture, and to promote the Leather Trade, by Tanning, Currying, and Shooe-making. He also in that Session pass'd a Law for Cohabitation, and Improvement of Trade.

In the General Court, he was a strict Observer of the Acts of Assembly, making them the sole Rule of his Judgment, where-ever they happen'd not to be silent.

But his Behaviour in Council at the same time, did not square with that Regularity; For, there he was so Arbitrary and Imperious, that they could not bear it, and several of the Councellors writ Letters to the Court of *England* against him. Where, instead of giving Redress to their Grievances, they sent their original Letters back to him.

Before the next Assembly he tack'd about, and was quite the Reverse of what he was in the first. Instead of encouraging Ports and Towns, he spread abroad his Dislike of them; and went among the People, finding fault with those Things, which he and the Assembly had unanimously agreed upon the preceding Session. Such a violent Change there was in him, that it surpriz'd every Body at first: But they soon found out, that it proceeded from some other Cause, than barely the Inconstancy of his Temper. Of this last Opinion he continued till his Removal, which happen'd soon after.

⁋.139. In *February*, 1692, Sir *Edmund Andros* arrived Governour. He began his Government with an Assembly, which overthrew the good Design of Ports and Towns: But the Ground-work of this Proceeding, was laid before Sir *Edmund*'s Arrival. However, this Assembly proceeded no further, than to suspend the Law, till their Majesties Pleasure should be known. But it seems the Merchants in *London* were dissatisfied, and made publick Complaints against it, which their Majesties were pleased to hear; and afterwards referr'd the Law back to the Assembly again, to consider, if it were suitable to the Circumstances of the Country, and to regulate it accordingly. But the Assembly never proceeded any further in it, and so it lies at this Day.

C.140. At this Session Mr. *Neal*'s Project[21] for a Post-Office, and his Patent of Post-Master-General in those Parts of *America*, were presented. The Assembly made an Act to promote that Design; but by reason of the inconvenient Distance of their Habitations, this Project fell to nothing.

C.141. Sir *Edmund Andros*, by a mistaken Zeal, brought an Innovation into their Courts, which was a Hardship upon the Country. He caused all the Statutes of *England*, even those made since their last Charter, notwithstanding they did not mention the Plantations, even such as particularly related to Usages and Customs peculiar to *England*, to be Law in their Courts. He set up the Statutes of *England* to be the sole Rule of his Judgment, as the Lieutenant-Governour had made the Acts of Assembly, of his. This gave them a new Distraction; so that they knew not what was Law, nor when they were secure in their Estates. He was likewise frequently pleased to say, they had no Title to their Lands, for a Reason which neither himself, nor any Body else knew. These Things caused great Heart-burnings in his Time.

C.142. With Sir *Edmund Andros* was sent over the College Charter; and the subsequent Assembly declared, that the Subscriptions which had been made to the College, were due, and immediately demandable. They likewise gave a Duty on the Exportation of Skins, and Furs, for its more plentiful Endowment.

The Subscription-Money did not come in with the same Readiness, with which it had been underwritten. However, there was enough given by their Majesties, and gather'd from the People, to keep all Hands at Work, and carry on the Building, the Foundation whereof they then laid.

₡.143. Sir *Edmund Andros* was a great Encourager of Manufactures. In his Time Fulling-Mills were set up by Act of Assembly. He also gave particular Marks of his Favour towards the Propagating of Cotton, which since his Time has been much neglected. He was likewise a great Lover of Method, and Dispatch in all sorts of Business, which made him find fault with the Management of the Secretaries Office. And, indeed, with very good Reason; for from the Time of *Bacon*'s Rebellion, till then, there never was any Office in the World more negligently kept. Several Patents of Land were enter'd blank upon Record; many Original Patents, Records, and Deeds of Land, with other Matters of great Consequence, were thrown loose about the Office, and suffer'd to be dirted, torn, and eaten by the Moths, and other Insects. But upon this Gentleman's Accession to the Government, he immediately gave Directions, to reform all these Irregularities; he caused the loose and torn Records of Value to be transcribed into new Books; and order'd Conveniencies to be built within the Office, for preserving the Records from being lost and confounded, as before. He prescribed Methods to keep the Papers dry and clean, and to reduce them into such Order, as that any thing might be turn'd to immediately. But all these Conveniencies were burnt soon after they were finished, in *October*, 1698, together with the Office it self, and the whole State-House. But his Diligence was so great in that Affair, that tho' his Stay afterward in the Country was very short; yet he caused all the Records, and Papers, which had been sav'd from the Fire, to be sorted again, and register'd in Order, and indeed in much better Order, than ever they had been before. In this Condition he left 'em at his quitting the Government.

He made several Offers to rebuild the State-House in the same Place; and had his Government continued but Six Months longer, 'tis probable he would have effected it after such a manner, as might have been least burdensome to the People.

⟦.144. Sir *Edmund Andros* being upon a Progress one Summer, call'd at a poor Man's House in *Stafford* County for Water. There came out to him an ancient Woman, and with her, a lively brisk Lad about Twelve Years old. The Lad was so ruddy, and fair, that his Complection gave the Governour a Curiosity to ask some Questions concerning him; and to his great Surprize was told, That he was the Son of that Woman at 76 Years of Age. His Excellency, smiling at this Improbability, enquir'd what sort of Man had been his Father? To this the good Woman made no Reply, but instantly ran, and led her Husband to the Door, who was then above 100 Years old. He confirm'd all that the Woman had said about the Lad, and, notwithstanding his great Age, was strong in his Limbs, and Voice; but had lost his Sight. The Woman for her part was without Complaint, and seem'd to retain a Vigour very uncommon at her Years. Sir *Edmund* was so well pleas'd with this extraordinary Account, that, after having made himself known to them, he offer'd to take care of the Lad: But they would by no means be perswaded to part with him. However, he gave them 20 Pounds.

⟦.145. In *November*, 1698. *Francis Nicholson*, Esq; was removed from *Maryland*, to be Governour of *Virginia*. But he went not then with that Smoothness on his Brow, he had carry'd with him, when he was appointed Lieutenant-Governour. He talk'd then no more of improving of Manufactures, Towns, and Trade. Neither was he pleased to make the Acts of Assembly the Rule of his Judgments, as formerly: But his own All-sufficient Will and Pleasure. Instead of encouraging the Manufactures, he sent over inhuman Memorials against them, which were so opposite to all Reason, that they refuted themselves. In one of these, he remonstrates, *That the Tobacco of that Country often bears so low a Price, that it will not yield Cloaths to the People that make it;* and yet presently after, in the same Memorial, he recommends it to the Parliament, *to pass an Act, forbidding the Plantations to make their own Cloathing;* which, in other Words, *is desiring a charitable Law, that the Planters shall go naked.* In a late Memorial concerted between him and his Creature Col. *Quarrey*,[22] 'tis most humbly proposed, *That all the* English *Colonies on the Continent of North* America, *be reduced under one Government, and under one Vice-Roy; and that a standing Army be there kept on foot, to subdue the Queen's Enemies;* which in plain *English*, is imploring Her Majesty, to put the Plantations under Martial Law, and in the Consequence, to give the Vice-Roy a fair Opportunity of shaking off his Dependance upon *England.*

¶.146. He began his Government with a pompous Shew of Zeal for the Church; tho' his Practice was not of a Piece with his pious Pretensions. It must be confess'd, that he has bestow'd some Liberalities upon the Clergy: But always upon Condition, that they should proclaim his Charity, either by signing Addresses dictated by himself, in his own Commendation, or at least by writing Letters of it to the Bishops in *England.* And he wou'd ever be so careful to hinder these Representations from miscarrying, that he constantly took Copies of them, and sent 'em with his own Letters.

He likewise gave himself Airs of encouraging the College: But he used this Pretext for so many By-Ends, that at last the Promoters of that good Work, grew weary of the Mockery. They perceiv'd his View was to gain himself a Character, and if he cou'd but raise that, the College might sink. And in Truth he has been so far from advancing it, that now after the Six Years of his Government, the Scholars are fewer than at his Arrival.

¶.147. Soon after his Accession to the Government, he caused the Assembly, and Courts of Judicature, to be remov'd from *James-Town*, where there were good Accommodations for People, to *Middle-Plantation*, where there were none. There he flatter'd himself with the fond Imagination, of being the Founder of a new City. He mark'd out the Streets in many Places, so as that they might represent the Figure of a *W*, in Memory of his late Majesty King *William*, after whose Name the Town was call'd *Williamsburg*. There he procur'd a stately Fabrick to be erected, which he placed opposite to the College, and graced it with the magnificent Name of the *Capitol*.

This imaginary City is yet advanced no further, than only to have a few Publick Houses, and a Store-House, more than were built upon the Place before. And by the Frequency of Publick Meetings, and the Misfortune of his Residence, the Students are interrupted in their Study, and make less Advances than formerly.

To defray the Charge of building the *Capitol*, he suggested the pernicious Duty of 15 Shillings for each Christian Servant imported, except *English*, and 20 Shillings for each Negro. I call this a pernicious Duty, because 'tis a great Hindrance to the Increase of that young Colony, as well as a very unequal Tax upon their Labour.

¶.148. It has been the constant Maxim of this Gentleman to set the People at Variance as much as possible amongst themselves. Whether this proceed from his great Fondness to the *Machevellian* Principle, *Divide & Impera*, or from his exceeding good Nature, I won't pretend to determine. But 'tis very certain, that by his Management, he has divided the most friendly, and most united People in the World, into very unhappy Factions. And, what is still worse, he has been heard to declare publickly to the Populace, *That the Gentlemen imposed upon them, and that the Servants had been all kidnapp'd, and had a lawful Action against their Masters.*

And that these Things may make the more effectual Impression, he takes care to vilifie the Gentlemen of the Council in publick Places, by the grossest and most injurious Language. He is frequently pleased to send vexatious Commands, to summon People in Her Majesty's Name, to attend him at some general Meeting, and when they come, all the Business perhaps he has with them, is to affront them before all the Company.

€.149. In the General Court, of which he is chief Judge, he has often behaved himself in that boisterous manner, that neither the rest of the Judges on the Bench, nor the Lawyers at the Bar, cou'd use their just Freedom. There 'tis usual with him to fall into excessive Passions, and utter the most abusive Language against those that presume to oppose his Arbitrary Proceedings. If the Attorney-General be so scrupulous, as to excuse himself from executing his illegal Commands, he runs a great Risque of being ill used. For in the Year 1700, Mr. *Fowler*,[23] who was then the King's Attorney, declining some hard Piece of Service, as being against Law, his Excellency in a Fury took him by the Collar, and swore, *That he knew of no Laws they had, and that his Commands should be obey'd without Hesitation or Reserve.* He often commits Gentlemen to Gaol, without the least Shadow of Complaint against them, and that without Bail, or Mainprize, to the great Oppression of the Queen's loyal

Subjects. Some of those have taken the Liberty to tell him, that such Proceedings were illegal, and not to be justify'd in any Country, that had the Happiness to be govern'd by the Laws of *England*. To whom he has been heard to reply, *That they had no Right at all to the Liberties of* English *Subjects, and that he wou'd hang up those that should presume to oppose him, with* Magna Charta *about their Necks.*

¶.150. He often mentions the absolute Government of *Fess* and *Morocco* with great Pleasure, and extols the inhuman Cruelties of that Prince towards his Subjects. And particularly one Day at a Meeting of the Governours of the College; upon some Opposition they made against one of his violent Proceedings, he vouchsafed to tell them, *That they were Dogs, and their Wives were Bitches; that he knew how to govern the* Moors, *and would beat them into better Manners.*

Neither does this Gentleman treat the Assemblies with more Gentleness, than particular People; for he has said very publickly, *That he knew how to govern the Country without Assemblies; and if they should deny him any thing, after he had obtain'd a standing Army, he wou'd bring them to Reason, with Halters about their Necks.*

¶.151. But no Wonder that he deals so freely with the People there, since neither Her Majesty's Instructions, nor the Laws of that Country can restrain him. Thus he takes upon him to transact Matters of the greatest Moment, without Advice of the Council: As for Example, he has appointed several Officers, without their Advice, which he ought not to do. Sometimes he has brought his Orders in his Hand, into the Council, and sign'd them at the Board, without so much as acquainting the Council what they were; tho' at the same time, they ought not to pass without their Advice; and after he had done this, he order'd the Clerk to enter them into the Minutes, as if they had been acted by the Consent of the Council.

If any of the Council happen to argue, or vote any thing contrary to this Gentleman's Inclinations, he instantly flies out into the most outragious Passions, and treats them with Terms very unbecoming his Station. By this means he takes away all Freedom of Debate, and makes the Council of no other Use, than to palliate his Arbitrary Practices. Sometimes, when he finds he can't carry Matters there as he desires, he makes no Scruple, of entring them in the Council-Books by his own Authority; he likewise causes many Things to be raz'd out, and others put in, by his own absolute Will and Pleasure. Nay, sometimes too, he has caused an Abstract of the Journals to be sent to *England*, instead of the Journals themselves; by which Artifice he leaves out, or puts in, just as much as he thinks fit.

¶.152. He is very sensible how unwarrantable and unjust these Proceedings are, and therefore has been always jealous, lest some of the many that have been injured, should send over their Complaints to *England*. This has put him upon a Practice most destructive to all Trade and Correspondence, which is, the Intercepting, and Breaking open of Letters. His Method was, to give Directions to some of his Creatures, dwelling near the Mouths of the Rivers, to send on Board the several Ships, that happen'd to arrive, and in the Governour's Name, demand the Letters. Thus he used to get them, and open as many as he thought fit, after which sometimes he would cause 'em to be sent where they were directed, and sometimes keep them. By this Management many People have not only suffer'd the Loss of their Letters, and of their Accounts, Invoices, *&c.* but likewise have miss'd great Advantages, for want of timely Advice, occasion'd by the Stopping of their Letters.

℃.153. Another Effect of his Jealousie was, to set Spies upon such People, as he suspected. These were to give him an Account of all the Words and Actions of those, which were most likely to complain. Nay, his Excellency has condescended to act the low Part of an Evesdropper himself, and to stand under a Window to listen for Secrets, that would certainly displease him. This Practice has made every Man afraid of his Neighbour, and destroy'd the mutual Confidence of the dearest Friends.

But the most extraordinary Method of learning Secrets, that ever was used in an *English* Government, was a kind of Inquisition, which this Gentleman has been pleased to erect frequently in that Country. He would call Courts at unusual Times, to enquire into the Life, and Conversation of those Persons, that had the Misfortune to be out of his Favour; tho' there was not the least publick Accusation against them. To these Courts he summon'd all the Neighbours of the Party he intended to expose, especially those that he knew were most intimate with him. Upon their Appearance, he administer'd an Oath to them, to answer truly, to all such Interrogatories, as he should propose. Then he would ask them endless Questions, concerning the particular Discourse and Behaviour of [t]he Party, in order to find out something that might be the Ground of an Accusation.

℃.154. In the 2d Year of this Gentleman's Government, there happen'd an Adventure very fortunate for him, which gave him much Credit with those, who rely'd on his own Account of the Matter; and that was the Taking of a Pyrate within the Capes of that Country.

It fell out that several Merchant Ships were got ready, and fallen down to *Lynhaven* Bay, near the Mouth of *James* River, in order for sailing. A Pyrate being inform'd of this, and hearing that there was no Man of War there, except a Sixth Rate, ventured within the Capes, and took several of the Merchant Ships. But a small Vessel happen'd to come down the Bay, and seeing an Engagement between the Pyrate, and a Merchant-man, made a Shift to get into the Mouth of *James* River, where the *Shoram*, a Fifth Rate Man of War, was newly arriv'd. The Sixth Rate, commanded by Capt. *John Aldred*, was then on the Carine in *Elizabeth* River, in order for her Return to *England*.

The Governour happen'd to be at that Time at *Kiquotan*, sealing up his Letters, and Capt. *Passenger*, Commander of the *Shoram*, went ashoar, to pay his Respects to him. In the mean while News was brought, that a Pyrate was got within the Capes; upon which the Captain was in Haste to go aboard his Ship: But the Governour would have stay'd him, promising to go along with him. The Captain soon after ask'd his Excuse, and went off, leaving him another Boat, if he pleased to follow. It was about One a Clock in the Afternoon, when the News was brought; but 'twas within Night, before his Excellency went aboard, staying all that while ashoar, upon some weighty Pretences. However, at last he follow'd, and by Break of Day, the Man of War was fairly out between the Capes, and the Pyrate; where after Ten Hours sharp Engagement, the Pyrate was obliged to strike, and surrender, upon the Terms of being left to the King's Mercy.

Now it happen'd, that Three Men of this Pyrate's Gang, were not on Board their own Ship at the time of the Surrender, and so were not included in the Articles of Capitulation, but were try'd in that Country. In summing up the Charge against them, (the Governour being present) the Attorney-General extoll'd his Excellency's mighty Courage, and Conduct, as if the Honour of taking the Pyrate had been due to him. Upon this, Capt. *Passenger* took the Freedom to interrupt Mr. Attorney in open Court, and said, that he was Commander of the *Shoram;* that the Pyrates were his Prisoners; and that no Body had pretended to command in that Engagement but himself: He further desir'd, that the Governour would do him the Justice to confess, whether he had given the least Word of Command all that Day, or directed any one thing during the whole Fight. Upon this, his Excellency tamely acknowledged, that what the Captain said was true; and so fairly yielded him all the Honour of that Exploit.

C.155. This Governour likewise gain'd some Reputation by another Instance of his Management, whereby he has let the World know, the violent Passion he has to publish his own Fame.

He had zealously recommended to the Court of *England*, the Necessity that *Virginia* shou'd contribute a certain *Quota* of Men, or else a Sum of Money, towards the Building, and Maintaining a Fort at *New-York*. The Reason he gave for this, was, because *New-York* was their Barrier, and as such it was but Justice, they shou'd help to defend it. This was by Order of his late Majesty K. *William* proposed to the Assembly: But upon the most solid Reasons, they humbly remonstrated, *That neither the Forts then in being, nor any other that might be built in the Province of* New-York, *cou'd in the least avail to the Defence and Security of* Virginia, *for that either the* French, *or the* Indians *might invade that Colony, and not come within an Hundred Miles of any such Fort*. The Truth of these Objections is obvious to any one, that ever look'd on the Maps of that Part of the World. But the Secret of the whole Business in plain Terms was this; Those Forts were necessary for *New-York*, to enable that Province to engross the Trade of the Neighbour *Indians;* which being highly to the Disadvant[a]ge of *Virginia*, 'twas unreasonable, that Country shou'd pay a Tribute towards its own Ruine. And since *New York* wou'd reap all the Benefit of such Forts, 'twas but just, it shou'd bear all the Charge of building them.

Now the Glory Col. *Nicholson* got in that Affair, was this; after he had represented *Virginia* as Republican, and Rebellious, for not complying with his Proposal, he said publickly, That *New-York* should not want the 900 Pounds, tho' he paid it out of his own Pocket, and soon after took a Journey to that Province.

When he arrived there, he gave his own Bills of Exchange for 900 Pounds, to the aforesaid Use, boasting, that he only rely'd on Her Majesty's Goodness to reimburse him out of the Quit-Rents of *Virginia*. But this was nothing but Grimace; for at the same time that he pass'd the Bills, he prudently took a Defeasance from the Gentleman, to whom they were given, specifying, *That till Her Majesty shou'd be graciously pleased, to remit him the Money out of the Quit Rents, those Bills shou'd never be made use of.* This was an admirable Piece of Sham-Generosity, and worthy of the great Pains he took to proclaim it. I my self have frequently heard him boast, that he gave this Money out of his own Pocket, and only depended on the Queen's Bounty to repay him.

Neither was he contented to spread abroad this Untruth there; but he also foisted it into a Memorial of Col. *Quarry*'s to the Council of Trade, in which are these Words: *As soon as Governour* Nicholson *found the Assembly of* Virginia *wou'd not see their own Interest, nor comply with Her Majesty's Orders, he went immediately to* New-York; *and out of his great Zeal to the Queen's Service, and the Security of Her Province, he gave his own Bills for* 900 *Pounds, to answer the Quota of* Virginia, *wholly depending on Her Majesty's Favour, to reimburse him out of the Revenues in that Province.*

Certainly his Excellency, and Col. *Quarry*, by whose joint Wisdom and Sincerity this Memorial was composed, must believe, that the *Council of Trade* have very imperfect Intelligence, how Matters pass in that Part of the World, or else they would not presume to impose such a Banter upon them.

But this is nothing, if compar'd to some other Passages of that unjust Representation, wherein they take upon them to describe the People of *Virginia, to be both numerous and rich, of Republican Notions and Principles, such as ought to be corrected, and lower'd in time; and that now or never is the only Time to maintain the Queen's Prerogative, and put a Stop to those wrong pernicious Notions, which are improving daily, not only in* Virginia, *but in all Her Majesty's other Governments. A Frown now from Her Majesty, will do more than an Army hereafter, &c.*

With those inhuman Reflections do those Gentlemen afterwards introduce the Necessity of a standing Army, the Truth of which is equal to that of the precedent Paragraph. Thus are that loyal People privately, and basely misrepresented; because they struggle against the Oppression, which this Governour practices, in Contempt of Her Majesty's Instructions, and the Laws of the Country. But I challenge the Authors of that Memorial, to give one single Instance, wherein the Inhabitants of *Virginia*, have shown the least Want of Loyalty to the Queen, or the least Disaffection to *England*.

The End of the First Book.

BOOK II.

Of the NATURAL
Product and Conveniencies
OF
VIRGINIA;
IN ITS
Unimprov'd STATE, before the
English went thither.

CHAP. I.

Of the Bounds and Coast of Virginia.

¶.1. *V*IRGINIA, as you have heard before, was a Name at first given, to all the Northern Part of the Continent of *America;* and when the Original Grant was made, both to the First and Second Colonies, that is, to those of *Virginia*, and *New-England*, they were both granted under the Name of *Virginia*. And afterwards, when Grants for other new Colonies were made, by particular Names, those Names for a long time served only to distinguish them, as so many Parts of *Virginia:* And until the Plantations became more familiar to *England*, it was so continued. But in Process of Time, the Name of *Virginia* was lost to all, except to that Tract of Land lying along the Bay of *Chesapeak*, and a little to the Southward, in which are included *Virginia* and *Maryland;* both which, in common Discourse, are still very often meant by the Name of *Virginia*.

The least Extent of Bounds in any of the Grants made to *Virginia*, since it was settled, and which we find upon Record there, is Two Hundred Miles North from Point *Comfort*, and Two Hundred Miles South; binding upon the Sea-Coast to the Eastward, and including all the Land West and North-West, from Sea to Sea; with the Islands on both Seas, within an Hundred Miles of the Main. But the Bounds of that Country being now under the Consideration of the General Assembly there, I shall not presume to offer any thing farther about them.

¶.2. The Entrance into *Virginia* for Shipping, is by the Mouth of *Chesapeak* Bay, which is indeed more like a

River, than a Bay: For it runs up into the Land about Two Hundred Miles, being every where near as wide, as it is at the Mouth, and in many places much wider. The Mouth thereof is about Seven Leagues over, through which all Ships must pass to go to *Maryland*.

The Coast is a bold and even Coast, with regular Soundings, and is open all the Year round: So that having the Latitude, which also can hardly be wanted, upon a Coast where so much clear Weather is, any Ship may go in by Soundings alone, by Day or Night, in Summer or in Winter; and need not fear any Disaster, if the Mariners understand any thing; for, let the Wind blow how it will, and chop about as suddenly as it pleases, any Master, tho' his Ship be never so dull, has Opportunity (by the Evenness of the Coast) either of standing off, and clearing the Shore; or else of running into safe Harbour within the Capes. A bolder and safer Coast is not known in the Universe; to which Conveniencies, there's the Addition of good Anchorage all along upon it, without the Capes.

¶.3. *Virginia*, in the most restrain'd Sense, distinct from *Maryland*, is the Spot to which I shall altogether confine this Description; tho' you may consider at the same time, that there cannot be much Difference between this, and *Maryland*, they being contiguous one to the other, lying in the same Bay, producing the same sort of Commodities, and being fallen into the same unhappy Form of Settlements, altogether upon Country Seats, without Towns. *Virginia* thus consider'd, is bounded on the South by North *Carolina;* on the North by *Patowmeck* River, which divides it from *Maryland;* on the East by the main Ocean, called the *Virginia* Seas; and on the West and North-West by the *California* Sea, whenever the Settlements shall be extended so far.

This Part of *Virginia* now inhabited, if we consider the Improvements in the Hands of the *English*, it cannot upon that Score be commended; but if we consider its natural Aptitude to be improv'd, it may with Justice be accounted, one of the finest Countries in the World. Most of the natural Advantages of it therefore, I shall endeavour to discover, and set in their true Light, together with its Inconveniencies; and afterwards proceed to the Improvements.

CHAP. II.

Of the Waters.

§.4. THE Largeness of the Bay of *Chesapeak* I have mention'd already. From one End of it to the other, there's good Anchorage, and so little Danger of a Wreck, that many Masters, who have never been there before, venture up to the Head of the Bay, upon the slender Knowledge of a common Sailor. But the Experience of one Voyage teaches any Master to go up afterwards, without a Pilot.

Besides this Bay, the Country is water'd with Four great Rivers, *viz. James, York, Rappahannock,* and *Patowmeck* Rivers; all which are full of convenient and safe Harbours. There are also abundance of lesser Rivers, many of which are capable of receiving the biggest Merchant-Ships, *viz. Elizabeth* River, *Nansamond, Chickahomony, Pocoson, Pamunky, Mattapony,* (which Two last are the Two upper Branches of *York* River) *North* River, *Eastermost* River, *Corotoman, Wiccocomoco, Pocomoke, Chissenessick, Pungotegue,* and many others: But because they are so well describ'd in the large Maps of *Virginia,* I shall forbear any farther Description of them.

These Rivers are of such Convenience, that, for almost every Half Dozen Miles of their Extent, there's a commodious and safe Road for a whole Fleet; which gives Opportunity to the Masters of Ships, to lie up and down straggling, according as they have made their Acquaintance, riding before that Gentleman's Door where they find the best Reception, or where 'tis most suitable to their Business.

¶.5. These Rivers are made up, by the Conflux of an infinite Number of Chrystal Springs of cool and pleasant Water, issuing every-where out of the Banks, and Sides of the Valleys. These Springs flow so plentifully, that they make the River Water fresh Fifty, Threescore, and sometimes an Hundred Miles below the Flux and Reflux of the Tides; And sometimes within 30, or 40 Miles of the Bay it self. The Conveniencies of these Springs are so many, they are not to be number'd: I shall therefore content my self to mention that one of supplying the Country every-where, except in the low Lands, with as many Mills as they can find Work for: And some of these send forth such a Glut a Water, that in less than Half a Mile below the Fountain-head, they afford a Stream sufficient to supply a Grist-Mill; of which there are several Instances.

¶.6. The only Mischief I know belonging to these Rivers is, that in the Month of *June* Annually, there rise up in the Salts, vast Beds of Seedling-Worms, which enter the Ships, Sloops, or Boats where-ever they find the Coat of Pitch, Tar, or Lime worn off the Timber; and by degrees eat the Plank into Cells like those of an Honey-comb. These Worms continue thus upon the Surface of the Water, from their Rise in *June*, until the first great Rains, after the Middle of *July;* but after that, do no other Damage till the next Summer-Season, and never penetrate farther than the Plank or Timber they first fix upon.

The Damage occasion'd by these Worms, may be Four several Ways avoided.

1. By keeping the Coat, (of Pitch, Lime and Tallow, or whatever else it is,) whole upon the Bottom of the Ship or Vessel, for these Worms, never fasten nor enter, but where the Timber is naked.

2. By Anchoring the larger Vessels in the Strength of

the Tide, during the Worm-Season, and haling the Smaller ashore, for in the Currant of a strong Tide, the Worm cannot fasten.

3. By Burning and Cleaning immediately after the Worm-Season is over, for then they are but just stuck into the Plank, and have not buried themselves in it; so that the least Fire in the World destroys them entirely, and prevents all Damage, that would otherwise ensue from them.

4. By running up into the Freshes with the Ship or Vessel during the Five or Six Weeks, that the Worm is thus above Water: For they never bite, nor do any Damage in Fresh Water, or where it is not very salt.

CHAP. III.

Of the Earths, and Soil.

C.7. THE Soil is of such Variety, according to the Difference of Situation, that one Part or other of it, seems fitted to every sort of Plant, that is requisite either for the Benefit or Pleasure of Mankind. And, were it not for the high Mountains to the North-West, which are supposed to retain vast Magazines of Snow, and by that means cause the Wind from that Quarter to descend a little too cold upon them, 'tis believed, that many of those delicious Summer Fruits, growing in the hotter Climates, might be kept there green all the Winter, without the Charge of Housing or any other Care, than what is due to the natural Plants of the Country, when transplanted into a Garden. But, as that would be no considerable Charge, any Man that is curious might, with all the Ease imaginable, preserve as many of them as would gratifie a moderate Luxury; and the Summer affords genial Heat enough, to ripen them to Perfection.

There are Three different kinds of Land, according to the Difference of Situation, either in the lower Parts of the Country, the Middle, or that on the Heads of the Rivers.

1. The Land towards the Mouth of the Rivers is generally of a low, moist and fat Mould, such as the heavier sort of Grain delight in, as Rice, Hemp, *Indian* Corn, *&c.* This also is varied here and there with Veins of a cold, hungry, sandy Soil, of the same Moisture, and very often lying under Water. But this also has its Advantages; for on such Land, generally grow the Huckle-berries, Cran-berries, Chincapins, *&c.* These low Lands are for the most part, well stor'd with Oaks,

Poplars, Pines, Cedars, Cypress, and Sweet-Gums; the Trunks of which are often Thirty, Forty, Fifty, some Sixty or Seventy Foot high, without a Branch or Limb. They likewise produce great Variety of Evergreens, unknown to me by Name, besides the beauteous Holly, Sweet-Myrtle, Cedar, and the Live Oak, which for Three Quarters of the Year is continually dropping its Acorns, and at the same time budding, and bearing others in their Stead.

2. The Land higher up the Rivers throughout the whole Country, is generally a level Ground, with shallow Vallies, full of Streams and pleasant Springs of clear Water, having interspers'd here and there among the large Levels, some small Hills, and extensive Vales. The Mould in some Places is black, fat, and thick laid; in others looser, lighter, and thin. The Foundation of the Mould is also various; sometimes Clay, then Gravel, and Rocky Stones; and sometimes Marle. The Middle of the Necks, or Ridges between the Rivers, is generally poor, being either a light Sand, or a white or red Clay, with a thin Mould: Yet even these Places are stored with Chestnuts, Chinkapins, Acorns of the Shrub-Oak, and a Reedy Grass in Summer, very good for Cattle. The rich Lands lie next the Rivers and Branches, and are stored with large Oaks, Walnuts, Hickories, Ash, Beech, Poplar, and many other Sorts of Timber, of surprizing Bigness.

3. The Heads of the Rivers afford a Mixture of Hills, Vallies and Plains, some richer than other, whereof the Fruits and Timber-Trees are also various. In some Places lie great Plats of low and very rich Ground, well Timber'd; in others, large Spots of Meadows and Savanna's, wherein are Hundreds of Acres without any Tree at all; but yield Reeds and Grass of incredible Height: And in the Swamps and sunken Grounds grow Trees, as vastly big, as I believe the World affords, and stand so close together, that the Branches or Boughs of many of them,

lock into one another; but what lessens their Value is, that the greatest Bulk of them are at some Distance from Water-Carriage. The Land of these upper Parts affords greater Variety of Soil, than any other, and as great Variety in the Foundations of the Soil or Mould, of which good Judgment may be made, by the Plants and Herbs that grow upon it. The Rivers and Creeks do in many Places form very fine large Marshes, which are a convenient Support for their Flocks and Herds.

¶.8. There is likewise found great Variety of Earths for Physick, Cleansing, Scouring, and making all Sorts of Potters-Ware; such as Antimony, Talk, yellow and red Oker, Fullers-Earth, Pipe-Clay, and other fat and fine Clays, Marle, &c. In a Word, there are all kinds of Earth fit for Use.

They have besides in those upper Parts, Coal for Firing, Slate for Covering, and Stones for Building, and Flat-Paving in vast Quantities, as likewise Pibble-Stones. Nevertheless, it has been confidently affirm'd by many, who have been there, that there is not a Stone in all the Country. If such Travellers knew no better than they said, my Judgment of them is, that either they were People of extream short Memories, or else of very narrow Observation. For tho' generally the lower Parts are flat, and so free from Stones, that People seldom Shoe their Horses; yet in many Places, and particularly near the Falls of the Rivers, are found vast Quantities of Stone, fit for all kind of Uses. However, as yet there is seldom any Use made of them, because commonly Wood is to be had at much less Trouble. And as for Coals, it is not likely they should ever be used there in any thing, but Forges and great Towns, if ever they happen to have any; for, in their Country Plantations, the Wood grows at every Man's Door so fast, that after it has been cut down, it will in Seven Years time, grow up again from Seed, to substantial Fire-Wood; and in Eighteen or Twenty Years 'twill come to be very good Board-Timber.

¶.9. For Mineral Earths, 'tis believ'd, they have great Plenty and Variety, that Country being in a good Latitude, and having great Appearances of them. It has been proved too, that they have both Iron and Lead, as appears by what was said before, concerning the Iron-Work, set up at *Falling-Creek*, in *James* River, where the Iron proved reasonably good: But before they got into the Body of the Mine, the People were cut off in that fatal Massacre; and the Project has never been set on Foot since. However, Col. *Byrd*, who is Proprietor of that Land, is at this Time boring, and searching after the richest Veins, near the Place of the former Work; which is very commodious for such an Undertaking, by reason of the Neighbourhood of abundance of Wood, running Water, Fire-Stone, and other Necessaries for that Purpose.

It is also said, that there is found good Iron Ore at *Corotoman*, and in several other Parts of the Country.

The Gold-Mine, of which there was lately so much Noise, may, perhaps, be found hereafter to be some good Metal, when it comes to be fully examined. But, be that as it will, the Stones, that are found near it in great Plenty, are valuable; their Lustre approaching nearer to that of the Diamond, than those of *Bristol* or *Kerry*. There is no other Fault in them, but their Softness, which the Weather hardens, when they have been some time exposed to it, they being found under the Surface of the Earth. This Place is about a Day's Journey from the Frontier Inhabitants of *James* River.

This I take to be the Place in *Purchase*'s Fourth Book of Pilgrimage,[24] called *Uttamussack*, where was formerly the principal Temple of the Country, and the Metropolitan Seat of the Priests, in *Powhatan's* Time. There stood the Three great Houses, near Sixty Foot in Length, which he reports to have been fill'd with the Images of their Gods; there were likewise preserved the Bodies of their Kings. These Houses they counted so holy, that none but their Priests and Kings durst go into them, the common People not presuming, without their particular Direction, to approach the Place.

There also was their great *Pawcorance*, or Altar-Stone, which, the *Indians* tell us, was a solid Chrystal, of between Three and Four Foot Cube, upon which, in their greatest Solemnities, they used to sacrifice. This, they would make us believe, was so clear, that the Grain of a Man's Skin might be seen through it; and was so heavy too, that when they remov'd their Gods and Kings, not being able to carry it away, they buried it thereabouts: But the Place has never been yet discover'd.

Mr. *Alexander Whittaker*, Minister of *Henrico*, on *James* River, in the Company's Time, writing to them,[25] says thus: Twelve Miles from the Falls, there is a Chrystal Rock, wherewith the *Indians* do head many of their Arrows; and Three Days Journey from thence, there is a Rock and Stony Hill found, which is on the Top covered over with a perfect and most rich Silver Ore. Our Men that went to discover those Parts, had but Two Iron Pickaxes with them, and those so ill temper'd, that the Points of them turn'd again, and bow'd at every Stroke; so that we could not search the Entrails of the Place: Yet some Trial was made of that Ore with good Success.

¶.10. Some People that have been in that Country, without knowing any thing about it, have affirm'd, that it is all a Flat, without any Mixture of Hills, because they see the Coast to Seaward perfectly level: Or else they have made their Judgment of the whole Country, by the Lands lying on the lower Parts of the Rivers (which, perhaps, they had never been beyond) and so conclude it to be throughout plain and even. When in truth, upon the Heads of the great Rivers, there are vast high Hills; and even among the Settlements, there are some so topping, that I have stood upon them, and view'd the Country all around over the Tops of the highest Trees, for many Leagues together; particularly, there are *Mawborn* Hills in the Freshes of *James* River; a Ridge of Hills about Fourteen or Fifteen Miles up *Mattapony* River; *Tolivers* Mount, upon *Rappahannock* River; and the Ridge of Hills in *Stafford* County, in the Freshes of *Patòwmeck* River; all which are within the Bounds of the *English* Inhabitants. But a little farther backward, there are Mountains, which indeed deserve the Name of Mountains, for their Height and Bigness. But since I have not seen them my self, I shall not pretend to give an Account of them, but refer you to *Batt*'s Report, *Pag.* 64. of the First Book.

These Hills are not without their Advantages; for, out of almost every rising Ground, throughout the Country, there issue Abundance of most pleasant Streams, of Pure and Chrystal Water, than which certainly the World does not afford any more delicious. These are every-where to be found in the upper Parts of this Country; and many of them flow out of the Sides of Banks very high above the Vales, which are the most suitable Places for Gardens: Where the finest Waterworks in the World may be made, at a very small Expence.

There are likewise several Mineral Springs, easily discoverable by their Taste, as well as by the Soil, which they drive out with their Streams. But I am not Naturalist skilful enough, to describe them with the Exactness they deserve.

CHAP. IV.

Of the wild Fruits of the Country.

¶.11. OF Fruits natural to the Country there is great Abundance, but the several Species of them, are produced according to the Difference of the Soil, and the various Situation of the Country: It being impossible that one Piece of Ground, should produce so many different Kinds intermix'd. Of the better Sorts of the wild Fruits, that I have met with, I will barely give you the Names, not designing a Natural History. And when I have done that, possibly I may not mention one half of what the Country affords, because I never went out of my Way, to enquire after any Thing of this Nature.

¶.12. Of stoned Fruits, I have met with Three good Sorts, *viz.* Cherries, Plums, and Persimmons.

1. Of Cherries natural to the Country, and growing wild in the Woods, I have seen Three Sorts. Two of these grow upon Trees, as big as the common *English* white Oak, whereof one grows in Bunches like Grapes. Both these Sorts are black without, and but one of them red within; that which is red within, is more palatable than the *English* black Cherry, as being without its bitterness. The Other, which hangs on the Branch like Grapes, is Water-colour'd within, of a faintish Sweet, and greedily devour'd by the small Birds. The Third sort is call'd the *Indian* Cherry, and grows higher up in the Country, than the Others do. It is commonly found by the Sides of Rivers, and Branches, on small slender Trees, scarce able to support themselves, about the Bigness of the Peach-Trees in *England*. This is certainly the

most delicious Cherry in the World; it is of a dark Purple when ripe, and grows upon a single Stalk, like the *English* Cherry, but is very small; though, I suppose, it may be made larger by Cultivation, if any Body wou'd mind it. These too are so greedily devour'd by the small Birds, that they won't let them remain on the Tree, long enough to ripen; by which Means, they are rarely known to any, and much more rarely tasted; though perhaps at the same time, they grow just by the Houses.

2. The Plums which I have observ'd to grow wild there, are of Two sorts, the Black, and the Murrey Plum, both which are small, and have much the same Relish with the Damasine.

3. The Persimmon is by *Hariot* call'd the *Indian* Plum; and so *Smith*, *Purchase*, and *Du Lake*, call it after him;[26] but I can't perceive that any of those Authors, had ever heard of the Sorts I have just now mention'd, they growing high up in the Country. These Persimmons amongst them retain their *Indian* Name. They are of several Sizes, between the Bigness of a Damasine and a Burgamot Pear. The Taste of them is so very rough, it is not to be endured, till they are fully ripe, and then they are a pleasant Fruit. Of these some *Vertuosi* make an agreeable kind of Beer; to which Purpose they dry them in Cakes, and lay them up for Use. These, like most other Fruits there, grow as thick upon the Trees, as Ropes of Onions; the Branches very often break down by the mighty Weight of the Fruit.

¶.13. Of Berries there is a great Variety, and all very good in their Kinds. Our Mulberries are of Three sorts, two Black and one White; the long Black sort are the best, being about the Bigness of a Boy's Thumb; the other Two sorts are of the Shape of the *English* Mulberry, short and thick, but their Taste does not so generally please, being of a faintish Sweet, without any Tartness. They grow upon well spread, large bodied

Trees, which run up surprizingly fast. These are the proper Food of the Silk-Worm.

2. There grow naturally Two Sorts of Currants, one red, and the other black, far more pleasant than those of the same Colour in *England*. They grow upon small Bushes.

3. There are Three Sorts of Hurts, or Huckleberries, upon Bushes, from Two to Ten Foot high. They grow in the Vallies and sunken Grounds, having different Relishes; but are all pleasing to the Taste. The largest sort grow upon the largest Bushes, and, I think, are the best Berries.

4. Cranberries grow in the low Lands, and barren sunken Grounds, upon low Bushes, like the Gooseberry, and are much of the same Size. They are of a lively Red, when ripe, and make very good Tarts. I believe, these are the Berries, which Capt. *Smith* compared to the *English* Gooseberry, and called *Raxcomens;* having, perhaps, seen some of them green, but none ripe.

5. The wild Raspberry is by some there, preferr'd to those, that were transplanted thither from *England;* but I cannot be of their Opinion.

6. Strawberries they have, as delicious as any in the World, and growing almost every where in the Woods, and Fields. They are eaten almost by all Creatures; and yet are so plentiful, that very few Persons take care to transplant them, but can find enough to fill their Baskets, when they have a mind, in the deserted old Fields.

¶.14. There grow wild several Sorts of good Nuts, *viz.* Chesnuts, Chinkapins, Hasel-nuts, Hickories, Walnuts, *&c.*

1. Chesnuts are found upon very high Trees, growing in barren Ridges. They are something less than the *French* Chesnut; but, I think, not differing at all in Taste.

2. Chinkapins have a Taste something like a Chesnut,

and grow in a Husk or Bur, being of the same sort of Substance, but not so big as an Acorn. They grow upon large Bushes, about as high as the common Apple-Trees in *England*, and either in the high or low, but always barren Ground.

3. Hasel-nuts are there in infinite Plenty, in all the Swamps; and towards the Heads of the Rivers, whole Acres of them are found upon the high Land.

4. Hickory-nuts are of several Sorts, all growing upon great Trees, and in an Husk, like the *French* Walnut, except that the Husk is not so thick, and more apt to open. Some of these Nuts are inclosed in so hard a Shell, that a light Hammer will hardly crack them; and when they are crack'd, their Kernel is fasten'd with so firm a Web, that there's no coming at it. Several other Sorts I have seen with thinner Shells, whose Kernel may be got with less Trouble. There are also several Sorts of Hickories, call'd Pig-nuts, some of which have as thin a Shell as the best *French* Walnuts, and yield their Meat very easily.

5. They have a sort of Walnut they call, Black-Walnuts, which are as big again as any I ever saw in *England*, but are very rank and oily, having a thick, hard, foul Shell, and come not clear of the Husk, as the Walnut in *France* doth.

6. Their Woods likewise afford a vast Variety of Acorns, Seven Sorts of which have fallen under my Observation. That which grows upon the Live Oak, buds, ripens, and drops off the Tree, almost the whole Year round. All their Acorns are very fat and oily; but the Live-Oak Acorn is much more so than the rest; and I believe the making Oil of them, would turn to a good Account: But now they only serve as Maste for the Hogs, and other wild Creatures, as do all the other Fruits afore-mention'd; together with several other sorts of Maste growing upon the Beech, Pine, and other Trees. The same Use is made also of divers Sorts of Pulse, and

other Fruits, growing upon wild Vines; such as Peas, Beans, Vetches, Squashes, Maycocks, Maracocks, Melons, Cucumbers, Lupines, and an Infinity of other Sorts of Fruits, which I cannot name.

¶.15. Grapes grow wild there in an incredible Plenty, and Variety; some of which are very sweet, and pleasant to the Taste, others rough and harsh, and, perhaps, fitter for Wine or Brandy. I have seen great Trees covered with single Vines, and those Vines almost hid with the Grapes. Of these wild Grapes, besides those large ones in the Mountains, mention'd by *Batt* in his Discovery, I have observed Six very different Kinds, *viz*.

1. Two of these Sorts grow among the Sand-banks, upon the Edges of the low Grounds, and Islands next the Bay, and Sea. They grow thin in small Bunches, and upon very low Vines. These are noble Grapes; and tho' they are wild in the Woods, are as large as the *Dutch* Gooseberry. One Species of them is white, the other purple, but both much alike in Flavour.

2. A Third Kind is produced throughout the whole Country, in the Swamps and Sides of Hills. These also grow upon small Vines, and in small Bunches; but are themselves as big as the *English* Bullace, and of a rank Taste when ripe, resembling the Smell of a Fox, from whence they are called Fox-Grapes. All these Three Sorts, when ripe, make admirable Tarts, being of a fleshy Substance, and, perhaps, if rightly managed, might make good Raisins.

3. There are Two Species more, that are common to the whole Country, some of which are black, and some blue on the Outside, but are both red within. They grow upon vast large Vines, and bear very plentifully. The nice Observer might, perhaps, distinguish them into several Kinds, because they differ in Colour, Size, and Relish; but I shall divide them only into Two, *viz*. The early, and the late ripe. The early ripe common

Grape is much larger, sweeter and better than the other. Of these some are quite black, and others blue; some also ripen Three Weeks, or a Month before the other. The Distance of their Ripening, is from the latter End of *August*, to the latter End of *October*. The late ripe common Grapes are less than any of the other, neither are they so pleasant to the Taste. They hang commonly till the latter End of *November*, or till *Christmas*. Of the former of these Two Sorts, the *French* Refugees at the *Monacan* Town have lately made a sort of Clarret, tho' they were gather'd off of the wild Vines in the Woods. I was told by a very good Judge, who tasted it, that it was a pleasant, strong, and full body'd Wine. From which we may conclude, that if the Wine was but tolerably good, when made of the wild Grape, which is shaded by the Woods, from the Sun, it would be much better, if produc'd of the same Grape cultivated in a regular Vineyard.

But here I find an Objection thrown in my Way, that Vineyards have been attempted both in *Virginia* and *Carolina;* and that several *French* Men went over to *Carolina*, on purpose to make Wine; and yet they could not succeed in it, but miscarried in all their Attempts. This I readily own: But I'll tell you what Progress they made, and why at last it came to nothing.

The Pine-Tree and Fir are naturally very noxious to the Vine; and the Vine is observed never to thrive, where it is any ways influenced by them. Now, all the lower Parts of their Rivers naturally produce these Trees; insomuch, that if a Man clear the Land there, of the Wood, he will certainly find that the Pine is the first Tree that will grow up again, tho' perhaps there was not a Pine in that Spot of Ground before. Again; the Vine thrives best on the Sides of Hills, Gravelly Ground, and in the Neighbourhood of fresh Streams. But the Experiments that have been made of Vineyards, both in *Virginia* and *Carolina*, have not only been near the malignant Influence of the Salt-Water, but also upon the low Lands, that are naturally subject to the Pine. The Experiment that Mr. *Isaac Jamart*, a *French* Merchant, made below *Archers-Hope-Creek*, on *James* River, in *Virginia*, was attended with these Disadvantages. And so was that of Sir *William Berkeley*, tho' his Project had a further bad Circumstance: For, to save Labour, he planted Trees for the Vines to run upon. But as he was full of Projects, so he was always very fickle, and set them on Foot, only to shew us what might be done, and not out of Hopes of any Gain to himself; so never minded to bring them to Perfection.

With the same Inconveniencies, the *French* in *Carolina* went about their Vineyards. They planted them near the salt Rivers, in Piney Ground, and made use of low Land into the Bargain, they having no other clear'd at that Time. Mr. *Nathaniel Johnson*, the present Governour of *Carolina*, has indeed of late made some likely Essays towards a Vineyard, having planted it upon the Hills: But he being now involv'd in Differences with the People, I am afraid that will be also neglected.

4. The Sixth Sort is far more palatable than the rest, and of the Size of the white Muscadine in *England;* but these are peculiar to the Frontiers, on the Heads of the Rivers. They grow upon very small Vines, which climb not higher than the Shrub, or smallest Bushes, on which they generally rest, or on the Plants, which annually spring out of the Ground: But these are so greedily eaten by the small Birds, and other wild Creatures, to whom they hang convenient, by the Lowness of their Vine, that (as it was said of the *Indian* Cherry) it is a great Rarity to find any of them ripe; though they are in great Plenty to be met with, while they are green. These, in all Likelihood, would make admirable Wine; unless the Earliness of their Ripening, may be an Objection.

The Year before the Massacre, *Anno* 1622, which destroy'd so many good Projects for *Virginia;* some *French*

Vignerons were sent thither, to make an Experiment of their Vines. These People were so in Love with the Country, that the Character they then gave of it, in their Letters to the Company in *England*, was very much to its Advantage; namely, That it far excell'd their own Country of *Languedoc:* The Vines growing in great abundance and Variety all over the Land: That some of the Grapes were of that unusual Bigness, that they did not believe them to be Grapes, until by opening them, they had seen their Kernels: That they had planted the Cuttings of their Vines at *Michaelmas*, and had Grapes from those very Cuttings, the Spring following. Adding in the Conclusion, That they had not heard of the like in any other Country: Neither was this out of the Way; for I have made the same Experiment both of their natural Vine, and of the Plants sent thither from *England*.[27]

The Copies of the Letters here quoted to the Company in *England*, are still to be seen; and *Purchase* in his 4th Volume of Pilgrims, has very justly quoted some of them.

₡.16. The Honey and Sugar-Trees are likewise spontaneous, near the Heads of the Rivers. The Honey-Tree bears a thick swelling Pod, full of Honey, appearing at a Distance like the bending Pod of a Bean or Pea. The Sugar-Tree yields a kind of Sap or Juice, which by boiling is made into Sugar. This Juice is drawn out, by wounding the Trunk of the Tree, and placing a Receiver under the Wound. The *Indians* make One Pound of Sugar, out of Eight Pounds of the Liquor. Some of this Sugar I examined very carefully. It was bright and moist, with a large full Grain; the Sweetness of it being like that of good Muscovada.

Though this Discovery has not been made by the *English* above Twelve or Fourteen Years; yet it has been known among the *Indians*, longer than any now living can remember. It was found out by the *English* after this manner. The Soldiers which were kept on the Land Frontiers, to clear them of the *Indians*, taking their Range through a Piece of low Ground, about Forty Miles above the inhabited Parts of *Patowmeck* River, and resting themselves in the Woods of those low Grounds, observ'd an inspissate Juice, like Molasses, distilling from the Tree. The Heat of the Sun had candied some of this Juice, which gave the Men a Curiosity to taste it. They found it sweet, and by this Process of Nature, learn'd to improve it into Sugar. But these Trees growing so far above the Christian Inhabitants, it hath not yet been tried, whether for Quantity, or Quality it may be worth while to cultivate this Discovery.

Thus the *Canada Indians* make Sugar of the Sap of a Tree. And *Peter Martyr*[28] mentions a Tree that yields the like Sap, but without any Description. The *Eleomeli* of the Ancients, a sweet Juice like Honey, is said to be got by wounding the Olive-Tree: And the *East-Indians* extract a sort of Sugar, they call *Jagra*, from the Juice, or potable Liquor, that flows from the Coco-Tree: The whole Process of Boiling, Graining and Refining of which, is accurately set down by the Authors of *Hortus Malabaricus*.[29]

¶.17. At the Mouth of their Rivers, and all along upon the Sea and Bay, and near many of their Creeks and Swamps, grows the Myrtle, bearing a Berry, of which they make a hard brittle Wax, of a curious green Colour, which by refining becomes almost transparent. Of this they make Candles, which are never greasie to the Touch, nor melt with lying in the hottest Weather: Neither does the Snuff of these ever offend the Smell, like that of a Tallow-Candle; but, instead of being disagreeable, if an Accident puts a Candle out, it yields a pleasant Fragrancy to all that are in the Room; insomuch, that nice People often put them out, on purpose to have the Incense of the expiring Snuff.

The Melting of these Berries, is said to have been first found out by a Surgeon in *New-England*, who perform'd wonderful Things, with a Salve made of them. This Discovery is very modern, notwithstanding these Countries have been so long settled.

The Method of managing these Berries, is by boiling them in Water, till they come to be intirely dissolv'd, except the Stone, or Seed, in the Middle, which amounts in Quantity to about half the Bulk of the Berry; the Biggest of which is something less than a Corn of Pepper.

The Cedar-Berries also have been experienced, to yield the same sort of Wax as the Myrtle, their Berries being as much larger than Pepper, as those of the Myrtle are less.

There are also in the Planes, and rich Grounds of the Freshes, abundance of Hops, which yield their Product without any Labour of the Husbandman, in Weeding, Hilling, or Poling.

¶.18. All over the Country, is interspers'd here and there, a surprizing Variety of curious Plants and Flowers. They have a sort of Brier, growing something like the Sarsaparilla. The Berry of this is as big as a Pea, and as round, being of a bright Crimson Colour. It is very hard, and finely polish'd by Nature; so that it might be put to divers Ornamental Uses.

There are several Woods, Plants and Earths, which have been fit for the Dying of curious Colours. They have the Puccoon and Musquaspen, Two Roots, with which the *Indians* use to paint themselves red: There's the Shumack and the Sassafras, which make a deep Yellow. Mr. *Heriot* tells us of several others, which he found at *Pamtego*, and gives the *Indian* Names of them: But that Language being not understood by the *Vir-*

ginians, I am not able to distinguish which he means. Particularly he takes Notice of *Wasebur*, an Herb; *Chapacour*, a Root; and *Tangomockonominge*, a Bark.

There's the Snake-Root, so much admired in *England* for a Cordial, and for being a great Antidote in all Pestilential Distempers.

There's the Rattle-Snake-Root, to which no Remedy was ever yet found comparable; for it effectually cures the Bite of a Rattle-Snake, which sometimes has been mortal in Two Minutes. If this Medicine be early applied, it presently removes the Infection, and in Two or Three Hours, restores the Patient to as perfect Health, as if he had never been hurt. This operates by violent Vomit; and Sweat.

The *James-Town* Weed (which resembles the Thorny Apple of *Peru*, and I take to be the Plant so call'd) is supposed to be one of the greatest Coolers in the World. This being an early Plant, was gather'd very young for a boil'd Salad, by some of the Soldiers sent thither, to pacifie the Troubles of *Bacon;* and some of them eat plentifully of it, the Effect of which was a very pleasant Comedy; for they turn'd natural Fools upon it for several Days: One would blow up a Feather in the Air; another wou'd dart Straws at it with much Fury; and another stark naked was sitting up in a Corner, like a Monkey, grinning and making Mows at them; a Fourth would fondly kiss, and paw his Companions, and snear in their Faces, with a Countenance more antick, than any in a *Dutch* Droll. In this frantick Condition they were confined, lest they should in their Folly destroy themselves; though it was observed, that all their Actions were full of Innocence and good Nature. Indeed, they were not very cleanly; for they would have wallow'd in their own Excrements, if they had not been prevented. A Thousand such simple Tricks they play'd, and after Eleven Days, return'd to themselves again, not remembring any thing that had pass'd.

Of spontaneous Flowers they have an unknown Variety: The finest Crown Imperial in the World; the Cardinal-Flower, so much extoll'd for its Scarlet Colour, is almost in every Branch; the Moccasin Flower, and a Thousand others, not yet known, to *English* Herbalists. Almost all the Year round, the Levels and Vales are beautified with Flowers of one Kind or other, which make their Woods as fragrant as a Garden. From these Materials their wild Bees make vast Quantities of Honey, but their Magazines are very often rifled, by Bears, Raccoons, and such like liquorish Vermine.

About Two Years ago, walking out to take the Air, I found, a little without my Pasture Fence, a Flower as big as a Tulip, and upon a Stalk resembling the Stalk of a Tulip. The Flower was of a Flesh Colour, having a Down upon one End, while the other was plain. The Form of it resembled the *Pudenda* of a Man and Woman lovingly join'd in one. Not long after I had discover'd this Rarity, and while it was still in Bloom, I drew a grave Gentleman, about an Hundred Yards, out of his Way, to see this Curiosity, not telling him any thing more, than that it was a Rarity, and such, perhaps, as he had never seen, nor heard of. When we arrived at the Place, I gather'd one of them, and put it into his Hand, which he had no sooner cast his Eye upon, but he threw it away with Indignation, as being asham'd of this Waggery of Nature. It was impossible to perswade him to touch it again, or so much as to squint towards so immodest a Representation. Neither would I presume to mention such an Indecency, but that I thought it unpardonable, to omit a Production so extraordinary.

There is also found, the fine Tulip-bearing Lawrel-Tree, which has the pleasantest Smell in the World, and keeps Blossoming and Seeding several Months together: It delights much in Gravelly Branches of Chrystal Streams, and perfumes the very Woods with its Odour. So also do the large Tulip-Tree, which we call a Poplar, the Locust, which resembles much the Jasmine, and the Perfuming Crab-Tree, during their Season. With one sort or other of these, as well as many other Sweet-flowering Trees not named, the Woods are almost everywhere adorn'd, and yield a surprizing Variety to divert the Traveller.

They find a World of Medicinal Plants likewise in that Country; and amongst the rest, the Planters pretend to have a Swamp-Root, which infallibly cures all Fevers, and Agues. The Bark of the Sassafras-Tree has been experimented to partake very much of the Virtue of the *Cortex Peruviana*. The Bark of the Root, of that which we call the Prickly Ash, being dried and powder'd, has been found to be a Specifick, in old Ulcers, and Long-running Sores. Infinite is the Number of other valuable Vegetables of every Kind: But Natural History not having been much my Study, I am unwilling to do Wrong to my Subject, by an unskilful Description.

ℭ.19. Several Kinds of the Creeping Vines bearing Fruit, the *Indians* planted in their Gardens or Fields, because they wou'd have Plenty of them always at hand; such as, Musk-melons, Water-melons, Pompions, Cushaws, Macocks, and Gourds.

1. Their Musk-melons resemble the large *Italian* Kind, and generally fill Four or Five Quarts.

2. Their Water-melons were much more large, and of several Kinds, distinguished by the Colour of their Meat and Seed; some are red, some yellow, and others white meated, and so of the Seed, some are yellow, some red, and some black; but these are never of different Colours in the same Melon. This Fruit the *Muscovites* call *Arpus;* the *Turks* and *Tartars*, *Karpus*, because they are extreamly cooling: The *Persians* call them, *Hindnanes*, because they had the first Seed of them from the *Indies*. They are excellently good, and very pleasant to the Taste, as also to the Eye; having the Rind of a lively

green Colour, streak'd and water'd, the Meat of a Carnation, and the Seed black, and shining, while it lies in the Melon.

3. Their Pompions I need not describe, but must say they are much larger and finer, than any I ever heard, of in *England*.

4. Their *Cushaws* are a kind of Pompion, of a bluish green Colour, streaked with White, when they are fit for Use. They are larger than the Pompions, and have a long narrow Neck: Perhaps this may be the *Ecushaw* of *T. Harriot*.

5. Their *Macocks* are a sort of *Melopepones*, or lesser sort of Pompion, of these they have great Variety, but the *Indian* Name *Macock* serves for all, which Name is still retain'd among them. Yet the *Clypeatæ* are sometimes call'd *Cymnels* (as are some others also) from the *Lenten* Cake of that Name, which many of them very much resemble. *Squash*, or *Squanter-Squash*, is their Name among the Northern *Indians*, and so they are call'd in *New-York*, and *New-England*. These being boil'd whole, when the Apple is young, and the Shell tender, and dished with Cream or Butter, relish very well with all sorts of Butcher's Meat, either fresh or salt. And whereas the Pompion is never eaten till it be ripe, these are never eaten after they are ripe.

6. The *Indians* never eat the Gourds, but plant them for other Uses. Yet the *Persians*, who likewise abound with this sort of Fruit, eat the *Cucurbita Lagenaris*, which they call *Kabach*, boiling it while it is green, before it comes to it's full Maturity; For, when it is ripe, the Rind dries, and grows as hard as the Bark of a Tree, and the Meat within is so consumed, and dried away, that there is then nothing left but the Seed, which the *Indians* take clean out, and afterwards use the Shells instead of Flagons and Cups; as is done also in several other Parts of the World.

The *Maracock*, which is the Fruit of what we call the

Passion Flower, our Natives did not take the Pains to plant, having enough of it growing every where; tho' they eat it with a great deal of Pleasure; this Fruit is about the Size of a Pullet's Egg.

€.20. Besides all these, our Natives had originally amongst them, *Indian* Corn, Peas, Beans, Potatoes, and Tobacco.

This *Indian* Corn was the Staff of Food, upon which the *Indians* did ever depend; for when Sickness, bad Weather, War, or any other ill Accident kept them from Hunting, Fishing and Fowling; this, with the Addition of some Peas, Beans, and such other Fruits of the Earth, as were then in Season, was the Families Dependance, and the Support of their Women and Children.

There are Four Sorts of *Indian* Corn, Two of which are early ripe, and Two, late ripe; all growing in the same manner; every single Grain of this when planted, produces a tall upright Stalk, which has several Ears hanging on the Sides of it, from Six to Ten Inches long. Each Ear is wrapt up in a Cover of many Folds, to protect it from the Injuries of the Weather. In every one of these Ears, are several Rows of Grain, set close to one another, with no other Partition, but of a very thin Husk. So that oftentimes the Increase of this Grain amounts to above a Thousand for one.

The Two Sorts which are early ripe, are distinguish'd only by the Size, which shows it self as well in the Grain, as in the Ear, and the Stalk. There is some Difference also in the Time of ripening.

The lesser Size of Early ripe Corn, yields an Ear not much larger than the Handle of a Case Knife, and grows upon a Stalk, between Three and Four Foot high. Of this are commonly made Two Crops in a Year, and, perhaps, there might be Heat enough in *England* to ripen it.

The larger Sort differs from the former only in Largeness, the Ear of this being Seven or Eight Inches long, as thick as a Child's Leg, and growing upon a Stalk Nine or Ten Foot high. This is fit for eating about the latter End of *May*, whereas the smaller Sort (generally speaking) affords Ears fit to roast by the Middle of *May*. The Grains of both these Sorts, are as plump and swell'd, as if the Skin were ready to burst.

The late ripe Corn is diversify'd by the Shape of the Grain only, without any Respect to the accidental Differences in Colour, some being blue, some red, some yellow, some white, and some streak'd. That therefore which makes the Distinction, is the Plumpness or Shrivelling of the Grain; the one looks as smooth, and as full as the early ripe Corn, and this they call *Flint-Corn;* the other has a larger Grain, and looks shrivell'd with a Dent on the Back of the Grain, as if it had never come to Perfection; and this they call *She-Corn*. This is esteem'd by the Planters, as the best for Increase, and is universally chosen by them for planting; yet I can't see, but that this also produces the Flint-Corn, accidentally among the other.

All these Sorts are planted alike, in Rows, Three, Four or Five Grains in a Hill, the larger Sort at Four or Five Foot Distance, the lesser Sort nearer. The *Indians* used to give it One or Two Weedings, and make a Hill about it, and so the Labour was done. They likewise plant a Bean in the same Hill with the Corn, upon whose Stalk it sustains it self.

The *Indians* sow'd Peas sometimes in the Intervals of the Rows of Corn, but more generally in a Patch of Ground by themselves. They have an unknown Variety of them, (but all of a Kidney-Shape) some of which I have met with wild; but whence they had their *Indian* Corn, I can give no Account; for I don't believe that it was spontaneous in those Parts.

Their Potatoes are either red or white, about as long as a Boy's Leg, and sometimes as long and big as both the Leg and Thigh of a young Child, and very much resembling it in Shape. I take these Kinds to be the same with those, which are represented in the Herbals, to be *Spanish* Potatoes. I am sure, those call'd *English* or *Irish* Potatoes are nothing like these, either in Shape, Colour, or Taste. The Way of propagating Potatoes there, is by cutting the small ones to Pieces, and planting the Cuttings in Hills of loose Earth: But they are so tender, that it is very difficult to preserve them in the Winter; for the least Frost coming at them, rots and destroys them; and therefore People bury 'em under Ground, near the Fire-Hearth, all the Winter, until the Time comes, that their Seedings are to be set.

How the *Indians* order'd their Tobacco, I am not certain, they now depending chiefly upon the *English*, for what they smoak: But I am inform'd, they used to let it all run to Seed, only succouring the Leaves, to keep the Sprouts from growing upon, and starving them; and when it was ripe, they pull'd off the Leaves, cured them in the Sun, and laid them up for Use. But the Planters make a heavy Bustle with it now, and can't please the Market neither.

CHAP. V.

Of the Fish.

¶.21. AS for Fish, both of Fresh and Salt-Water, of Shell-Fish, and others, no Country can boast of more Variety, greater Plenty, or of better in their several Kinds.

In the Spring of the Year, Herrings come up in such abundance into their Brooks and Foards, to spawn, that it is almost impossible to ride through, without treading on them. Thus do those poor Creatures expose their own Lives to some Hazard, out of their Care to find a more convenient Reception for their Young, which are not yet alive. Thence it is, that at this Time of the Year, the Freshes of the Rivers, like that of the *Broadruck*, stink of Fish.

Besides these Herrings, there come up likewise into the Freshes from the Sea, Multitudes of Shads, Rocks, Sturgeon, and some few Lampreys, which fasten themselves to the Shad, as the *Remora* of *Imperatus* is said to do to the Shark of *Tiburone*. They continue their stay there about Three Months. The Shads at their first coming up, are fat and fleshy; but they waste so extreamly in Milting and Spawning, that at their going down they are poor, and seem fuller of Bones, only because they have less Flesh. It is upon this Account, (I suppose) that those in the *Severn*, which in *Gloucester* they call *Twaits*, are said at first to want those intermuscular Bones, which afterwards they abound with. As these are in the Freshes, so the Salts afford at certain Times of the Year, many other Kinds of Fish in infinite Shoals, such as the Old-Wife, a Fish not much unlike an Herring, and the Sheep's-Head, a Sort of Fish, which they esteem in the Number of their best.

¶.22. There is likewise great Plenty of other Fish all the Summer long; and almost in every Part of the Rivers and Brooks, there are found of different Kinds: Wherefore I shall not pretend to give a Detail of them; but venture to mention the Names only of such as I have eaten and seen my self, and so leave the rest to those, that are better skill'd in Natural History. However, I may add, that besides all those that I have met with my self, I have heard of a great many very good sorts, both in the Salts and Freshes; and such People too, as have not always spent their Time in that Country have commended them to me, beyond any they had ever eat before.

Those which I know of my self, I remember by the Names. Of Herrings, Rocks, Sturgeons, Shads, Old-Wives, Sheep's-Heads, Black and red Drums, Trouts, Taylors, Green-Fish, Sun-Fish, Bass, Chub, Place, Flounders, Whitings, Fatbacks, Maids, Wives, Small-Turtle, Crabs, Oisters, Mussels, Cockles, Shrimps, Needle-Fish, Breme, Carp, Pike, Jack, Mullets, Eels, Conger-Eels, Perch, and Cats, &c.

Those which I remember to have seen there, of the Kinds that are not eaten, are the Whale, Porpus, Shark, Dog-Fish, Garr, Stingray, Thornback, Saw-Fish, Toad-Fish, Frog-Fish, Land-Crabs, Fidlers, and Periwinckles. One Day as I was halling a Sain upon the Salts, I caught a small Fish, about Two Inches and an Half long, in Shape something resembling a Scorpion, but of a Dirty dark Colour; I was a little shie of handling it, tho', I believe, there was no Hurt in it. This I judged to be that Fish, which Mr. *Purchase* in his *Pilgrims*, and Capt. *Smith* in his General History, Pag. 28. affirm to be extreamly like St. *George*'s Dragon, except only that it wants Feet and Wings.

¶.23. Before the Arrival of the *English* there, the *Indians* had Fish in such vast Plenty, that the Boys and Girls wou'd take a pointed Stick, and strike the lesser sort, as they Swam upon the Flats. The larger Fish, that kept in deeper Water, they were put to a little more Difficulty to take; But for these they made Weyrs; that is, a Hedge of small riv'd Sticks, or Reeds, of the Thickness of a Man's Finger, these they wove together in a Row, with Straps of Green Oak, or other tough Wood, so close that the small Fish cou'd not pass through. Upon High-Water Mark, they pitched one End of this Hedge, and the other they extended into the River, to the Depth of Eight or Ten Foot, fastening it with Stakes, making Cods out from the Hedge on one side, almost at the End, and leaving a Gap for the Fish to go into them, which were contrived so, that the Fish could easily find their Passage into those Cods, when they were at the Gap, but not see their Way out again, when they were in: Thus if they offered to pass through, they were taken.

Sometimes they made such a Hedge as this, quite a-cross a Creek at High-Water, and at Low wou'd go into the Run, so contracted into a narrow Compass, and take out what Fish they pleased.

At the Falls of the Rivers, where the Water is shallow, and the Current strong, the *Indians* use another kind of Weir, thus made: They make a Dam of loose Stone, whereof there is plenty at hand, quite a-cross the River, leaving One, Two, or more Spaces or Trunnels, for the Water to pass thro'; at the Mouth of which they set a Pot of Reeds, wove in Form of a Cone, whose Base is about Three Foot, and perpendicular Ten, into which the Swiftness of the Current carries the Fish, and wedges them so fast, that they cannot possibly return.

The *Indian* Way of Catching Sturgeon, when they came into the narrow part of the Rivers, was by a Man's clapping a Noose over their Tail, and by keeping fast his hold. Thus a Fish finding it self intangled, wou'd flounce, and often pull him under Water, and then that Man was counted a *Cockarouse*, or brave Fellow, that wou'd not let go; till with Swimming, Wading, and Diving, he had tired the Sturgeon, and brought it ashore. These Sturgeons would also often leap into their Canoes, in crossing the River, as many of them do still every Year, into the Boats of the *English*.

They have also another Way of Fishing like those on the *Euxine* Sea, by the Help of a blazing Fire by Night. They make a Hearth in the Middle of their Canoe, raising it within Two Inches of the Edge; upon this they lay their burning Light-Wood, split into small Shivers, each Splinter whereof will blaze and burn End for End, like a Candle: 'Tis one Man's Work to tend this Fire and keep it flaming. At each End of the Canoe stands an *Indian*, with a Gig, or pointed Spear, setting the Canoe forward with the Butt-end of the Spear, as gently as he can, by that Means stealing upon the Fish, without any Noise, or disturbing of the Water. Then they with great Dexterity, dart these Spears into the Fish, and so take 'em. Now there is a double Convenience in the Blaze of this Fire; for it not only dazzles the Eyes of the Fish, which will lie still, glaring upon it, but likewise discovers the Bottom of the River clearly to the Fisherman, which the Day-light does not.

The following Print, (as all the others in this Book,) was drawn by the Life, and I may justly affirm it, to be a very true Representation of the *Indian* Fishery.

Tab. I. *Represents the* Indians *in a Canoe with a Fire in the Middle, tended by a Boy and a Girl. In one End is a Net made of Silk Grass, which they use in Fishing their Weirs. Above is the Shape of their Weirs, and the Manner of setting a Weir-Wedge, across the Mouth of a Creek.*

☙ Note, *That in Fishing their Weirs, they lay the Side of the Canoe to the Cods of the Weir, for the more convenient coming at*

Indians in a Canoe with a Fire in the Middle

them, and not with the End going into the Cods, as is set down in the Print: But we could not otherwise represent it here, lest we should have confounded the Shape of the Weir, with the Canoe.

In the Air you see a Fishing-Hawk flying away with a Fish, and a Bald-Eagle pursuing, to take it from him; the Bald-Eagle has always his Head and Tail white, and they carry such a Lustre with them, that the white whereof may be discern'd as far as you can see the Shape of the Bird.

¶.24. 'Tis a good Diversion to observe the Manner of the Fishing-Hawks preying upon Fish, which may be seen every fair Day all the Summer long, and especially in a Morning. At the first coming of the Fish in the Spring, these Birds of Prey are surprizingly eager. I believe, in the Dead of Winter, they Fish farther off at Sea, or remain among the craggy uninhabited Islands, upon the Sea Coast. I have often been pleasantly entertain'd, by seeing these Hawks take the Fish out of the Water, and as they were flying away with their Quarry, the bald Eagles take it from them again. I have often observ'd the first of these hover over the Water, and rest upon the Wing, some Minutes together, without the least change of Place, and then from a vast Height, dart directly into the Water, and there plunge down for the Space of Half a Minute, or more, and at last bring up with him a Fish, which he could hardly rise with; then, having got upon the Wing again, he wou'd shake himself so powerfully, that he threw the Water like a Mist about him; afterwards away he'd fly to the Woods with his Game, if he were not overlook'd by the Bald-Eagle, and robb'd by the Way, which very frequently happens. For the Bald-Eagle no sooner perceives a Hawk that has taken his Prey, but he immediately pursues, and strives to get above him in the Air, which if he can once attain, the Hawk for fear of being torn by him, lets the Fish drop, and so by the Loss of his Dinner, compounds for his own Safety. The poor Fish is no sooner loosed from the Hawk's Tallons, but the Eagle shoots himself, with wonderful Swiftness, after it, and catches it in the Air, leaving all further Pursuit of the Hawk, which has no other Remedy, but to go and fish for another.

Walking once with a Gentleman in an Orchard by the River-side, early in the Spring, before the Fish were by us perceiv'd to appear in Shoal-Water, or near the Shores, and before any had been caught by the People; we heard a great Noise in the Air just over our Heads, and looking up, we see an Eagle in close pursuit of a Hawk, that had a great Fish in his Pounces. The Hawk was as low as the Apple-Trees, before he wou'd let go his Fish, thinking to recover the Wood, which was just by, where the Eagles dare never follow, for fear of bruising themselves. But, notwithstanding the Fish was dropp'd so low, and tho' it did not fall above Thirty Yards from us, yet we with our Hollowing, Running, and casting up our Hats, could hardly save the Fish from the Eagle, and if it had been dropp'd Two Yards higher, he wou'd have got it: But we at last took Possession of it alive, carried it Home, and had it dressed forthwith. It serv'd Five of us very plentifully, without any other Addition, and some to the Servants. This Fish was a Rock near Two Foot long, very fat, and a great Rarity for the Time of Year, as well as for the Manner of its being taken.

These Fishing-Hawks, in more plentiful Seasons, will catch a Fish, and loiter about with it in the Air, on purpose to have a Chace with an Eagle; and when he does not appear soon enough, the Hawk will make a sawcy Noise, and insolently defie him. This has been frequently seen, by Persons who have observ'd their Fishings.

CHAP. VI.

Of wild Fowl, and hunted Game.

¶.25. AS in Summer, the Rivers and Creeks are fill'd with Fish, so in Winter they are in many Places cover'd with Fowl. There are such a Multitude of Swans, Geese, Brants, Sheldrakes, Ducks of several Sorts, Mallard, Teal, Blewings, and many other Kinds of Water-Fowl, that the Plenty of them is incredible. I am but a small Sports-man, yet with a Fowling-Peice, have kill'd above Twenty of them at a Shot. In like manner are the Mill-Ponds, and great Runs in the Woods stor'd with these Wild-Fowl, at certain Seasons of the Year.

¶.26. The Shores, Marshy Grounds, Swamps, and Savanna's, are also stor'd with the like Plenty of other Game, of all Sorts, as Cranes, Curlews, Herons, Snipes, Woodcocks, Saurers, Ox-eyes, Plover, Larks, and many other good Birds for the Table that they have not yet found a Name for. Not to mention Beavers, Otters, Musk-Rats, Minxes, and an infinite Number of other wild Creatures.

¶.27. Altho' the Inner Lands want these Benefits, (which, however, no Pond or Slash is without,) yet even they, have the Advantage of Wild Turkeys, of an incridible Bigness, Pheasants, Partridges, Pigeons, and an Infinity of small Birds, as well as Deer, Hairs, Foxes, Raccoons, Squirrels, Possums. And upon the Frontier Plantations, they meet with Bears, Panthers, Wild-Cats, Elks, Buffaloes, and Wild Hogs, which yield Pleasure, as well as Profit to the Sports-man. And tho' some of these Names may seem frightful to the *English*, who hear not of them in their own Country; yet they are not so there; for all these Creatures ever fly from the Face of Man, doing no Damage but to the Cattle and Hogs, which the *Indians*, never troubled themselves about.

Here I can't omit a strange Rarity in the Female *Possum*, which I my self have seen. They have a false Belly, or loose Skin quite over the Belly; this never sticks to the Flesh of the Belly, but may be look'd into at all Times, after they have been concern'd in Procreation. In the Hinder-part of this, is an Overture big enough for a small Hand to pass into: Hither the young Ones, after they are full hair'd, and strong enough to run about, do fly when ever any Danger appears, or when they go to rest, or suck. This they continue till they have learn'd to live without the Dam: But, what is yet stranger, the young Ones are bred in this false Belly, without ever being within the true One. They are form'd at the Teat, and there they grow for several Weeks together into perfect Shape, becoming visibly larger, till at last they get Strength, Sight, and Hair; and then they drop off, and rest in this false Belly, going in and out at Pleasure. I have observed them thus fasten'd at the Teat, from the Bigness of a Flie, until they became as large as a Mouse. Neither is it any Hurt to the old One to open this Budget, and look in upon her Young.

¶.28. The *Indians* had no other Way of taking their Water or Land-Fowl, but by the Help of Bows, and Arrows: Yet, so great was their Plenty that with this Weapon only, they kill'd what Numbers they pleased. And when the Water-Fowl kept far from Shore, (as in warmer Weather they sometimes did,) they took their Canoes, and paddl'd after them.

But they had a better Way of killing the Elks, Buffaloes, Deer, and greater Game, by a Method which we call Fire-Hunting: That is, a Company of them wou'd go together back into the Woods, any time in the Winter, when the Leaves were fallen, and so dry, that they wou'd burn; and being come to the Place design'd, they wou'd Fire the Woods, in a Circle of Five or Six Miles Compass; and when they had compleated the first Round, they retreated inward, each at his due Distance, and put Fire to the Leaves and Grass afresh, to accelerate the Work, which ought to be finished with the Day. This they repeat, till the Circle be so contracted, that they can see their Game herded all together in the Middle, panting and almost stifled with Heat and Smoak; for the poor Creatures being frighten'd at the Flame, keep running continually round, thinking to run from it, and dare not pass through the Fire; by which Means they are brought at last into a very narrow Compass. Then the *Indians* let flie their Arrows at them, and (which is very strange) tho' they stand all round quite clouded in Smoak, yet they rarely shoot each other. By this means they destroy all the Beasts, collected within that Circle. They make all this Slaughter only for the sake of the Skins, leaving the Carcases to perish in the Woods.

Father *Verbiast*,[30] in his Description of the Emperor of *China's* Voyage into the Eastern *Tartary*, Anno 1682, gives an Account of a Way of Hunting the *Tartars* have, not much unlike this, only whereas the *Indians* surround their Game with Fire, the *Tartars* do it with a great Body of armed Men, who having environ'd the Ground they design to drive, march equally inwards, which, still as the Ring lessens, brings the Men nearer each other, till at length the wild Beasts are incompassed with a living Wall.

The *Indians* have many pretty Inventions, to discover and come up to the Deer, Turkeys and other Game undiscern'd; but that being an Art, known to very few *English* there, I will not be so accessary to the Destruction of their Game, as to make it publick. I shall therefore only tell you, that when they go a Hunting into the Out-lands, they commonly go out for the whole Season, with their Wives and Family. At the Place where they find the most Game, they build up a convenient Number of small Cabbins, wherein they live during that Season. These Cabbins are both begun, and finished in Two or Three Days, and after the Season is over, they make no further Account of them.

€.29. This and a great deal more was the natural Production of that Country, which the Native *Indians* enjoy'd, without the Curse of Industry, their Diversion alone, and not their Labour, supplying their Necessities. The Women and Children indeed, were so far provident, as to lay up some of the Nuts, and Fruits of the Earth, in their Season, for their further Occasions: But none of the Toils of Husbandry were exercised by this happy People; except the bare planting a little Corn, and Melons, which took up only a few Days in the Summer, the rest being wholly spent in the Pursuit of their Pleasures. And indeed all that the *English* have done, since their going thither, has been only to make some of these Native Pleasures more scarce, by an inordinate and unseasonable Use of them; hardly making Improvements equivalent to that Damage.

I shall in the next Book give an Account of the *Indians* themselves, their Religion, Laws, and Customs; that so, both the Country, and its primitive Inhabitants may be consider'd together, in that original State of Nature, in which the *English* found them. Afterwards I will treat of the present State of the *English* there, and the Alterations, I can't call them Improvements, they have made at this Day.

The End of the Second Book.

THE
HISTORY
AND
Present STATE
OF
VIRGINIA.

BOOK III.
Of the Indians, *their Religion, Laws, and Customs, in War and Peace.*[31]

CHAP. I.

Of the Persons of the Indians, and their Dress.

¶.1. THE *Indians* are of the middling and largest stature of the *English:* They are straight and well proportion'd, having the cleanest and most exact Limbs in the World: They are so perfect in their outward frame, that I never heard of one single *Indian*, that was either dwarfish, crooked, bandy-legg'd, or otherwise mis-shapen. But if they have any such practice among them, as the *Romans* had, of exposing such Children till they dyed, as were weak and mis-shapen at their Birth, they are very shy of confessing it, and I could never yet learn that they had.

Their Colour, when they are grown up, is a Chesnut brown and tawny; but much clearer in their Infancy. Their Skin comes afterwards to harden and grow blacker, by greasing and Sunning themselves. They have generally coal black Hair, and very black Eyes, which are most commonly grac'd with that sort of Squint which many of the *Jews* are observ'd to have. Their Women are generally Beautiful, possessing an uncommon delicacy of Shape and Features, and wanting no Charm, but that of a fair Complexion.

¶.2. The Men wear their Hair cut after several fanciful Fashions, sometimes greas'd, and sometimes painted. The Great Men, or better sort, preserve a long Lock behind for distinction. They pull their Beards up by the roots with a Muscle-shell; and both Men and Women do the same by the other parts of their Body for Cleanliness sake. The Women wear the Hair of the Head very long, either hanging at their Backs, or brought before

An Indian Man in His Summer Dress

Tab. 2. Is an *Indian* man in his Summer Dress.

The upper part of his Hair is cut short, to make a ridge, which stands up like the Comb of a Cock, the rest is either shorn off, or knotted behind his Ear. On his Head are stuck three Feathers of the Wild Turkey, Pheasant, Hawk, or such like. At his Ear is hung a fine Shell with Pearl Drops. At his Breast is a Tablet or fine Shell, smooth as polish'd Marble, which sometimes also has etched on it, a Star, Half Moon, or other Figure, according to the makers fancy. Upon his Neck, and Wrists, hang Strings of Beads, Peak[32] and Roenoke.[33] His Apron is made of a Deer skin, gashed round the edges, which hang like Tassels or Fringe; at the upper end of the Fringe is an edging of Peak, to make it finer. His Quiver is of a thin Bark; but sometimes they make it of the Skin of a Fox, or young Wolf, with the Head hanging to it, which has a wild sort of Terror in it; and to make it yet more Warlike, they tye it on with the Tail of a Panther, Buffaloe, or such like, letting the end hang down between their Legs. The prickt lines on his Shoulders, Breast and Legs, represent the Figures painted thereon. In his Left Hand he holds a Bow, and in his Right an Arrow. The mark upon his Shoulder Blade, is a distinction used by the Indians in Travelling, to shew the Nation they are of. And perhaps is the same with that which Baron Lahontan[34] calls the Arms and Heraldry of the Indians. Thus the several letter'd marks, are used by several other Nations about Virginia, when they make a journey to their Friends and Allies.

The Landskip is a natural representation of an Indian Field.

Tab. 3. Is two *Indian* Men in their Winter Dress.

Seldom any but the Elder people wore the Winter Cloaks, (which they call Match-coats,) till they got a supply of European goods; and now most have them of one sort or other in the cold Winter Weather. Fig. 1. wears the proper Indian Match-coat, which is made of Skins, drest with the Furr on, *sowed together, and worn with the Furr inwards, having the edges also gashed for beauty sake. On his Feet are* Moccasins. *By him stand some* Indian *Cabins on the Banks of the River. Fig.* 2. *wears the* Duffield *Match-coat bought of the* English, *on his Head is a Coronet of Peak, on his Legs are Stockings made of Duffields: That is, they take a length to reach from the Ankle to the Knee, so broad as to wrap round the Leg; this they sow together, letting the edges stand out an Inch beyond the Seam. When this is on, they Garter below Knee, and fasten the lower end in the* Moccasin.

in a single Lock, bound up with a Fillet of Peak, or Beads; sometimes also they wear it neatly tyed up in a Knot behind. It is commonly greased, and shining black, but never painted.

The People of Condition of both Sexes, wear a sort of Coronet on their Heads, from 4 to 6 inches broad, open at the top, and composed of Peak, or Beads, or else of both interwoven together, and workt into Figures, made by a nice mixture of the Colours. Sometimes they wear a Wreath of Dyed Furrs; as likewise Bracelets on their Necks and Arms. The Common People go bareheaded, only sticking large shining Feathers about their Heads, as their fancies lead them.

¶.3. Their Cloaths are a large Mantle, carelessly wrapped about their Bodies, and sometimes girt close in the middle with a Girdle. The upper part of this Mantle is drawn close upon the Shoulders, and the other hangs below their Knees. When that's thrown off, they have only for Modesty sake a piece of Cloath, or a small Skin, tyed round their Waste, which reaches down to the middle of the Thigh. The common sort tye only a String round their Middle, and pass a piece of Cloath or Skin round between their Thighs, which they turn at each end over the String.

Their Shoes, when they wear any, are made of an

Tab. 3. Book 3. Pag: 5.

fig: 2. fig: 1.

Two Indian Men in Their Winter Dress

entire piece of Buck-Skin; except when they sow a piece to the bottom, to thicken the Soal. They are fasten'd on with running Strings, the Skin being drawn together like a Purse on the top of the Foot, and tyed round the Ankle. The *Indian* name of this kind of Shoe is *Moccasin*.

But because a Draught of these things will inform the Reader more at first view, than a description in many words, I shall present him with the following Prints; wherein he is to take notice, that the air of the Face, as well as the ornaments of the Body, are exactly represented, being all drawn by the Life.

Tab. 4. Is a Priest and a Conjurer in their proper Habits. The Priest's Habit is sufficiently describ'd above.

The Conjurer shaves all his Hair off, except the Crest on the Crown, upon his Ear he wears the skin of some dark colour'd Bird; he, as well as the Priest, is commonly grim'd with Soot or the like; to save his modesty he hangs an Otter-skin at his Girdle, fastning the Tail between his Legs; upon his Thigh hangs his Pocket, which is fastn'd by tucking it under his Girdle, the bottom of this likewise is fring'd with Tassils for ornament sake. In the middle between them is the Huskanawing spoke of §.32.

C.4. I don't find that the *Indians* have any other distinction in their dress, or the fashion of their Hair, than only what a greater degree of Riches enables them to make; except it be their Religious persons, who are known by the particular cut of the Hair, and the unusual figure of their Garments; as our Clergy are distinguisht by their Canonical Habit.

The Habit of the *Indian* Priest, is a Cloak made in the form of a Woman's Petticoat; but instead of tying it about their middle, they fasten the gatherings about their Neck, and tye it upon the Right Shoulder, always keeping one Arm out to use upon occasion. This Cloak

Book 3. Pag: 6.

Tab: 4.

a Huskanaw pen.

fig: 2. a Preist.   a Conjurer. fig: 1.

hangs even at the bottom, but reaches no lower than the middle of the Thigh; but what is most particular in it, is, that it is constantly made of a skin drest soft, with the Pelt or Furr on the outside, and revers'd; insomuch, that when the Cloak has been a little· worn, the hair falls down in flakes, and looks very shagged, and frightful.

The cut of their Hair is likewise peculiar to their Function; for 'tis all shaven close except a thin Crest, like a Cocks-comb which stands bristling up, and runs in a semi-circle from the Forehead up along the Crown to the nape of the Neck: They likewise have a border of Hair over the Forehead, which by its own natural strength, and by the stiffning it receives from Grease and Paint, will stand out like the peak of a Bonnet.

¶.5. The dress of the Women is little different from that of the Men, except in the tying of their Hair. The Ladies of Distinction wear deep Necklaces, Pendants and Bracelets, made of small Cylinders of the *Conque* shell, which they call *Peak:* They likewise keep their Skin clean, and shining with Oyl, while the Men are commonly bedaub'd all over with Paint.

They are remarkable for having small round Breasts, and so firm, that they are hardly ever observ'd to hang down, even in old Women. They commonly go naked as far as the Navel downward, and upward to the middle of the Thigh, by which means they have the advantage of discovering their fine Limbs, and compleat Shape.

Tab. 5. Is a couple of Young Women.

The first wearing a Coronet, Necklace, and Bracelet of Peak; the second a wreath of Furs on her Head, and her Hair is bound with a Fillet of Peak and Beads. Between the two, is a Woman under a Tree, making a Basket of Silk-Grass, after their own manner.

Pag. 9. Book 3.

fig. 1.

Tab. 5.

fig. 2.

A Couple of Young Women

Tab. 6. Is a Woman, and a Boy running after her.

One of her Hands rests in her Necklace of Peak, and the other holds a Gourd, in which they put Water, or other liquid.

The Boy wears a Necklace of Runtees,[35] *in his right hand is an Indian Rattle, and in his left a roasting Ear of Corn. Round his Waste is a small string, and another brought cross thro his Crotch, and for decency a soft skin is fastn'd before.*

A Woman and a Boy Running after Her

CHAP. II.

Of the Marriages amongst the Indians, *and management of their Children.*

¶.6. THE *Indians* have their solemnities of Marriage, and esteem the Vows made at that time, as most sacred and inviolable. Notwithstanding they allow both the Man and the Wife to part upon disagreement; yet so great is the disreputation of a Divorce, that Marry'd people, to avoid the Character of Inconstant and Ungenerous, very rarely let their Quarrels proceed to a Separation. However, when it does so happen, they reckon all the ties of Matrimony dissolv'd, and each hath the liberty of marrying another. But Infidelity is accounted the most unpardonable of all Crimes in either of the Parties, as long as the Contract continues.

In these Separations, the Children go, according to the affection of the Parent, with the one or the other; for Children are not reckon'd a Charge among them, but rather Riches, according to the blessing of the Old Testament; and if they happen to differ about dividing their Children, their method is then, to part them equally, allowing the Man the first choice.

¶.7. Tho the young *Indian* Women are said to prostitute their bodies for *Wampom* Peak, Runtees, Beads, and other such like fineries; yet I never could find any ground for the accusation, and believe it only to be an unjust scandal upon them. This I know, that if ever they have a Child while they are single, it is such a disgrace to them, that they never after get Husbands. Besides, I must do 'em the justice to say, I never heard of a Child any of them had before Marriage, and the *Indians* themselves disown any such custom; tho they acknowledge at the same time, that the Maidens are entirely at their own disposal, and may manage their persons as they think fit.

Indeed I believe this Story to be an aspersion cast on those innocent Creatures, by reason of the freedom they take in Conversation, which uncharitable Christians interpret as Criminal, upon no other ground, than the guilt of their own Consciences.

The *Indian* Damsels are full of spirit, and from thence are always inspir'd with Mirth and good Humour. They are extreamly given to laugh, which they do with a Grace not to be resisted. The excess of Life and Fire, which they never fail to have, makes them frolicksom, but without any real imputation to their Innocence. However, this is ground enough for the *English*, who are not very nice in distinguishing betwixt guilt, and harmless freedom, to think them Incontinent: Tho it be with as little justice, as the jealous *Spaniards* condemn the liberty us'd by the Women of *France*, which are much more chast than their own Ladies, which they keep under the strictest confinement.

¶.8. The manner of the *Indians* treating their young Children is very strange, for instead of keeping them warm, at their first entry into the World, and wrapping them up, with I don't know how many Cloaths, according to our fond custom; the first thing they do, is to dip the Child over Head and Ears in cold Water, and then to bind it naked to a convenient Board, having a hole fitly plac'd for evacuation; but they always put Cotton, Wool, Furr, or other soft thing, for the Body to rest easy on, between the Child and the Board. In this posture they keep it several months, till the Bones begin to harden, the Joynts to knit, and the Limbs to

How Indian Mothers Carry Their Children

grow strong; and then they let it loose from the Board, suffering it to crawl about, except when they are feeding, or playing with it.

While the Child is thus at the Board, they either lay it flat on its back, or set it leaning on one end, or else hang it up by a string fasten'd to the upper end of the Board for that purpose. The Child and Board being all this while carry'd about together. As our Women undress their Children to clean them and shift their Linnen, so they do theirs to wash and grease them.

The method the Women have of carrying their Children after they are suffer'd to crawl about, is very particular; they carry them at their backs in Summer, taking one Leg of the Child under their Arm, and the Counter-Arm of the Child in their Hand over their Shoulder; the other Leg hanging down, and the Child all the while holding fast with its other Hand; but in Winter they carry them in the hollow of their Match-coat at their back, leaving nothing but the Child's Head out, as appears by the Figure.

CHAP: III.

Of the Towns, Buildings and Fortifications of the Indians.

¶.9. THE method of the *Indian* Settlements is altogether by Cohabitation, in Townships, from fifty to five hundred Families in a Town, and each of these Towns is commonly a Kingdom. Sometimes one King has the command of several of these Towns, when they happen to be united in his Hands, by Descent or Conquest; but in such cases there is always a Viceregent appointed in the dependent Town, who is at once Governour, Judge, Chancellour, and has the same Power and Authority which the King himself has in the Town where he resides. This Viceroy is oblig'd to pay to his Principal some small Tribute, as an acknowledgment of his submission, as likewise to follow him to his Wars, whenever he is requir'd.

¶.10. The manner the *Indians* have of building their Houses, is very slight and cheap; when they would erect a *Wigwang*, which is the *Indian* name for a House, they stick Saplins into the ground by one end, and bend the other at the top, fastening them together by strings made of fibrous Roots, the rind of Trees, or of the green Wood of the white Oak, which will rive into Thongs. The smallest sort of these Cabbins are conical like a Bee-hive; but the larger are built in an oblong form, and both are cover'd with the Bark of Trees, which will rive off into great flakes. Their Windows are little holes left open for the passage of the Light, which in bad weather they stop with Shutters of the same Bark, opening the Leeward Windows for Air and Light. Their

Village Showing Palisades

Chimney, as among the true Born *Irish*, is a little hole in the top of the House, to let out the Smoak, having no sort of Funnel, or any thing within, to confine the Smoke from ranging through the whole Roof of the Cabbins, if the vent will not let it out fast enough. The Fire is always made in the middle of the Cabbin. Their Door is a Pendent Mat, when they are near home; but when they go abroad, they barricado it with great Logs of Wood set against the Mat, which are sufficient to keep out Wild Beasts. There's never more than one Room in a House, except in some Houses of State, or Religion, where the Partition is made only by Mats, and loose Poles.

¶.11. Their Houses or Cabbins, as we call them, are by this ill method of Building, continually Smoaky, when they have Fire in them; but to ease that inconvenience, and to make the Smoak less troublesome to their Eyes, they generally burn Pine, or Lightwood, (that is, the fat knots of dead Pine) the Smoak of which does not offend the Eyes, but smuts the Skin exceedingly, and is perhaps another occasion of the darkness of their Complexion.

¶.12. Their Seats, like those in the Eastern part of the World, are the ground itself; and as the People of Distinction amongst them used Carpets, so cleanliness has taught the better sort of these, to spread Match-coats and Mats, to sit on.

They take up their Lodging in the sides of their Cabbins upon a Couch made of Board, Sticks, or Reeds, which are rais'd from the Ground upon Forks, and cover'd with Mats or Skins. Sometimes they lye upon a Bear Skin, or other thick Pelt drest with the Hair on, and laid upon the Ground near a Fire, covering themselves with their Match-coats. In warm weather a single Mat is their only Bed, and another roll'd up, their

Pillow. In their Travels, a Grass-plat under the covert of a shady Tree, is all the lodgings they require, and is as pleasant and refreshing to them, as a Down Bed and fine *Holland* Sheets are to us.

€.13. Their Fortifications consist only of a Palisado, of about ten or twelve foot high; and when they would make themselves very safe, they treble the Pale. They often encompass their whole Town: But for the most part only their Kings Houses, and as many others as they judge sufficient to harbour all their People, when an Enemy comes against them. They never fail to secure within their Palisado, all their Religious Reliques, and the Remains of their Princes. Within this Inclosure, they likewise take care to have a supply of Water, and to make a place for a Fire, which they frequently dance round with great solemnity.

CHAP. IV.

Of their Cookery and Food.

¶ 14. THeir Cookery has nothing commendable in it, but that it is perform'd with little trouble. They have no other Sauce but a good Stomach, which they seldom want. They boil, broil, or tost all the Meat they eat, and it is very common with them to boil Fish as well as Flesh with their *Homony;* This is *Indian* Corn soaked, broken in a Mortar, husked, and then boil'd in Water over a gentle Fire, for ten or twelve hours, to the consistence of Furmity: The thin of this is, what my Lord *Bacon* calls Cream of Maize, and highly commends for an excellent sort of nutriment.

They have two ways of Broyling, *viz.* one by laying the Meat itself upon the Coals, the other by laying it upon Sticks rais'd upon Forks at some distance above the live Coals, which heats more gently, and drys up the Gravy; this they, and we also from them, call Barbacueing.

They skin and paunch all sorts of Quadrupeds; they draw, and pluck their Fowl; but their Fish they dress with their Scales on, without gutting; but in eating they leave the Scales, Entrails and Bones to be thrown away.

They never serve up different sorts of Victuals in one Dish; as Roast and Boyl'd, Fish and Flesh; but always serve them up in several Vessels.

They bake their Bread either in Cakes before the Fire, or in Loaves on a warm Hearth, covering the Loaf first with Leaves, then with warm Ashes, and afterwards with Coals over all.

Methods of Broiling Fish

Tab. 9. *Represents the manner of their Roasting and Barbacueing, with the form of their Baskets for common uses, and carrying Fish.*

¶.15. Their Food is Fish and Flesh of all sorts, and that which participates of both; as the Beavor, a small kind of Turtle, or *Tarapins*, (as we call them) and several Species of Snakes. They likewise eat Grubs, the *Nymphæ* of Wasps, some kinds of *Scarabæi*, *Cicadæ*, *&c*. These last are such as are sold in the Markets of *Fess*, and such as the *Arabians*, *Lybians*, *Parthians* and *Æthiopians* commonly eat; so that these are not a new Dyet, tho a very slender one; and we are inform'd, that St. *John* was dyeted upon Locusts, and Wild Honey.

They make excellent Broth, of the Head and Umbles of a Deer, which they put into the Pot all bloody. This seems to resemble the *jus nigrum* of the *Spartans*, made with the Blood and Bowels of a Hare. They eat not the Brains with the Head, but dry, and reserve them to dress their Leather with.

They eat all sorts of Peas, Beans, and other Pulse, both parched and boiled. They make their Bread of the *Indian* Corn, Wild Oats, or the Seed of the Sunflower. But when they eat their Bread, they eat it alone, and not with their Meat.

They have no Salt among them, but for seasoning, use the Ashes of Hiccory, Stickweed, or some other Wood or Plant, affording a Salt ash.

They delight much to feed on Roasting-ears; that is, the *Indian* Corn, gathered green and milky, before it is grown to its full bigness, and roasted before the Fire, in the Ear. For the sake of this Dyet, which they love exceedingly, they are very careful to procure all the several sorts of *Indian* Corn before mentioned, by which means they contrive to prolong their Season. And indeed this is a very sweet and pleasing Food.

They have growing near their Towns, Peaches, Strawberries, Cushawes, Melons, Pompions, Macocks, &c. The Cushaws and Pompions they lay by, which will keep several months good after they are gather'd; the Peaches they save, by drying them in the Sun; they have likewise several sorts of the *Phaseoli*.

In the Woods, they gather Chincapins, Chesnuts, Hiccories, and Walnuts. The Kernels of the Hiccories they beat in a Mortar with Water, and make a White Liquor like Milk, from whence they call our Milk *Hickory*. Hazlenuts they will not meddle with, tho they make a shift with Acorns sometimes, and eat all the other Fruits mentioned before, but they never eat any sort of Herbs or Leaves.

They make Food of another Fruit call'd *Cuttanimmons*, the Fruit of a kind of Arum, growing in the Marshes: They are like Boyl'd Peas, or Capers to look on, but of an insipid earthy taste. Captain *Smith* in his History of *Virginia* calls them *Ocoughtanamnis*, and *Theod. de Bry* in his Translation, *Sacquenummener*.

Out of the Ground they dig Trubbs, Earth-nuts, Wild Onions, and a Tuberous Root they call *Tuckahoe*, which while crude is of a very hot and virulent quality: but they can manage it so as in case of necessity, to make Bread of it, just as the *East Indians* and those of *Egypt*, are said to do of *Colocassia*. It grows like a Flagg in the miry Marshes, having Roots of the magnitude and taste of *Irish* Potatoes, which are easy to be dug up.

¶.16. They accustom themselves to no set Meals, but eat night and day, when they have plenty of Provisions, or if they have got any thing that is a rarity. They are very patient of Hunger, when by any accident they happen to have nothing to eat; which they make more easy to them by girding up their Bellies, just as the wild *Arabs* are said to do, in their long marches; by which means they are less sensible of the impressions of Hunger.

¶.17. Among all this variety of Food, Nature hath not taught them the use of any other Drink than Water; which tho they have in cool and pleasant Springs every where, yet they will not drink that, if they can get Pond Water, or such as has been warm'd by the Sun and Weather. *Baron Lahontan* tells of a sweet juice of Maple, which the *Indians* to the Northward gave him, mingl'd with Water; but our *Indians* use no such Drink. For their Strong drink, they are altogether beholding to us, and are so greedy of it, that most of them will be drunk as often as they find an opportunity; notwithstanding which, it is a prevailing humour among them, not to taste any Strong drink at all, unless they can get enough to make them quite drunk, and then they go as solemnly about it, as if it were part of their Religion.

¶.18. Their fashion of sitting at Meals, is on a Mat spread on the ground, with their Legs lying out at length before them, and the Dish between their Legs, for which reason, they seldom or never, sit more than two together at a Dish, who may with convenience mix their Legs together, and have the Dish stand commodiously to them both. As appears by the Figure.

The Spoons which they eat with, do generally hold half a pint; and they laugh at the *English* for using small ones, which they must be forc'd to carry so often to their Mouths, that their Arms are in danger of being tir'd, before their Belly.

Tab. 10. Is a Man and his Wife at Dinner.

No. *1. Is their Pot boiling with* Homony *and Fish in it.
2. Is a Bowl of Corn, which they gather up with their Fingers, to feed themselves.*

A Man and His Wife at Dinner

3. *The* Tomahawk, *which he lays by at Dinner.*
4. *His Pocket, which is likewise stript off, that he may be at full liberty.*
5. *A Fish* } *both ready for*
6. *A heap of roasting Ears.* } *dressing.*
7. *The Gourd of Water.*
8. *A Cockle shell, which they sometimes use instead of a Spoon.*
9. *The Mat they sit on. All other matters in this Figure, are understood by the foregoing, and following Descriptions.*

CHAP. V.

Of the Travelling, Reception, and Entertainment of the Indians.

¶.19. THeir Travels they perform altogether on foot, the fatigue of which they endure to admiration. They make no other provision for their Journey, but their Gun or Bow, to supply them with Food for many hundreds miles together. If they carry any Flesh in their marches, they barbicue it, or rather dry it by degrees, at some distance, over the clear Coals of a Wood fire; just as the *Charibees* are said, to preserve the Bodies of their Kings and Great men from Corruption. Their Sauce to this dry Meat, (if they have any besides a good Stomach) is only a little Bears Oyl, or Oyl of Acorns; which last they force out, by boyling the Acorns in a strong Lye. Sometimes also in their Travels, each man takes with him a pint or quart of *Rockahomonie*, that is, the finest *Indian* Corn, parched, and beaten to powder. When they find their Stomach empty, (and cannot stay for the tedious Cookery of other things), they put about a spoonful of this into their Mouths, and drink a draught of Water upon it, which stays their Stomachs, and enables them to pursue their Journey without delay. But their main dependance is upon the Game they kill by the way, and the natural Fruits of the Earth. They take no care about Lodging in these Journeys: but content themselves with the shade of a Tree, or a little High Grass.

When they fear being discover'd, or follow'd by an Enemy in their Marches; they, every morning, having first agreed where they shall rendezvouze at night, disperse themselves into the Woods, and each takes a several way, that so the Grass or Leaves being but singly prest, may rise again, and not betray them. For the *Indians* are very artful in following a track, even where the Impressions are not visible to other People, especially if they have any advantage from the looseness of the Earth, from the stiffness of the Grass, or the stirring of the Leaves, which in the Winter Season lye very thick upon the ground; and likewise afterwards, if they do not happen to be·burned.

When in their Travels, they meet with any Waters, which are not fordable, they make Canoas of Birch Bark, by slipping it whole off the Tree, in this manner. First, they gash the Bark quite round the Tree, at the length they wou'd have the Canoe of, then slit down the length from end to end; when that is done, they with their *Tomahawks* easily open the Bark, and strip it whole off. Then they force it open with Sticks in the middle, slope the underside of the ends, and sow them up, which helps to keep the Belly open; or if the Birch Trees happen to be small, they sow the Bark of two together; The Seams they dawb with Clay or Mud, and then pass over in these Canoes, by two, three, or more at a time, according as they are in bigness. By reason of the lightness of these Boats, they can easily carry them over Land, if they foresee that they are like to meet with any more Waters, that may impede their March; or else they leave them at the Water-side, making no farther account of them; except it be to repass the same Waters in their return. See the resemblance Tab. 6.

C.20. They have a peculiar way of receiving Strangers, and distinguishing whether they come as Friends or Enemies; tho they do not understand each others Language: and that is by a singular method of smoking Tobacco; in which these things are always observ'd.

1. They take a Pipe much larger and bigger than the common Tobacco Pipe, expressly made for that purpose,

with which all Towns are plentifully provided; they call them the Pipes of Peace.

2. This Pipe they always fill with Tobacco, before the Face of the Strangers, and light it.

3. The chief Man of the *Indians*, to whom the Strangers come, takes two or three Whiffs, and then hands it to the chief of the Strangers.

4. If the Stranger refuses to Smoke in it, 'tis a sign of War.

5. If it be Peace, the chief of the Strangers takes a Whiff or two in the Pipe, and presents it to the next Great Man of the Town, they come to visit; he, after taking two or three Whiffs, gives it back to the next of the Strangers, and so on alternately, until they have past all the persons of Note on each side, and then the Ceremony is ended.

After a little discourse, they march together in a friendly manner into the Town, and then proceed to explain the Business upon which they came. This Method is as general a Rule among all the *Indians* of those parts of *America*, as the Flag of Truce is among the *Europeans*. And tho the fashion of the Pipe differ, as well as the ornaments of it, according to the humour of the several Nations, yet 'tis a general Rule, to make these Pipes remarkably bigger, than those for common use, and to adorn them with beautiful Wings, and Feathers of Birds, as likewise with Peak, Beads, or other such Foppery. Father *Lewis Henepin* gives a particular description of one, that he took notice of, among the *Indians*, upon the Lakes wherein he Travell'd. He describes it by the Name of *Calumet* of Peace, and his words are these, Book I. Chap. 24.[36]

"This *Calumet* is the most mysterious thing in the World, among the Salvages of the Continent of the Northern *America;* for it is used in all their important transactions: However, it is nothing else but a large Tobacco pipe, made of red, black or white Marble: The

Head is finely polished, and the Quill, which is commonly two foot and an half long, is made of a pretty strong Reed, or Cane, adorn'd with Feathers of all Colours, interlac'd with Locks of Womens Hair. They tye it to two Wings of the most curious Birds they can find, which makes their *Calumet* not much unlike *Mercury*'s Wand, or that Staff Ambassadors did formerly carry, when they went to treat of Peace. They sheath that Reed into the Neck of Birds they call *Huars*, which are as big as our Geese, and spotted with black and white; or else of a sort of Ducks, which make their Nests upon Trees, tho the Water be their ordinary element; and whose Feathers be of many different colours. However, every Nation adorns their *Calumet* as they think fit, according to their own genius, and the Birds they have in their Country.

"Such a Pipe is a Pass and Safe Conduct among all the Allies of the Nation who has given it. And in all Embassies, the Ambassador carries that *Calumet*, as the Symbol of Peace, which is always respected: For, the Salvages are generally perswaded, that a great misfortune would befall them, if they violated the Publick Faith of the *Calumet*.

"All their Enterprizes, Declarations of War, or Conclusions of Peace, as well as all the rest of their Ceremonies, are Seal'd, (if I may be permitted to say so) with this *Calumet:* They fill that Pipe with the best Tobacco they have, and then present it to those, with whom they have concluded any great affair; and Smoke out of the same after them."

In Tab. 6. is seen the *Calumet* of Peace, drawn by *Lahontan*, and one of the sort which I have seen.

€.21. They have a remarkable way of entertaining all Strangers of Condition, which is perform'd after the following manner. First, the King or Queen, with a Guard, and a great Retinue, march out of the Town, a quarter or half a mile, and carry Mats for their accommodation; when they meet the Strangers, they invite them to sit down upon those Mats. Then they pass the Ceremony of the Pipe, and afterwards, having spent about half an hour in grave discourse, they get up all together, and march into the Town. Here the first Complement, is to wash the Courteous Travellers Feet; then he is treated at a Sumptuous Entertainment, serv'd up by a great number of Attendants. After which he is diverted with Antique *Indian* Dances, perform'd both by Men and Women, and accompany'd with great variety of Wild Musick. At this rate he is regal'd till Bed time; when a Brace of young Beautiful Virgins are chosen, to wait upon him that night, for his particular refreshment. These Damsels are to Undress this happy Gentleman, and as soon as he is in Bed, they gently lay themselves down by him, one on one side of him, and the other on the other. They esteem it a breach of Hospitality, not to submit to every thing he desires of them. This kind Ceremony is us'd only to Men of great Distinction: And the Young Women are so far from suffering in their Reputation for this Civility, that they are envy'd for it by all the other Girls, as having had the greatest Honour done them in the World.

After this manner perhaps many of the Heroes were begotten in old time, who boasted themselves to be the Sons of some Way-faring God.

CHAP. VI.

Of the Learning, and Languages of the Indians

¶.22. THese *Indians* have no sort of Letters to express their words by, but when they would communicate any thing, that cannot be deliver'd by Message, they do it by a sort of Hieroglyphick, or representation of Birds, Beasts or other things, shewing their different meaning, by the various forms describ'd, and by the different position of the Figures.

Baron *Lahontan* in his second Volume of new Voyages, has two extraordinary Chapters, concerning the Heraldry and Hieroglyphicks of the *Indians:* but I having had no opportunity of conversing with our *Indians*, since that Book came to my hands, nor having ever suspected them, to be acquainted with Heraldry, I am not able to say any thing upon that subject.

The *Indians* when they travel never so small a way, being much embroil'd in War one with another, use several marks painted upon their Shoulders, to distinguish themselves by, and show what Nation they are of. The usual mark is one, two or three Arrows; one Nation paints these Arrows upwards, another downwards, a third sideways, and others again use other distinctions, as in Tab. 2. from whence it comes to pass, that the *Virginia* Assembly took up the humour, of making Badges of Silver, Copper or Brass, of which they gave a sufficient number, to each Nation in amity with the *English*, and then made a Law, that the *Indians* should not travel among the *English* Plantations, without one of these Badges in their Company to show that they are Friends. And this is all the Heraldry, that I know is practis'd among the *Indians*.

℃.23. Their Language differs very much, as antiently in the several parts of *Britain;* so that Nations at a moderate distance, do not understand one another. However, they have a sort of general Language, like what *Lahontan* calls the *Algonkine*, which is understood by the Chief men of many Nations, as *Latin* is in most parts of *Europe*, and *Lingua Franca* quite thro the *Levant*.

The general Language here us'd, is said to be that of the *Occaneeches*, tho they have been but a small Nation, ever since those parts were known to the *English:* but in what this Language may differ from that of the *Algonkines*, I am not able to determin.

CHAP. VII.

Of the War, and Peace of the Indians.

¶.24. WHen they are about to undertake any War, or other solemn Enterprize, the King Summons a Convention of his Great men, to assist at a Grand Council, which in their Language is call'd a *Matchacomoco*. At these Assemblies 'tis the custom, especially when a War is expected, for the young men to paint themselves irregularly with black, red, white, and several other motly colours, making one half of their face red, (for instance) and the other half black or white, with great Circles of a different hue, round their Eyes; with monstrous Mustachoes, and a thousand fantastical Figures, all over the rest of their Body; and to make themselves appear yet more ugly and frightful, they strow Feathers, Down, or the hair of Beasts, upon the Paint while it is still moist, and capable of making those light substances stick fast on: When they are thus formidably equipt, they rush into the *Matchacomoco*, and instantly begin some very Grotesque Dance, holding their Arrows, or *Tomahawks* in their hands, and all the while singing the antient Glories of their Nation, and especially of their own Families; threatning, and making signs with their *Tomahawk*, what a dreadful havock they intend to make amongst their Enemies.

Notwithstanding these terrible Airs they give themselves, they are very timorous when they come to Action, and rarely perform any open or bold feats; but the execution they do, is chiefly by Surprize and Ambuscade.

¶.25. The fearfulness of their Nature, makes 'em very

jealous and implacable. Hence it is, that when they get a Victory, they destroy Man, Woman and Child, to prevent all future Resentments.

ℭ.26. I can't think it any thing but their Jealousy, that makes them exclude the Lineal Issue from succeeding immediately to the Crown: Thus if a King have several Legitimate Children, the Crown does not descend in a direct Line to his Children, but to his Brother by the same Mother, if he have any, and for want of such, to the Children of his eldest Sister, always respecting the Descent by the Female, as the surer side. But the Crown goes to the Male Heir (if any be) in equal degree, and for want of such, to the Female, preferably to any Male that is more distant.

ℭ.27. As in the beginning of a War, they have Assemblies for Consultation, so upon any Victory, or other great success, they have publick meetings again, for Processions and Triumphs. I never see one of these, but have heard that they are accompany'd with all the marks of a wild and extravagant Joy.

Captain *Smith* gives the particulars of one that was made upon his being taken Prisoner, and carry'd to their Town. These are his words, *pag.* 47.

"Drawing themselves all in File, the King in the midst had all their Pieces and Swords born before him. Captain *Smith* was led after him by 3 great Salvages, holding him fast by each Arm; and on each side six went in File, with their Arrows nock'd; but arriving at the Town (which was but thirty or forty Hunting-houses made of Mats, which they remove as often they please, as we our Tents) all the Women and Children staring to behold him, the Souldiers first all in File perform'd the form of a *Bissom* as well as could be; and on each Flank, Officers as Serjeants to see them keep their Order. A good time they continu'd this exercise, and then cast themselves in a Ring, dancing in such several postures, and singing and yelling out such hellish Notes and Screeches; being strangely painted, every one his Quiver of Arrows, and at his Back a Club, on his Arm a Fox or an Otters skin, or some such matter for his *Vambrace;* their Heads and Shoulders painted red with Oyl and *Puccoons*[37] mingl'd together, which Scarlet-like colour made an exceeding handsom shew; his Bow in his hand, and the skin of a Bird with the Wings abroad dry'd, ty'd on his Head, a piece of Copper, a white Shell, a long Feather, with a small Rattle growing at the tails of their Snakes, ty'd to it, or some such like Toy. All this while *Smith* and the King stood in the midst, guarded as before is said, and after three Dances they all departed."

I suppose here is something omitted, and that the Conjurer should have been introduc'd in his proper Dress, as the sequel of the Story seems to mean.

₡.28. They use formal Embassies for treating, and very ceremonious ways in concluding of Peace, or else some other memorable Action, such as burying a *Tomahawk*, and raising an heap of Stones thereon, as the *Hebrews* did over *Absalom*, or of planting a Tree, in token that all Enmity is bury'd with the *Tomahawk*, that all the desolations of War are at an end, and that Friendship shall flourish among them, like a Tree.

CHAP. VIII.

Concerning the Religion, and Worship of the Indians.

¶.29. I Don't pretend to have div'd into all the mysteries of the *Indian* Religion, nor have I had such opportunities of learning them, as Father *Henepin* and Baron *Lahontan* had, by living much among the *Indians* in their Towns; and because my rule is to say nothing but the naked Truth, I intend to be very brief upon this Head.

In the Writings of those two Gentlemen, I cannot but observe direct contradictions, altho they travell'd the same Country, and the accounts they pretend to give, are of the same *Indians.* One makes 'em have very refin'd notions of a Deity, and the other don't allow them so much as the name of a God. For which reason, I think my self oblig'd sincerely to deliver what I can warrant to be true upon my own knowledge; it being neither my Interest, nor any part of my Vanity to impose upon the World.

I have been at several of the *Indian* Towns, and conversed with some of the most sensible of them in that Country; but I cou'd learn little from them, it being reckon'd Sacriledge, to divulge the Principles of their Religion. However, the following Adventure discover'd something of it. As I was ranging the Woods, with some other Friends, we fell upon their *Quioccosan* (which is their House of Religious Worship) at a time, when the whole Town were gathered together in another place, to consult about the bounds of the Land given them by the *English*.

Thus finding our selves Masters of so fair an opportunity, (because we knew the *Indians* were engaged,) we resolved to make use of it, and to examine their *Quioccasan*, the inside of which, they never suffer any *English* Man to see; and having removed about fourteen Loggs from the Door, with which it was barricado'd, we went in, and at first found nothing but naked Walls, and a Fire place in the middle. This House was about eighteen foot wide, and thirty foot long, built after the manner of their other Cabbins, but larger, with a Hole in the middle of the Roof, to vent the Smoke, the Door being at one end: Round about the House, at some distance from it, were set up Posts, with Faces carved on them, and painted. We did not observe any Window, or passage for the Light, except the Door, and the vent of the Chimney. At last, we observ'd, that at the farther end, about ten foot of the Room, was cut off by a Partition of very close Mats; and it was dismal dark behind that Partition. We were at first scrupulous to enter this obscure place, but at last we ventur'd, and groping about, we felt some Posts in the middle; then reaching our hands up those Posts, we found large Shelves, and upon these Shelves three Mats, each of which was roll'd up, and sow'd fast. These we handed down to the light, and to save time in unlacing the Seams, we made use of a Knife, and ripp'd them, without doing any damage to the Mats. In one of these we found some vast Bones, which we judg'd to be the Bones of Men, particularly we measur'd one Thigh-bone, and found it two foot nine inches long: In another Mat, we found some *Indian Tomahawks* finely grav'd, and painted. These resembl'd the wooden Faulchion us'd by the Prize fighters in *England*, except that they have no guard to save the Fingers. They were made of a rough heavy Wood, and the shape of them is represented in the Tab. 10. No. 3. Among these *Tomahawks* was the largest that ever I saw; there was fasten'd to it a Wild Turky's Beard painted red, and two of the longest Feathers of his Wings hung dangling at it, by a string of about 6 Inches long, ty'd to the end of the *Tomahawk*. In the third Mat there was something, which we took to be their Idol, tho of an underling sort, and wanted putting together. The pieces were these, first a Board three foot and a half long, with one indenture at the upper end, like a Fork, to fasten the Head upon, from thence half way down, were Half hoops nail'd to the edges of the Board, at about four Inches distance, which were bow'd out, to represent the Breast and Belly; on the lower half was another Board of half the length of the other, fasten'd to it by Joynts or pieces of Wood, which being set on each side, stood out about 14 inches from the Body, and half as high; we suppos'd the use of these to be for the bowing out of the Knees, when the Image was set up. There were packt up with these things, red and blue pieces of Cotton Cloath, and Rolls made up for Arms, Thighs and Legs, bent to at the Knees, as is represented in the Figure of their Idol, which was taken by an exact Drawer in the Country. It wou'd be difficult to see one of these Images at this day, because the *Indians* are extreme shy of exposing them. We put the Cloaths upon the Hoops for the Body, and fasten'd on the Arms and Legs, to have a view of the representation: But the Head and rich Bracelets, which it is usually adorn'd with, were not there, or at least we did not find them. We had not leisure to make a very narrow search; for having spent about an hour in this enquiry, we fear'd the business of the *Indians* might be near over; and that if we staid longer, we might be caught offering an affront to their Superstition; for this reason we wrapt up these Holy materials in their several Mats again, and laid them on the Shelf, where we found them. This Image when drest up, might look very venerable in that dark place; where 'tis not possible to see it, but by the glimmering light, that is let in, by lifting up a piece of the Matting, which we observ'd to be conveniently hung for that purpose; for when the light of the Door and Chimney, glance in several directions, upon the Image thro that little passage, it must needs make a strange representation, which those poor people are taught to worship with a devout Ignorance. There are other things that contribute towards carrying on this Imposture; first the chief Conjurer enters within the Partition in the dark, and may undiscern'd move the Image as he pleases: Secondly, a Priest of Authority stands in the room with the people, to keep them from being too inquisitive, under the penalty of the Deity's displeasure, and his own censure.

Their Idol bears a several name in every Nation, as *Okee*, *Quioccos*, *Kiwasa*. They do not look upon it, as one single Being, but reckon there are many of them of the same nature; they likewise believe, that there are tutelar Deities in every Town.

Tab. 11. Their Idol in his Tarbernacle.

The Dark edging shews the Sides and Roof [of] the House, which consist of Saplins and Bark. The paler Edging shews the Mats, by which they make a Partition, of about ten foot, at the end of the House, for the Idols abode. The Idol is set upon his Seat of Mats, within his dark recess, above the peoples Heads, and the Curtain is drawn up before him.

☾.30. Father *Henepin* in his Continuation, pag. 60. will not allow that the *Indians* have any belief of a Deity, nor that they are capable of the Arguments, and Reasonings that are common to the rest of Mankind. He farther says, that they have not any outward Ceremony to denote their Worship of a Deity, nor have any word to express God by: That there's no Sacrifice, Priest, Temple, or any other token of Religion among them. Baron *Lahontan*, on the other hand, makes them have such refin'd Notions, as seem almost to confute his own belief of Christianity.

Tab. 11.   *Book* 3. *Pag:* 31.
                         S.G.

Idol call'd OKÈE, QUIÓCCOS, *or* KIWASÀ.

The first I cannot believe, tho written by the Pen of that Pious Father; because, to my own knowledge, all the *Indians* in these parts, are a Superstitious and Idolatrous people; and because all other Authors, who have written of the *American Indians*, are against him. As to the other account, of the just thoughts the *Indians* have of Religion, I must humbly intreat the Barons pardon, because I am very sure, they have some unworthy Conceptions of God, and another World. Therefore what that Gentleman tells the Publick, concerning them, is rather to show his own Opinions, than those of the *Indians*.

Once in my Travels, in very cold Weather, I met at an *English* man's House with an *Indian*, of whom an extraordinary Character had been given me, for his Ingenuity and Understanding. When I see he had no other *Indian* with him, I thought I might be the more free; and therefore I made much of him, seating him close by a large Fire, and giving him plenty of strong Cyder, which I hop'd wou'd make him good Company, and openhearted. After I found him well warm'd (for unless they be surprized some way or other, they will not talk freely of their Religion) I asked him concerning their God, and what their Notions of Him were? He freely told me, they believ'd God was universally beneficent, that his Dwelling was in the Heavens above, and that the Influences of his Goodness reach'd to the Earth beneath. That he was incomprehensible in his Excellence, and enjoy'd all possible Felicity: That his Duration was Eternal, his Perfection boundless, and that he possesses everlasting Indolence and Ease. I told him, I had heard that they Worshipped the Devil, and asked why they did not rather Worship God, whom they had so high an opinion of, and who wou'd give them all good things, and protect them from any Mischief that the Devil could do them? To this his answer was, That, 'tis true, God is the giver of all good things, but they flow naturally and promiscuously from him; that they are showr'd down upon all Men indifferently without distinction; that God do's not trouble himself, with the impertinent affairs of Men, nor is concern'd at what they do: but leaves them to make the most of their Free Will, and to secure as many as they can, of the good things that flow from him. That therefore it was to no, purpose either to fear, or Worship him: But on the contrary, if they did not pacify the Evil Spirit, and make him propitious, he wou'd take away, or spoil all those good things that God had given, and ruine their Health, their Peace and their Plenty, by sending War, Plague and Famine among them; for, said he, this Evil Spirit, is always busying himself with our affairs, and frequently visiting us, being present in the Air, in the Thunder, and in the Storms. He told me farther, That he expected Adoration and Sacrifice from them, on pain of his displeasure; and that therefore they thought it convenient to make their Court to him. I then asked him concerning the Image, which they Worship in their *Quioccasan;* and assur'd him, that it was a dead insensible Log, equipt with a bundle of Clouts, a meer helpless thing made by Men, that could neither hear, see, nor speak; and that such a stupid thing could no ways hurt, or help them. To this he answer'd very unwillingly, and with much hesitation; However, he at last deliver'd himself in these broken and imperfect sentences; *It is the Priests—they make the people believe*, *and*———Here he paus'd a little, and then repeated to me, that *it was the Priests*———and then gave me hopes that he wou'd have said something more, but a qualm crost his Conscience, and hinder'd him from making any farther Confession.

℃.31. The Priests and Conjurers have a great sway in every Nation. Their words are looked upon as Oracles, and consequently are of great weight among the common people. They perform their Adorations and Conjurations, in the general Language before spoken of, as the Catholicks of all Nations do their Mass in the *Latin*. They teach, that the Souls of Men survive their Bodies, and that those who have done well here, enjoy most transporting Pleasures in their *Elizium* hereafter; that this *Elizium* is stor'd with the highest perfection of all their Earthly Pleasures; namely, with plenty of all sorts of Game, for Hunting, Fishing and Fowling; that it is blest with the most charming Women, which enjoy an eternal bloom, and have an Universal desire to please. That it is deliver'd from excesses of Cold or Heat, and flourishes with an everlasting Spring. But that, on the contrary, those who are wicked, and live scandalously here, are condemn'd to a filthy stinking Lake after Death, that continually burns with Flames, that never extinguish; where they are persecuted and tormented day and night, with Furies in the Shape of Old Women.

They use many Divinations and Inchantments, and frequently offer Burnt Sacrifice to the Evil Spirit. The people annually present their first Fruits of every Season and Kind, namely, of Birds, Beasts, Fish, Fruits, Plants, Roots, and of all other things, which they esteem either of Profit or Pleasure to themselves. They repeat their Offerings, as frequently as they have great successes in their Wars, or their Fishing, Fowling or Hunting.

Captain *Smith* describes the particular manner of a Conjuration that was made about him, while he was a Prisoner amongst the *Indians*, at the *Pamaunkie* Town, in the first settlement of the Country; and after that, I'll tell you of another of a more modern date, which I had from a very good hand. *Smith*'s words are these.

"Early in the Morning a great Fire was made in a long House, and a Mat spread on the one side and on the other: On the one they caus'd him to sit, and all the Guard went out of the House; and presently there came skipping in a great grim Fellow, all painted over with Coal mingl'd with Oyl, and many Snakes and Weasel Skins stufft with Moss, and all their Tails ty'd together, so as they met in the Crown of his Head, like a Tossil, and round about the Tossil was a Coronet of Feathers, the Skins hanging round about his Head, Back and Shoulders, and in a manner covering his Face; with a hellish Voice, and a Rattle in his Hand, with most strange gestures and postures he began his Invocation, and environ'd the Fire with a Circle of Meal; which done, three more such like Devils came rushing in with the like Antick Tricks, painted half black, half red; but all their Eyes were painted white, and some great strokes, like Mostachoes along their Cheeks: Round about him these Fiends danced a pretty while; and then came in three more as ugly as the rest, with red Eyes and white strokes over their black Faces: At last they all sat down right against him, 3 of them on one hand of the Chief Priest, and three on the other. Then all of them with their Rattles began a Song; which ended, the Chief Priest laid down five Wheat Corns; then straining his Arms and Hands with such violence that he sweat, and his Veins swell'd, he began a short Oration: At the conclusion, they all gave a short groan, and then laid down three grains more; after that, began their Song again, and then another Oration, ever laying down so many Corns as before, till they had twice encircled the Fire: That done, they took a bunch of little Sticks prepar'd for that purpose, continuing still their Devotion; and at the end of every Song and Oration they laid down a Stick betwixt the divisions of Corn. Till night neither he nor they did eat or drink, and then they feasted merrily, with the best provisions they could make. Three days they used this Ceremony, the meaning whereof they told him, was to know, if he intended them well or no. The Circle of Meal signified their Country, the Circles of Corn, the bounds of the Sea, and the Sticks his Country. They imagined the World to be flat and round like a Trencher, and they in the midst."

Thus far is *Smith*'s Story of Conjuration concerning himself, but when he says they encircled the Fire with Wheat, I am apt to believe, he means their *Indian* Corn; which some, contrary to the custome of the rest of Mankind, will still call by the name of *Indian* Wheat.

The later Story of Conjuration is this, Some few years ago, there happen'd a very dry time, towards the heads of the Rivers, and especially on the upper parts of *James River*, where Collonel *Byrd* had several Quarters of Negroes. This Gentleman has for a long time been extreamly respected, and fear'd by all the *Indians* round about, who, without knowing the Name of any Governour, have ever been kept in order by Him. During this drowth, an *Indian*, well known to one of the Collonel's Overseers, came to him, and ask'd if his Tobacco was not like to be spoyl'd? The Overseer answer'd Yes, if they had not Rain very suddenly: The *Indian*, who pretended great kindness for his Master, told the Overseer, if he would promise to give him two Bottles of Rum, he would bring him Rain enough: The Overseer did not believe any thing of the matter, not seeing at that time the least appearance of Rain, nor so much as a Cloud in the Sky; however, he promis'd to give him the Rum, when his Master came thither, if he wou'd be as good as his word: Upon this the *Indian* went immediately a *Pauwawing*,[38] as they call it; and in about half an hour, there came up a black Cloud into the Sky, that shower'd down Rain enough upon this Gentlemans Corn and Tobacco, but none at all upon any of the Neighbours, except a few drops of the Skirt of the Shower. The *Indian* for that time went away, without returning to the Overseer again, till he heard of his Masters arrival at the *Falls*, and then he came to him, and demanded the two Bottles of Rum. The Collonel at first seem'd to know nothing of the matter, and ask'd the *Indian*, for what reason he made that demand? (altho his Overseer had been so overjoy'd at what had happen'd that he could not rest till he had taken a Horse and rid near forty Miles to tell his Master the story.) The *Indian* answer'd with some concern, that he hop'd the Overseer had let him know the service he had done him, by bringing a Shower of Rain to save his Crop. At this the Collonel, not being apt to believe such Stories, smil'd, and told him, he was a Cheat, and had seen the Cloud a coming, otherwise he could neither have brought the Rain, nor so much as foretold it. The *Indian* at this seeming much troubl'd, reply'd, Why then had not such a one, and such a one, (naming the next Neighbours) Rain as well as your Overseer, for they lost their Crops; but I lov'd you, and therefore I sav'd yours? The Collonel made sport with him a little while, but in the end order'd him the two Bottles of Rum, letting him understand however, that it was a free Gift, and not the consequence of any Bargain with his Overseer.

€.32. The *Indians* have their Altars and places of Sacrifice. Some say they now and then sacrifice young Children: but they deny it, and assure us, that when they withdraw these Children, it is not to Sacrifice them, but to Consecrate them to the service of their God. *Smith* tells of one of these Sacrifices in his time, from the Testimony of some people, who had been Eye-witnesses. His words are these.

"Fifteen of the properest young Boys between ten and fifteen years of Age they painted white, having brought them forth, the people spent the Forenoon in Dancing and Singing about them with Rattles. In the Afternoon they put these Children to the Root of a Tree. By them all the Men stood in a Guard, every one having a *Bastinado* in his Hand, made of Reeds bound together; they made a Lane between them all along, through which there were appointed five Young Men to fetch these Children: So every one of the five went through the Guard, to fetch a Child each after other by turns; the Guard fiercely beating them with their *Bastinadoes*, and they patiently enduring and receiving all, defending the Children with their naked Bodies from the unmerciful blows, that pay them soundly, though the Children escape. All this while the Women weep and cry out very passionately, providing Mats, Skins, Moss, and dry Wood, as things fitting for their Childrens Funeral. After the Children were thus past the Guard, the Guards tore down the Tree, Branches and Bows with such violence, that they rent the Body, made Wreaths for their Heads, and bedeck'd their Hair with the Leaves.

"What else was done with the Children was not seen, but they were all cast on a heap in a Valley as dead, where they made a great Feast for all the Company.

"The *Werowance* being demanded the meaning of this Sacrifice, answer'd, that the Children were not dead, but that the *Okee* or Devil did suck the Blood from the Left Breast of those, who chanc'd to be his by lot, till they were dead, but the rest were kept in the Wilderness by the young men, till nine months were expired, during which time they must not converse with any; and of these were made their Priests and Conjurers."

How far Captain *Smith* might be misinform'd in this account, I can't say, or whether their *Okee*'s sucking the Breast, be only a delusion or pretence of the Physician, (or Priest, who is always a Physician) to prevent all reflection on his skill, when any happen'd to dye under his discipline. This I choose rather to believe, than those Religious Romances concerning their *Okee*. For I take this story of *Smith*'s to be only an example of *Huskanawing*, which being a Ceremony then altogether unknown to him, he might easily mistake some of the circumstances of it.

The Solemnity of *Huskanawing* is commonly practis'd once every fourteen or sixteen years, or oftener, as their young men happen to grow up. It is an Institution or Discipline which all young men must pass, before they can be admitted to be of the number of the Great men, or *Cockarouses*[39] of the Nation; whereas by Captain *Smith*'s Relation, they were only set apart to supply the Priesthood. The whole Ceremony is performed after the following manner.

The choicest and briskest young men of the Town, and such only as have acquired some Treasure by their Travels and Hunting, are chosen out by the Rulers to be *Huskanawed;* and whoever refuses to undergo this Process, dare not remain among them. Several of those odd preparatory Fopperies are premis'd in the beginning, which have been before related; but the principal part of the business is to carry them into the Woods, and there keep them under confinement, and destitute of all Society, for several months; giving them no other sustenance, but the Infusion, or Decoction of some Poisonous Intoxicating Roots; by virtue of which Physick, and by the severity of the discipline, which they undergo, they become stark staring Mad: In which raving condition they are kept eighteen or twenty days. During these extremities, they are shut up, night and day, in a strong Inclosure made on purpose; one of which I saw, belonging to the *Paumaunkie Indians*, in the year 1694. It was in shape like a Sugar-loaf, and every way open like a Lattice, for the Air to pass through, as in Tab. 4. Fig. 3. In this Cage thirteen young Men had been *Huskanaw'd*, and had not been a month set at liberty, when I saw it. Upon this occasion it is pretended, that these poor Creatures drink so much of that Water of *Lethe*, that they perfectly lose the remembrance of all former things, even of their Parents, their Treasure, and their Language. When the Doctors find that they have drank sufficiently of the *Wysoccan*, (so they call this mad Potion) they gradually restore them to their Sences again, by lessening the Intoxication of their Diet; but before they are perfectly well, they bring them back into their Towns, while they are still wild and crazy, through the Violence of the Medicine. After this they are very fearful of discovering any thing of their former remembrance; for if such a thing should happen to any of them, they must immediately be *Huskanaw'd* again; and the second time the usage is so severe, that seldom any one escapes with Life. Thus they must pretend to have forgot the very use of their Tongues, so as not to be able to speak, nor understand any thing that is spoken, till they learn it again. Now whether this be real or counterfeit, I don't know; but certain it is, that they will not for some time take notice of any body, nor any thing, with which they were before acquainted, being still under the guard of their Keepers, who constantly wait upon them every where, till they have learnt all things perfectly over again. Thus they unlive their former lives, and commence Men, by forgetting that they ever have been Boys. If under this Exercise any one should dye, I suppose the Story of *Okee*, mention'd by *Smith*, is the Salvo for it: For (says he) *Okee* was to have such as were his by lot; and such were said to be Sacrificed.

Now this Conjecture is the more probable, because we know that *Okee* has not a share in every *Huskanawing;* for tho two young men happen'd to come short home, in that of the *Pamaunkie Indians*, which was perform'd in the year 1694, yet the *Appamattucks*, formerly a great Nation, tho now an inconsiderable people, made an *Huskanaw* in the year 1690, and brought home the same number they carried out.

€.33. I can account no other way for the great pains and secrecy of the Keepers, during the whole process of this discipline, but by assuring you, that it is the most meritorious thing in the World, to discharge that trust well, in order to their preferment to the greatest posts in the Nation, which they claim as their undoubted right, in the next promotion. On the other hand, they are sure of a speedy Passport into the other World, if they should by their Levity or Neglect, show themselves in the least unfaithful.

Those which I ever observ'd to have been *Huskanawed*, were lively handsome well timber'd young men, from fifteen to twenty years of age or upward, and such as were generally reputed rich.

I confess, I judged it at first sight to be only an Invention of the Seniors, to engross the young mens Riches to themselves; for, after suffering this operation, they never pretended to call to mind any thing of their former property: But their Goods were either shared among the old men, or brought to some publick use; and so those Younkers were oblig'd to begin the World again.

But the *Indians* detest this opinion, and pretend that this violent method of taking away the Memory, is to release the Youth from all their Childish impressions, and from that strong Partiality to persons and things, which is contracted before Reason comes to take place. They hope by this proceeding, to root out all the prepossessions and unreasonable prejudices which are fixt in the minds of Children. So that, when the Young men come to themselves again, their Reason may act freely, without being byass'd by the Cheats of Custom and Education. Thus also they become discharg'd from the remembrance of any tyes by Blood, and are establisht in a state of equality and perfect freedom, to order their actions, and dispose of their persons, as they think fit, without any other Controul, than that of the Law of Nature. By this means also they become qualify'd, when they have any Publick Office, equally and impartially to administer Justice, without having respect either to Friend or Relation.

§.34. The *Indians* offer Sacrifice almost upon every new occasion; as when they travel or begin a long Journey, they burn Tobacco instead of Incense, to the Sun, to bribe him to send them fair Weather, and a prosperous Voyage: When they cross any great Water, or violent Fresh, or Torrent, they throw Tobacco, Puccoon, Peak, or some other valuable thing, that they happen to have about them, to intreat the Spirit presiding there, to grant them a safe passage. It is call'd a Fresh, when after very great Rains, or (as we suppose) after a great Thaw of the Snow and Ice lying upon the Mountains to the North West, the Water descends, in such abundance into the Rivers, that they overflow the Banks which bound their Streams at other times.

Likewise when the *Indians* return from War, from Hunting, from great Journeys, or the like, they offer some proportion of their Spoils, of their chiefest Tobacco, Furs and Paint, as also the fat, and choice bits of their Game.

§.35. I never could learn that they had any certain time or set days for their Solemnities: but they have appointed Feasts that happen according to the several Seasons. They solemnize a day for the plentiful coming of their Wild Fowl, such as Geese, Ducks, Teal, *&c.* for the returns of their Hunting Seasons, and for the ripening of certain Fruits: but the greatest Annual Feast they have, is at the time of their Corn-gathering, at which they revel several days together. To these they universally contribute, as they do to the gathering in the Corn. On this occasion they have their greatest variety of Pastimes, and more especially of their War-Dances, and Heroick Songs; in which they boast, that their Corn being now gather'd, they have store enough for their Women and Children; and have nothing to do, but to go to War, Travel, and to seek out for New Adventures.

¶.36. They make their Account by units, tens, hundreds, &c. as we do; but they reckon the Years by the Winters, or *Cohonks*, as they call them; which is a name taken from the note of the Wild Geese, intimating so many times of the Wild Geese coming to them, which is every Winter. They distinguish the several parts of the Year, by five Seasons, *viz.* The budding or blossoming of the Spring; the earing of the Corn, or roasting ear time; the Summer, or highest Sun; the Corn-gathering, or fall of the Leaf; and the Winter, or *Cohonks*. They count the Months likewise by the Moons, tho not with any relation to so many in a year, as we do: but they make them return again by the same name, as the Moon of Stags, the Corn Moon, the first and second Moon of *Cohonks*, &c. They have no distinction of the hours of the Day, but divide it only into three parts, the Rise, Power, and lowering of the Sun. And they keep their account by knots on a string, or notches on a Stick, not unlike the *Peruvian Quippoes*.

¶.37. In this state of Nature, one would think they should be as pure from Superstition, and overdoing matters in Religion, as they are in other things: but I find it is quite the contrary; for this Simplicity gives the cunning Priest a greater advantage over them, according to the *Romish* Maxim, *Ignorance is the Mother of Devotion*. For, no bigotted Pilgrim appears more zealous, or strains his Devotion more at the Shrine, than these believing *Indians* do, in their Idolatrous Adorations. Neither do the most refin'd Catholicks undergo their pennance with so much submission as these poor Pagans do the severities, which their Priests inflict upon them.

They have likewise in other cases many fond and idle Superstitions, as for the purpose, by the falls of *James* River upon Collonel *Byrd*'s Land, there lies a Rock which I have seen, about a mile from the River, wherein is fairly imprest several marks like the footsteps of a Gigantick Man, each step being about five foot asunder: These they aver to be the track of their God.

This is not unlike what the Fathers of the *Romish* Church tell us, that our Lord left the print of his Feet on the Stone, whereon he stood while he talkt with St. *Peter;* which Stone was afterward preserv'd as a very Sacred Relique, and after several translations, was at last fix'd in the Church of *St. Sebastian* the Martyr, where it is kept, and visited with great expressions of Devotion. So that the *Indians*, as well as these, are not without their pious frauds.

€.38. As this people have a great reverence for the Priest, so the Priest very oddly endeavours to preserve their respect, by being as hideously ugly as he can, especially when he appears in publick; for besides, that the cut of his Hair is peculiar to his Function, as in Tab. 4. Pag. 6. and the hanging of his Cloak, with the Fur reverst and falling down in flakes, looks horridly shagged, he likewise bedaubs himself in that frightful manner with Paint, that he terrifies the people into a veneration for him.

The Conjurer is a Partner with the Priest, not only in the Cheat, but in the advantages of it, and sometimes they officiate for one another. When this Artist is in the Act of Conjuration, or of *Pauwawing*, as they term it, he always appears with an air of Haste, or else in some Convulsive posture, that seems to strain all the faculties, like the *Sybils*, when they pretended to be under the Power of Inspiration. At these times, he has a black Bird with expanded Wings fasten'd to his Ear, differing in nothing but colour, from *Mahomet*'s Pidgeon. He has no cloathing but a small skin before, and a Pocket at his Girdle, as in Tab. 4. Pag. 6.

The *Indians* never go about any considerable Enterprize, without first consulting their Priests and Conjurers; for the most ingenious amongst them are brought up to those functions, and by that means become better instructed in their Histories, than the rest of the people. They likewise engross to themselves all the knowledge of Nature, which is handed to them by Tradition from their Forefathers; by which means they are able to make a truer judgment of things, and consequently are more capable of advising those that consult them upon all occasions. These Reverend Gentlemen are not so entirely given up to their Religious Austerities, but they sometimes take their pleasure (as well as the Laity) in Fishing, Fowling and Hunting.

¶.39. The *Indians* have Posts fix'd round their *Quioccasan*, which have Mens Faces carved upon them, and are painted. They are likewise set up round some of their other celebrated places, and make a Circle for them to dance about, on certain solemn occasions. They very often set up Pyramidical Stones, and Pillars, which they colour with *Puccoon*, and other sorts of Paint, and which they adorn with *Peak*, *Roenoke*, *&c*. To these they pay all outward signs of Worship and Devotion; not as to God, but as they are Hieroglyphicks of the permanency and immutability of the Deity; because these, both for figure and substance, are, of all Sublunary Bodies, the least subject to decay or change; they also for the same reason keep Baskets of Stones in their Cabbins. Upon this account too, they offer Sacrifice to Running Streams, which by the perpetuity of their Motion, typifie the Eternity of God.

They erect Altars where-ever they have any remarkable occasion; and because their principal Devotion consists in Sacrifice, they have a profound respect for these Altars. They have one particular Altar, to which, for some mystical reason, many of their Nations pay an extraordinary Veneration; of this sort was the Crystal Cube, mention'd Book II. Chap. 3. ¶.8. The *Indians* call this by the name of *Pawcorance*, from whence proceeds the great Reverence they have for a small Bird that uses the Woods, and in their note continually sound that name. This Bird flys alone, and is only heard in the twilight. They say this is the Soul of one of their Princes; and on that score, they wou'd not hurt it for the World. But there was once a profane *Indian* in the upper parts of *James* River, who, after abundance of fears and scruples, was at last brib'd to kill one of them with his Gun; but the *Indians* say he paid dear for his presumption, for in few days after he was taken away, and never more heard of.

When they travel by any of these Altars, they take great care to instruct their Children and Young people in the particular occasion and time of their erection, and recommend the respect which they ought to have for them; so that their careful observance of these Traditions, proves as good a Memorial of such Antiquities, as any Written Records; especially for so long as the same people continue to inhabit in, or near the same place.

I can't understand that their Women ever pretended to intermeddle with any Offices, that relate to the Priesthood, or Conjuration.

¶.40. The *Indians* are Religious in preserving the Corpses of their Kings and Rulers after Death, which they order in the following manner. First, they neatly flay off the Skin as entire as they can, slitting it only in the Back; then they pick all the Flesh off from the Bones as clean as possible, leaving the Sinews fastned to the Bones, that they may preserve the Joynts together; then they dry the Bones a little in the Sun, and put them into the Skin again, which in the mean time has been kept from drying or shrinking; when the Bones are placed right in the Skin, they nicely fill up the vacuities, with a very fine white Sand. After this they sew up the Skin

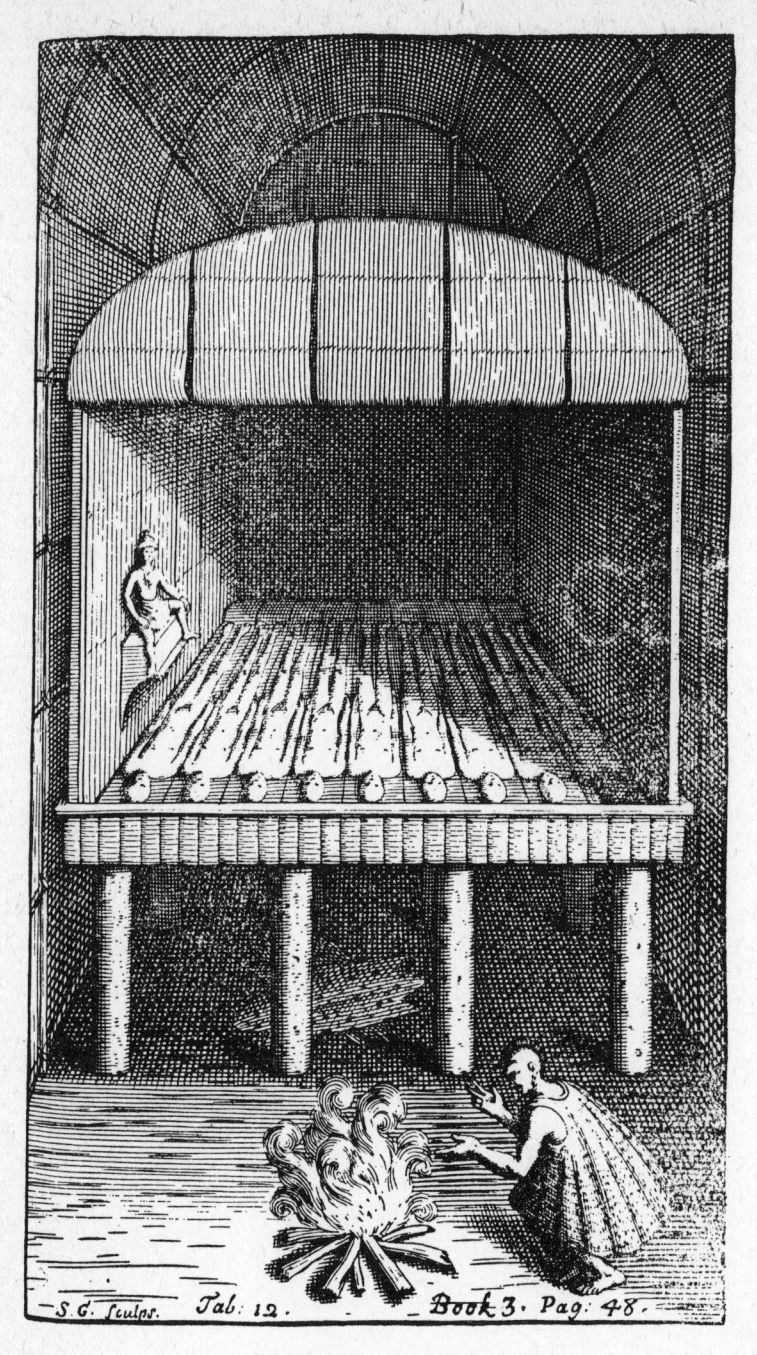

The Burial of the Kings

again, and the Body looks as if the Flesh had not been removed. They take care to keep the Skin from shrinking, by the help of a little Oyl or Grease, which saves it also from Corruption. The Skin being thus prepar'd, they lay it in an Apartment for that purpose, upon a large Shelf rais'd above the Floor. This Shelf is spread with Mats, for the Corps to rest easie on, and skreen'd with the same, to keep it from the Dust. The Flesh they lay upon Hurdles in the Sun to dry, and when it is throughly dryed, it is sewed up in a Basket, and set at the Feet of the Corps, to which it belongs. In this place also they set up a *Quioccos*, or Idol, which they believe will be a Guard to the Corps. Here night and day one or other of the Priests must give his Attendance, to take care of the Dead Bodies. So great an Honor and Veneration have these ignorant and unpolisht people for their Princes, even after they are dead.

The Mat is suppos'd to be turn'd up in the Figure, that the Inside may be viewed.

Tab. 12. Represents the Burial of the Kings.

CHAP. IX.

Of the Diseases, and Cures of the Indians.

¶.41. THE *Indians* are not subject to many Diseases, and such as they have, generally come from excessive Heats, and sudden Colds, which they as suddenly get away by Sweating. But if the Humour happen to fix, and make a pain in any particular Joynt, or Limb, their general cure then is by burning, if it be in any part that will bear it; their method of doing this, is by little Sticks of Light-wood, the Coal of which will burn like a hot Iron; the sharp point of this they run into the Flesh, and having made a Sore, keep it running till the Humour be drawn off: Or else they take Punck, (which is a sort of a soft Touch-wood, cut out of the knots of Oak or Hiccory Trees, but the Hiccory affords the best,) this they shape like a Cone, (as the *Japoneses* do their *Moxa* for the Gout) and apply the Basis of it to the place affected. Then they set fire to it, letting it burn out upon the part, which makes a running Sore effectually.

They use Sucking frequently and Scarrifying, which, like the *Mexicans*, they perform with a Rattle-Snakes Tooth. They seldom cut deeper than the *Epidermis*, by which means they give passage to those sharp waterish Humours, that lye between the two Skins, and cause Inflamations. Sometimes they make use of Reeds for Cauterizeing, which they heat over the Fire, till they are ready to flame, and then apply them upon a piece of thin wet Leather, to the place aggriev'd, which makes the Heat more pierceing.

Their Priests are always Physicians, and by the method of their Education in the Priesthood, are made very knowing in the hidden qualities of Plants, and other Natural things, which they count a part of their Religion to conceal from every body, but from those that are to succeed them in their holy Function. They tell us, their God will be angry with them, if they should discover that part of their knowledge; so they suffer only the Rattle Snake Root to be known, and such other Antidotes, as must be immediately apply'd; because their Doctors can't be always at hand to remedy those sudden misfortunes, which generally happen in their Hunting or Travelling.

They call their Physick *Wisoccan*, not from the name of any particular Root or Plant, but as it signifies Medicine in general. So that *Heriot*, *De Bry*,[40] *Smith*, *Purchass* and *De Laet*, seem all to be mistaken in the meaning of this word *Wighsacan*, which they make to be the name of a particular Root: And so is *Parkinson*[41] in the word *Woghsacan*, which he will have to be the name of a Plant. Nor do I think there is better authority for applying the word *Wisank* to the Plant *Vincetoxicum Indianum Germanicum*, or *Winank* to the *Sassafrass* Tree.

The Physick of the *Indians*, consists for the most part, in the Roots and Barks of Trees, they very rarely using the Leaves either of Herbs or Trees; what they give inwardly, they infuse in Water, and what they apply outwardly, they stamp or bruise, adding Water to it, if it has not moisture enough of it self; with the thin of this they bathe the part affected, then lay on the thick, after the manner of a Pultis, and commonly dress round, leaving the fore place bare.

¶.42. They take great delight in Sweating, and therefore in every Town they have a Sweating-House, and a Doctor is paid by the Publick to attend it. They commonly use this to refresh themselves, after they have been fatigu'd with Hunting, Travel, or the like, or else when they are troubl'd with Agues, Aches, or Pains in their Limbs. Their method is thus, the Doctor takes three or four large Stones, which after having heated red hot, he places 'em in the middle of the Stove, laying on them some of the inner Bark of Oak beaten in a Mortar, to keep them from burning. This being done, they creep in six or eight at a time, or as many as the place will hold, and then close up the mouth of the Stove, which is usually made like an Oven, in some Bank near the Water side. In the mean while, the Doctor, to raise a Steam, after they have been stewing a little while, pours cold Water on the Stones, and now and then sprinkles the Men to keep them from fainting. After they have sweat as long as they can well endure it, they sally out, and (tho it be in the depth of Winter) forthwith plunge themselves over Head and Ears in cold Water, which instantly closes up the Pores, and preserves them from taking cold. The heat being thus suddenly driven from the extream parts to the Heart, makes them a little feeble for the present, but their Spirits rally again, and they instantly recover their Strength, and find their Joynts as supple and vigorous as if they never had travell'd, or been indispos'd. So that I may say as *Bellonius*[42] does in his Observations on the *Turkish* Bagnio's, All the Crudities contracted in their Bodies, are by this means evaporated and carry'd off. The *Muscovites* and *Finlanders* are said to use this way of Sweating also. "It is almost a Miracle, says *Olearius*,[43] to see how their Bodies, accustom'd to, and harden'd by Cold, can endure so intense a Heat, and how that when they are not able to endure it longer, they come out of the Stoves as naked as they were born, both Men and Women, and plunge into cold Water, or cause it to be pour'd on them." *Trav. into Musc.*, *1.* 3. *p.*67.

The *Indians* also pulverize the Roots of a kind of *Anchuse* or yellow *Alkanet*, which they call *Puccoon*, and of a sort of wild *Angelica*, and mixing them together with Bears Oyl, make a yellow Ointment, with which, after they have bath'd, they anoint themselves Capapee; this supples the Skin, renders them nimble and active, and withal so closes up the Pores, that they lose but few of their Spirits by Perspiration. *Piso*[44] relates the same of the *Brasilians*, and my Lord *Bacon*[45] asserts, that Oyl and fat things do no less conserve the substance of the Body, than Oyl colours, and Varnish do that of the Wood.

They have also a further advantage of this Oyntment, for it keeps all Lice, Fleas, and other troublesome Vermine from coming near them; which otherwise, by reason of the nastiness of their Cabbins, they would be very much infested with.

Smith talks of this *Puccoon*, as if it only grew on the Mountains, whereas it is common to all the Plantations of the *English*, except only to those situated in very low Grounds.

CHAP. X.

Of the Sports, and Pastimes of the Indians.

¶.43. THEIR Sports and Pastimes are Singing, Dancing, Instrumental Musick, and some boisterous Plays, which are perform'd by Running, Catching and Leaping upon one another; they have also one great Diversion, to the practising of which, are requisite whole handfuls of Sticks or hard Straws, which they know how to count as fast, as they can cast their Eyes upon them, and can handle with a surprizing dexterity.

Their Singing is not the most charming that I have heard, it consists much in exalting the voice, and is full of slow melancholy accents. However, I must allow even this Musick to contain some wild Notes that are agreeable.

Their Dancing is perform'd either by few or a great Company, but without much regard either to Time or Figure. The first of these is by one or two persons, or at most by three. In the mean while, the Company sit about them in a Ring upon the Ground, singing outrageously and shaking their Rattles. The Dancers sometimes Sing, and sometimes look menacing and terrible, beating their Feet furiously against the Ground, and showing ten thousand Grimaces and Distortions. The other is perform'd by a great number of people, the Dancers themselves forming a Ring, and moving round a Circle of carv'd Posts, that are set up for that purpose; or else round a Fire, made in a convenient part of the Town; and then each has his Rattle in his hand, or what other thing he fancies most, as his Bow and Arrows, or his *Tomahawk*. They also dress themselves up with Branches of Trees, or some other strange accoutrements. Thus they proceed, Dancing and Singing, with all the antick postures they can invent; and he's the bravest Fellow that has the most prodigious gestures. Sometimes they place three young Women in the middle of the Circle, as you may see in the Figure.

Tab. 13. Represents a solemn Festival Dance of the *Indians*, round their carv'd Posts.

Those which on each side are hopping upon their Hams, take that way of coming up to the Ring, and when they find an opportunity strike in among the rest.

Captain *Smith* relates the particulars of a Dance made for his Entertainment, by *Pocahontas*, Daughter of the Emperor *Powhatan*, to divert him, till her Father came, who happen'd not to be at home when *Smith* arriv'd at his Town. *Gen. Hist.* p. 67.
"In a fair plain Field they made a Fire, before which he sat down upon a Mat, when suddenly amongst the Woods was heard such a hideous noise and shrieking, that the *English* betook themselves to their Arms, and seized on two or three Old Men by them, supposing *Powhatan*, with all his Power, was coming to surprize them. But presently *Pocahontas* came, willing him to kill her, if any hurt were intended; and the beholders, which were Men, Women and Children, satisfied the Captain that there was no such matter. Then presently they were presented with this Antick, thirty young Women came naked out of the Woods, only cover'd behind and before with a few Green Leaves, their Bodies all painted, some of one colour, some of another, but all differing; their Leader had a fair pair of Bucks Horns on her Head, and an Otters Skin at her Girdle, and another at her Arm, a Quiver of Arrows at her Back, a Bow and Arrows in her Hand: The next had in her

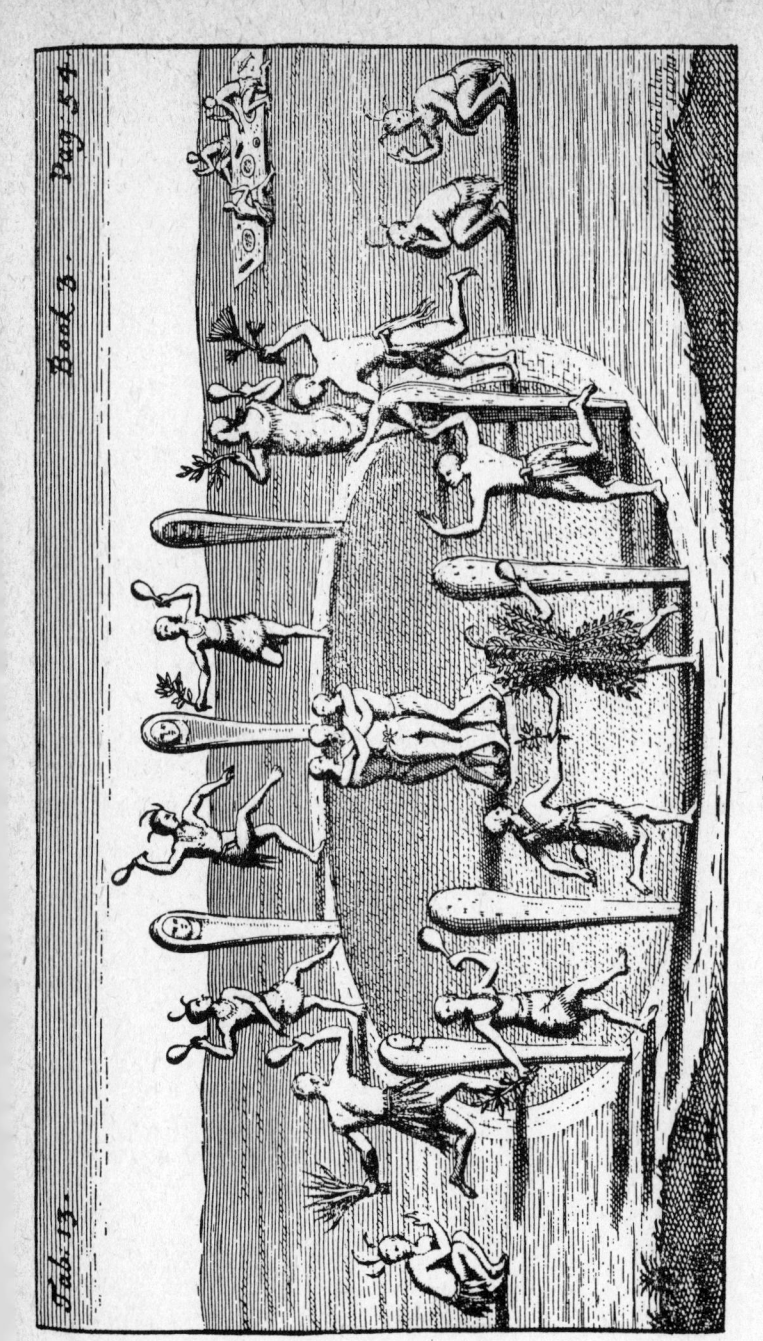

Solemn Festival Dance

Hand a Sword, another a Club, another a Potstick; all of 'em being Horned alike: The rest were all set out with their several Devices. These Fiends, with most Hellish Shouts and Cries, rushing from among the Trees, cast themselves in a Ring about the Fire, Singing and Dancing with most excellent ill variety, oft falling into their infernal passions, and then solemnly betaking themselves again to Sing and Dance; having spent near an hour in this *Mascarado*, as they enter'd, in like manner they departed."

They have a Fire made constantly every night, at a convenient place in the Town, whither all that have a mind to be merry, at the Publick Dance or Musick, resort in the Evening.

Their Musical Instruments are chiefly Drums and Rattles: Their Drums are made of a Skin, stretched over an Earthen Pot half full of Water. Their Rattles are the Shell of a small Gourd, or Macock of the creeping kind, and not of those call'd *Callibaches*, which grow upon Trees; Of which the *Brasilians* make their *Maraka*, or *Tamaraka*, a sort of Rattle also, as *Clusius*[46] seems to intimate.

CHAP. XI.

Of the Laws, and Authority of the Indians *among one another.*

¶.44. THe *Indians* having no sort of Letters among them, as has been before observ'd, they can have no Written Laws; nor did the Constitution in which we found them, seem to need many. Nature and their own convenience having taught them to obey one Chief, who is Arbiter of all things among them. They claim no property in Lands, but they are in Common to a whole Nation. Every one Hunts and Fishes, and gathers Fruits in all places. Their labour in tending Corn, Pompions, Melons, *&c.* is not so great, that they need quarrel for room, where the Land is so fertile, and where so much lyes uncultivated.

They bred no sort of Cattle, nor had any thing that could be call'd Riches. They valued Skins and Furs for use, and *Peak* and *Roenoke* for ornament.

They are very severe in punishing ill breeding, of which every *Werowance* is undisputed Judge, who never fails to lay a rigorous penalty upon it. An example whereof I had from a Gentleman that was an eye-witness; which was this.

In the time of *Bacon*'s Rebellion, one of these *Werowances*, attended by several others of his Nation, was treating with the *English* in *New Kent* County, about a Peace; and during the time of his Speech, one of his Attendants presum'd to interrupt him, which he resented as the most unpardonable affront that cou'd be offer'd him; and therefore he instantly took his *Tomahawk* from his Girdle, and split the Fellow's Head, for his presumption. The poor Fellow dying immediately upon the spot, he commanded some of his Men to carry him out, and went on again with his Speech where he left off, as unconcern'd as if nothing had happen'd.

The *Indians* never forget nor forgive an Injury, till satisfaction be given, be it National, or Personal: but it becomes the business of their whole Lives, and even after that, the Revenge is entail'd upon their Posterity, till full reparation be made.

¶ 45. The Titles of Honour that I have observ'd among them peculiar to themselves, are only *Cockarouse*, and *Werowance*, besides that of the King, and Queen: but of late they have borrow'd some Titles from us, which they bestow among themselves. A *Cockarouse* is one that has the Honour to be of the King or Queens Council, with relation to the affairs of the Government, and has a great share in the Administration. A *Werowance* is a Military Officer, who of course takes upon him the command of all Parties, either of Hunting, Travelling, Warring, or the like, and the word signifies a War Captain.

The Priests and Conjurers are also of great Authority, the people having recourse to them for Counsel and Direction, upon all occasions; by which means, and by help of the First Fruits and frequent Offerings, they riot in the fat of the Land, and grow rich upon the spoils of their ignorant Country-men.

They have also people of a Rank inferiour to the Commons, a sort of Servants among them. These are call'd Black Boys, and are attendant upon the Gentry, to do their servile Offices, which, in their state of Nature, are not many. For they live barely up to the present relief of their Necessities, and make all things easy and comfortable to themselves, by the indulgence of a kind Climate, without toiling and perplexing their mind for Riches, which other people often trouble themselves to provide for uncertain and ungrateful Heirs. In short, they seem, as possessing nothing, and yet enjoying all things.

CHAP. XII.

Of the Treasure or Riches of the Indians.

¶.46. THe *Indians* had nothing which they reckoned Riches, before the *English* went among them, except *Peak, Roenoke,* and such like trifles made out of the *Cunk* shell. These past with them instead of Gold and Silver, and serv'd them both for Money, and Ornament. It was the *English* alone that taught them first to put a value on their Skins and Furs, and to make a Trade of them.

Peak is of two sorts, or rather of two colours, for both are made of one Shell, tho of different parts; one is a dark Purple Cylinder, and the other a white; they are both made in size, and figure alike, and commonly much resembling the *English Buglas*, but not so transparent nor so brittle. They are wrought as smooth as Glass, being one third of an inch long, and about a quarter, diameter, strung by a hole drill'd thro the Center. The dark colour is the dearest, and distinguish'd by the name of *Wampom Peak*. The *English* men that are call'd *Indian* Traders, value the *Wampom Peak* at eighteen pence *per* Yard, and the white *Peak* at nine pence. The *Indians* also make Pipes of this, two or three inches long, and thicker than ordinary, which are much more valuable. They also make *Runtees* of the same Shell, and grind them as smooth as *Peak*. These are either large like an Oval Bead, and drill'd the length of the Oval, or else they are circular and flat, almost an inch over, and one third of an inch thick, and drill'd edgeways. Of this Shell they also make round Tablets of about four inches diameter, which they polish as smooth as the other, and sometimes they etch or grave thereon, Circles, Stars, a Half Moon, or any other figure suitable to their fancy. These they wear instead of Medals before or behind their Neck, and use the *Peak*, *Runtees* and Pipes for Coronets, Bracelets, Belts or long Strings hanging down before the Breast, or else they lace their Garments with them, and adorn their *Tomahawks*, and every other thing that they value.

They have also another sort which is as current among them, but of far less value; and this is made of the Cockleshell, broke into small bits with rough edges, drill'd through in the same manner as Beads, and this they call *Roenoke*, and use it as the *Peak*.

These sorts of Money have their rates set upon them as unalterable, and current as the values of our Money are.

The *Indians* have likewise some Pearl amongst them, and formerly had many more, but where they got them is uncertain, except they found 'em in the Oyster Banks, which are frequent in this Country.

CHAP. XIII.

Of the Handicrafts of the Indians.

¶.47. BEfore I finish my account of the *Indians*, it will not be amiss to inform you, that when the *English* went first among them, they had no sort of Iron or Steel Instruments: but their Knives were either Sharpen'd Reeds, or Shells, and their Axes sharp Stones bound to the end of a Stick, and glued in with Turpentine. By the help of these, they made their Bows of the Locust Tree, an excessive hard Wood when it is dry, but much more easily cut when it is green, of which they always took the advantage. They made their Arrows of Reeds or small Wands, which needed no other cutting, but in the length, being otherwise ready for Notching, Feathering and Heading. They fledged their Arrows with Turkey Feathers, which they fastned with Glue made of the Velvet Horns of a Deer, but it has not that quality it's said to have, of holding against all Weathers; they arm'd the Heads with a white transparent Stone, like that of *Mexico* mention'd by *Peter Martyr*, of which they have many Rocks; they also headed them with the Spurs of the Wild Turkey Cock.

They rubb'd Fire out of particular sorts of Wood (as the Antients did out of the Ivy and Bays) by turning the end of a hard piece upon the side of a piece that is soft and dry, like a Spindle on its Inke, by which it heats, and at length burns; to this they put sometimes also rotten Wood, and dry Leaves to hasten the Work.

¶.48. Under the disadvantage of such Tools they made a shift to fell vast great Trees, and clear the Land of Wood, in places where they had occasion.

They bring down a great Tree, by making a small Fire round the Root, and keeping the Flame from running upward, until they burn away so much of the basis, that the least puff of Wind throws it down. When it is prostrate, they burn it off to what length they would have it, and with their Stone *Tomahawks* break off all the Bark, which when the Sap runs, will easily strip, and at other times also, if it be well warm'd with Fire. When it is brought to a due length, they raise it upon a Bed to a convenient height for their working, and then begin by gentle Fires to hollow it, and with scrapers rake the Trunk, and turn away the Fire from one place to another, till they have deepen'd the Belly of it to their desire: Thus also they shape the ends, till they have made it a fit Vessel for crossing the Water, and this they call a Canoe, one of which I have seen thirty foot long.

When they wanted any Land to be clear'd of the Woods, they chopp'd a Notch round the Trees quite through the Bark with their Stone Hatchets, or *Tomahawks*, and that deaden'd the Trees, so that they sprouted no more, but in a few years fell down. However, the Ground was plantable, and would produce immediately upon the withering of the Trees: but now for all these uses they employ Axes, and little Hatchets, which they buy of the *English*. The occasions aforemention'd, and the building of their Cabbins, are still the greatest use they have for these Utensils, because they trouble not themselves with any other sort of Handicraft, to which such Tools are necessary. Their Houshold Utensils are Baskets made of Silk grass, Gourds, which grow to the shapes they desire them, and Earthen Pots to boil Victuals in, which they make of Clay.

Tab. 14. *Shews their manner of Felling great Trees (before they had Iron Instruments) by Fireing the Root; and bringing them to fit lengths, and shaping them for use, by Fire alone.*

Trees Being Felled by Fire and Made into Canoes

The *Indians* of *Virginia* are almost wasted, but such Towns, or People as retain their Names, and live in Bodies, are hereunder set down; All which together can't raise five hundred fighting men. They live poorly, and much in fear of the Neighbouring *Indians*. Each Town, by the Articles of Peace in 1677. pays 3 *Indian* Arrows for their Land, and 20 Beaver Skins for protection every year.

In *Accomack* are 8 Towns, *viz*.

Matomkin is much decreased of late by the Small Pox, that was carried thither.

Gingoteque. The few remains of this Town are joyn'd with a Nation of the *Maryland Indians*.

Kiequotank, is reduc'd to very few Men.

Matchopungo, has a small number yet living.

Occahanock, has a small number yet living.

Pungoteque. Govern'd by a Queen, but a small Nation.

Oanancock, has but four or five Families.

Chiconessex, has very few, who just keep the name.

Nanduye. A Seat of the Empress. Not above 20 Families, but she hath all the Nations of this Shore under Tribute.

In *Northampton*. *Gangascoe*, which is almost as numerous as all the foregoing Nations put together.

In *Prince George*. *Wyanoke*, is almost wasted, and now gone to live among other *Indians*.

In *Charles City*. *Appamattox*. These Live in Collonel *Byrd*'s Pasture, not being above seven Families.

In *Surry*. *Nottawayes*, which are about a hundred Bow men, of late a thriving and increasing People.

By *Nansamond*. *Menheering*, has about thirty Bowmen, who keep at a stand.

Nansamond. About thirty Bow-men: They have increased much of late.

In *King Williams County*, 2. *Pamunkie*, has about forty Bow-men, who decrease.

Chickahomonie, which had about sixteen Bow-men, but lately increas'd.

In *Essex. Rappahannock*, is reduc'd to a few Families, and live scatter'd upon the *English* Seats.

In *Richmond. Port-Tabago*, has [a]bout five Bow-men, but Wasting.

In *Northumberland. Wiccocomoco*, has but three men living, which yet keep up their Kingdom, and retain their Fashion; they live by themselves, separate from all other *Indians*, and from the *English*.

¶.49. Thus I have given a succinct account of the *Indians;* happy, I think, in their simple State of Nature, and in their enjoyment of Plenty, without the Curse of Labour. They have on several accounts reason to lament the arrival of the *Europeans*, by whose means they seem to have lost their Felicity, as well as their Innocence. The *English* have taken away great part of their Country, and consequently made every thing less plenty amongst them. They have introduc'd Drunkenness and Luxury amongst them, which have multiply'd their Wants, and put them upon desiring a thousand things, they never dreamt of before. I have been the more concise in my account of this harmless people, because I have inserted several Figures, which I hope have both supplied the defect of Words, and render'd the Descriptions more clear. I shall in the next place proceed to treat of Virginia, as it is now improv'd, (I should rather say alter'd,) by the *English;* and of its present Constitution and Settlement.

The End of the Third Book.

BOOK IV.

Of the Present State of VIRGINIA. *As this Book must consist of two Parts, First, The Polity of the Government; Secondly, The Husbandry and Improvements of the Country;* [47] *so I shall handle them separately.*

PART I.

Of the Civil Polity and Government of Virginia.

CHAP. I.

Of the Constitution of Government in Virginia.

¶.1. I Have already hinted, that the first Settlement of this Country, was under the direction of a Company of Merchants incorporated.

That the first Constitution of Government appointed by them, was by a President and Council, which Council was nominated by the Corporation, and the President annually chosen by the People.

That in the year 1610 this Constitution was altered, and the Company obtain'd a new Grant of his Majesty; whereby they themselves had the nomination of the Governor, who was oblig'd to act only by advice in Council.

That in the year 1620, an Assembly of Burgesses was first call'd, from all the inhabited parts of the Country, who sat in consultation with the Governor and Council, for setling the Publick Affairs of the Plantation; and so the form of Government became perfect.

That when the Company was dissolv'd, the King continued the same method of Government, by a Governour, Council, and Burgesses; which three being united, were call'd the General Assembly.

· That this General Assembly debated all the weighty Affairs of the Colony, and enacted Laws for the better government of the People; and the Governor and Council were to put them in execution.

That the Governor and Council were appointed by the King, and the Assembly chosen by the People.

Afterwards the Governor had a more extensive Power put into his hands, so that his Assent in all affairs became absolutely necessary; yet was he still bound to act by Advice of Council.

Until the Rebellion 1676, the Governor had no power to suspend the Councellors, nor to remove any of them from the Council-Board.

Then a power was given him of Suspending them, but with Proviso, that he gave substantial Reasons for so doing; and was answerable to his Majesty for the truth of the Accusation.

Then also this Model of Government by a Governor, Council and Assembly, was confirm'd to them [by] Charter, with a further Clause, That if the Governor should happen to die, or be removed, and no other Person in the Country nominated by the Crown to supply his Place; then the President, or eldest Councellor, with the assistance of any five of the Council, should take upon him the Administration of the Government.

Before the year 1680, the Council sat in the same House with the Burgesses of Assembly, much resembling the Model of the *Scots* Parliament; and then the Lord *Colepepper* taking advantage of some Disputes among them, procur'd the Council to sit apart from the Assembly; and so they became two distinct Houses, in imitation of the two Houses of Parliament in *England*, the Lords and Commons; and so is the Constitution at this day.

¶.2. The Governor is appointed by the Crown; his Commission is under the Privy Seal, and runs during Pleasure.

He represents the Queen's Person there in all things, and is subject to her Instructions, *viz.*

In assenting to, or dissenting from the Laws, agreed upon by the Council and Assembly.

In giving his Test to all Laws so assented to.

In Calling, Prorogueing, and Dissolving the Assembly.

In calling, and presiding in all Councils of State.

In appointing Commissioners and Officers for the administration of Justice.

In granting Commissions to all Officers of the Militia, under the degree of a Lieutenant-General, which Title he bears himself.

In ordering and disposing the Militia for the defence of the Country, according to Law.

In testing Proclamations.

In disposing of the Queens Land according to the Charter, and the Laws of that Country; for which end, and for other publick Occasions, the Seal of the Colony is committed to his keeping.

All Issues of the publick Revenue must bear his Test.

And by virtue of a Commission from the Admiralty, he takes upon himself the Office of Vice-Admiral.

The Governors Salary till within these thirty years last past, was no more than a Thousand pounds a year; besides which he had about five hundred more in Perquisites: Indeed, the General Assembly by a publick Act, made an Addition of two hundred pounds a year to Sir *William Berkeley* in particular, out of the great Respect and Esteem they bore to that Gentleman, who had been a long time a good and just Governor; and who had laid out the greatest part of his Revenue in Experiments, for the Advantage and Improvement of the Country; and who had besides suffered extremely in the time of the Usurpation. But this Addition was to determine with his Government.

Sir *William Berkley* after the short Interval of *Jeffery*'s and *Chichley*'s being Deputy-Governors, was succeeded by the Lord *Colepepper;* who under pretence of his being a Peer of *England*, obtain'd of King *Charles* II. a Salary of 2000 *l.* besides 150 *l.* a year for House-Rent, because there was no House appointed by the Country for the Governors Reception.

This Noble Lord made his advantage of the confusions, in which he found the Country, that had not recover'd the Calamities of *Bacons* Rebellion. He observ'd that abundance of People had been concern'd in those Troubles; and consequently, he concluded they wou'd not scruple to grant him any thing, to protect themselves from Prosecution. By this means he not only obtain'd the Concurrence of the Assembly to his Money-Grants, but likewise prevail'd with them to make the Imposition of two Shillings *per* Hogshead, and the Fort-Duties perpetual; and to make them subject to his Majesties direction, to be disposed of for the use of the Government. This increas'd Salary has been continued ever since, to all the succeeding Governors, and the Perquisites are now also increased.

If the Administration of the Government happen to fall into the hands of the President and Council, there is then usually allow'd to the President, the Addition of five hundred pounds a year only; and to the Council, no more than what is given them at other times.

¶.3. The Gentlemen of the Council are appointed by Letter or Instruction from her Majesty, which says no more, but that they be sworn of the Council.

The number of the Councellors when compleat, is Twelve; and if at any time by Death or Removal, there happen to be fewer than nine residing in the Country, then the Governor has Power to appoint and swear into the Council, such of the Gentlemen of the Country, as he shall think fit, to make up that number, without expecting any direction from *England*.

The business of the Council is to advise and assist the Governor in all Important Matters of Government, and to be a restraint upon him, if he should attempt to exceed the bounds of his Commission: They are enabled to do this, by having each of them an equal Vote with the Governor, in most things of Conseqence, *viz.*

In calling Assemblies.

In disposing of the Publick Revenue, and inspecting the Accounts thereof.

In placing, and displacing Naval Officers, and Collectors of all publick Duties.

In all Votes and Orders of Council.

In the nomination of all Commission-Officers, either of honorary or profitable Places.

In publishing Proclamations.

In making Grants, and passing all the Patents for Land.

In the General Assembly, the Council make the Upper-House, and claim an intire Negative Voice to all Laws, as the House of Lords in *England*.

The Salary of the Council is in all but 350 *l. per Ann.* to be proportion'd among them according to their Attendance on General Courts, and Assemblies.

¶.4. The Burgesses of Assembly are elected, and return'd from all parts of the Country, *viz.* from each County two, and from *James* City one; which make up in all fifty one Burgesses, besides one Burgess to be sent by the Colledge, as the Charter directs. They are conven'd by Writs issued from the Secretaries Office, under the Seal of the Colony, and the Test of the Governor. These are directed to the Sheriff of each County respectively, and ought to bear date at least forty days before the return. The Freeholders are the only Electors, and where-ever they have a Free-hold, (if they be not Women, or under Age) they have a Vote in the Election. The Method of summoning the Free-holders, is by publication of the Writ, together with the day appointed by the Sheriff for Election, at every Church and Chappel in the County, two several Sundays successively. The Election is concluded by plurality of Voices; and if either Party be dissatisfied, or thinks he has not fair Treatment, he may demand a Copy of the Poll, and upon Application to the House of Burgesses, shall have his Complaint inquired into. But to prevent undue Elections, many Acts have been there made agreeable to some lately enacted in *England*.

The first business of a Convention, is to make choice of a Speaker, and to present him in full House to the Governor. Upon this occasion the Speaker in the name of the House, petitions the Governor to confirm the usual Liberties, and Priviledges of Assembly, namely, Access to his Person, whenever they shall have occasion; a freedom of Speech, and Debate in the House, without being further accountable; and a Protection of their Persons and their Servants from Arrest, *&c.* And these being granted by the Governor, they proceed to do Business, choosing Committees, and in other things, imitating as near as they can, the Method of the Honourable House of Commons in *England*.

The Laws having duly past the House of Burgesses, the Council and the Governors Assent; they are transmitted to the Queen by the next Shipping, for her Approbation, her Majesty having another Negative Voice, on this Condition, that they immediately become Laws, and be in force upon the Governors first passing them, and so remain, if her Majesty don't actually repeal them, although she be not pleased to declare her Royal Assent.

There are no appointed times for their Convention, but the Custom hitherto has been once in a year, or once in two years; and indeed, seldom two intire years pass without an Assembly; They wisely keeping the power that is left them, in their own Hands, by the short continuation of the Imposition Acts. They are call'd together, whenever the Exigencies of the Country make it necessary, or her Majesty is pleas'd to order any thing to be proposed to them.

CHAP. II.
Of the Sub-divisions of Virginia.

€.5. THE Country is divided into twenty five Counties, and the Counties as they are in bigness, into fewer or more Parishes, as the Scheme at the latter end will show, as it will also several other things, to save a long account in Words.

The Method of bounding the Counties is at this time, with respect to the Convenience of having each County limited to one single River, for its Trade and Shipping: So that any one whose Concerns are altogether in one County, may not be obliged to seek his Freight and Shipping in more than one River. Whereas at first, they were bounded with respect to the Circuit, and the Propinquity of the extreams to one common Center; by which means, one County reached then quite a-cross a neck of Land from River to River. But this way of bounding the Counties being found more inconvenient than the other, it was changed by a Law, into what it is now.

Besides this Division into Counties, and Parishes, there are two other Sub-divisions, which are subject to the Rules and Alterations made by the County-Courts; namely, into Precincts or Burroughs, for the limits of Constables; and into Precincts or Walks, for the Surveyors of Highways.

€.6. There is another Division of the Country into necks of Land, which are the boundaries of the Escheators, *viz*.

The *Northern* Neck between *Patowmeck* and *Rappahannock* Rivers:

The Neck between *Rappahannock* and *York* Rivers, within which *Pamunky* Neck is included:

The Neck between *York* and *James* Rivers:

The Lands on the *South* side *James* River:

And the Land on the *Eastern* Shoar; in all, five Divisions.

¶.7. There is yet another Division of the Countrey, into Districts, according to the Rivers, with respect to the Shipping, and Navigation: These are the bounds appointed for the Naval Officers, and Collectors of the Publick Duties, and are as follow.

1. The Upper-parts of *James* River, from Hog-Island upwards.
2. The Lower-parts of *James* River, from Hog-Island downwards to the *Capes*, and round *Point-Comfort*, to *Back-River*.
3. *York*, *Poquoson*, *Mobjack-Bay*, and *Pieanketank* Rivers.
4. *Rappahannock* River.
5. From *Wicocomoco* upwards, on *Patowmeck* River.
6. From *Wicocomoco* downwards, on the same River, and down the Bay to the *Rappahannock* District.
7. *Pocomoke*, and the other parts on the *Eastern*, made formerly two Districts; but they are now united into one.

CHAP. III.

Of the Publick Offices of the Government.

§.8. BEsides the Governor and Council aforemention'd, there are two other General Officers in that Colony, bearing her Majesties immediate Commission, *viz.* The Auditor of the Revenue, and the Secretary of State.

The Auditors business is to audite the Accounts of the publick Money of the Government, and duly to transmit the state of them to *England;* such as the Quit-Rents, the Money arising by the two Shillings *per* Hogshead, Fort-Duties, the Fines and Forfeitures, and the Profits of Escheats. His Salary is 7½ *per Cent*, of all the publick Money.

The Secretaries business is to keep the publick Records of the Country, and to take care that they be regularly and fairly made up; namely, all Judgments of the General Court, as likewise all Deeds, and other Writings there proved; and further, to issue all Writs, both Ministerial, and Judicial relating thereto. To make out and record all Patents for Land, to file the Rights by which they issued, and to take the return of all Inquests of Escheat.

In his Office is kept a Register of all Commissions of Administration, and Probates of Wills, granted throughout the Colony; as also of all Births, Burials, Marriages, and Persons that go out of the Country: Of all Houses of publick Entertainment, and of all publick Officers in the Country; and of many other things, proper to be kept in so general an Office.

From this Office are likewise issued all Writs for

choosing of Burgesses, and in it are fil'd Authentick Copies of all Proclamations.

This Office was reduc'd into very good Order, after the burning of the State House at *James* Town; but for want of Conveniences, and due Care, it is growing a-pace into as great confusion as ever.

The Secretaries Income arises from Fees for all business done in his Office, which come (*Communibus annis*) to about 70,000 *l*. Tobacco *per Annum;* out of which he pays 12500 and Cask to the Clerks: His other Perquisites proceed out of the acknowledgements pay'd him annually by the County Clerks, and are besides about forty thousand pounds a year of Tobacco, and Cask.

¶.9. There are two other General Officers in the Country, who do not receive their Commis[si]on and Authority immediately from the Crown; and those are, 1. The Ecclesiastical Commissary, authorised by the Right Reverend Father in God, the Lord Bishop of *London*, Ordinary of all the Plantations: 2*ly*. The Countries Treasurer, authorised by the General Assembly.

The Commissaries business is to make Visitations of Churches, and have the Inspection of the Clergy. He is allowed 100 *l. per Ann.* out of the Quitrents.

The Treasurers business is to receive the Money from the several Collectors, and to make up the Accounts, of the Duties rais'd by some late Acts of Assembly, for extraordinary Occasions; his Salary is six *per Cent.* of all Money passing through his Hands.

These are all the General Officers belonging to that Government, except of the Court of Admiralty, which has no standing Officer.

¶.10. The other publick Commission-Officers in the Government, (except those of the Militia, for whom a Chapter is reserved) are Escheators, Naval Officers,

Collectors, Clerks of Courts, Sheriffs of Counties, Surveyors of Land, and Coroners.

The Escheators have their Precincts or Bounds, according to the several Necks of Land; for their Profits, they demand five Pound Sterling for each Office found, being paid only as business happens.

The Naval Officers have their bounds according to the Districts on the Rivers, and so have the Collectors. The Profits of the first arise from large Fees, upon the entering and clearing of all Ships and Vessels. The Collectors have each a Salary out of the Treasury in *England*, of Forty pounds, Sixty pounds, or an Hundred pounds, according to their several Districts, they being appointed by the Honourable the Commissioners of the Customs in *Eng.* Pursuant to a Statute made in the 25*th* year of King *Charles* the Second; and have moreover Salaries of 20 *per Cent.* on all the Duties they collect, by virtue of the same Statute, and also large Fees for every Entry and Clearing.

The Naval Officers other Profits, are ten *per Cent.* for all Money's by them receiv'd; both on the two Shillings *per* Hogshead, Fort-Duties, Skins and Furs, and also on the new Imposts on Servants and Liquors.

The Clerks of Courts, Sheriffs, and Surveyors, are limited according to the several Counties. The Clerks of Courts receive their Commissions from the Secretary of State; the Sheriffs theirs from the Governor, and the Surveyors of Land, theirs from the Governors of the Colledge, in whom the Office of Surveyor-General is vested by their Charter.

The Clerks Profits proceed from stated Fees, upon all Law-suits and business in their respective Courts, except the Clerk of the General Court, who is paid a Salary by the Secretary, who takes the Fees of that Court to himself. The large and populous Counties by these Fees allow a plentiful Maintenance to their Clerks; the Clerks at present exact what Fees they will, having none allow'd them by Law, because of the expiration of the Acts relating thereto.

The Sheriffs Profit is likewise by Fees on all business done in the County-Courts, to which he is the Ministerial Officer; but the best of his Income is by a Salary of 10 *per Cent.* on all his Collections; he has likewise several other Advantages, which make his place very profitable.

The Profits of the Surveyors of Land are according to the trouble they take: But because Men of Honour and Understanding, should be incouraged to undertake this Office, on whose Probity and Skill, the title and quiet of Estates depend, it were to be wisht, that these Officers were allow'd larger Fees.

The Coroner is a Commission-Officer also, but his Profits are not worth naming, though he has large Fees allowed him, when he does any Business. There are two or more of them appointed in each Parish, as occasion requires; but in the vacancy, or absence of any, upon an Exigency, the next Justice of Peace does the Business, and receives the Fee, which is 133 Pounds of Tobacco for an Inquest, and nothing for any other Business.

C.11. There are other Ministerial Officers that have no Commission; which are, Surveyors of the High-ways, Constables, and Headboroughs. These are appointed, reliev'd, and altered annually by the County-Courts, as they see occasion; and such bounds are given them, as those Courts think most convenient. Their business is all done without profit.

CHAP. IV.

Of the Standing Revenues or Publick Funds in Virginia.

¶.12. THere are five sorts of standing Publick Revenues in that Country, *viz.* 1*st* A Rent reserv'd by her Majesty upon all the Lands granted by Patent: 2*d* A Revenue granted to her Majesty by act of Assembly, for the Support and Maintenance of the Government. 3*d* A Revenue raised by the Assembly, and kept in their own disposal, for extraordinary Occasions: 4*th*, A Revenue rais'd by the Assembly, and granted to the College: And 5*th*, A Revenue raised by Act of Parliament in *England* upon the Trade there.

¶.13. 1*st*, The Rent reserved upon their Lands, is called her Majesties Revenue of Quit-rents, and is two Shillings for every hundred Acres of Land, Patented by any Person in that Country. This is paid into the Treasury there by all, except the Inhabitants of the *Northern* Neck, who pay nothing to the Queen; but the whole Quit-Rent of that Neck, is paid to certain Proprietors of the Lord *Colepepper*'s Family, who have assum'd the possession thereof to themselves, upon the pretensions before rehears'd in the first part of this Book.

This Revenue has been upwards of Twelve hundred pounds a Year, since Tobacco has held a good price. It is lodg'd in the Auditors Hands, to be dispos'd of by her Majesty, to the use and benefit of the Country. This Money is left in bank there, to be made use of upon any sudden, and dangerous Emergency: And for want of such a Bank, Sir *William Berkley* was not able to make any stand against *Bacon*, whom otherwise he might easily have subdu'd, and consequently have prevented above 100000 pounds expence, to the Crown of *England*, to pacifie those Troubles.

¶.14. 2*d*, The Revenue granted to her Majesty by act of Assembly, for the Support and Maintenance of the Government, arises first out of a Duty of two Shillings *per* Hogshead, which is paid for every Hogshead of Tobacco exported out of that Colony: 2*dly*, By a rate of fifteen pence *per* Tun, for every Ship, upon each return of her Voyage, whether she be empty or full. 3*dly*, By a Duty of Sixpence *per* Poll for every Passenger bond or free, going into that Country: 4*thly*, By the Fines and Forfeitures impos'd by several Acts of Assembly. 5*thly*, By Waifs and Strayes happening to be taken up within that Government: And 6*thly*, By Escheats of Land, and Personal Estate, for want of a lawful Heir; all which are paid into the hands of the Auditor, and disposed of by the Governor and Council, (with liberty for the Assembly to inspect the Accounts when they meet) for defraying the publick charges of the Government.

This Revenue, *Communibus Annis*, amounts to more than three thousands pounds a year.

¶.15. 3*dly*, The Revenue arising by Act of Assembly, and reserv'd to their own disposal, is of two sorts, *viz.* a Duty upon Liquors imported from the Neighbouring Plantations, and a Duty upon all Slaves and Servants imported, except *English*.

The Duty on Liquors is 4 *d. per* Gallon on all Wines, Rum, and Brandy; and 1 *d. per* Gallon on Beer, Syder, and other Liquors, discounting 20 *per Cent.* upon the Invoyce.

The Duty on Servants and Slaves, is fifteen Shillings for each Servant, not being a Native of *England* or *Wales*, and twenty Shillings for each Slave, or Negro.

The former of these Duties amounts *Communibus Annis*,

to six hundred pounds a year, and the latter to more or less, as the Negro Ships happen to arrive.

The charge of building and adorning the Capitol, was defray'd by the last of these Duties, and so was the erecting of the publick Prison. By both these, several great Claimers from the Assembly are paid, which would ease the Levy by the Poll, if the Duty were raised any other way, than upon the Servants: But the latter of these being a Duty of 15 or 20 Shillings *per* Head, makes it advance to 40 or 50 in the Sale, as hath been experienc'd; and so there's five or six years Levy paid before the Servant can be purchas'd.

These Funds are gather'd into the hands of the Treasurer of the Country, and are disposed of only by order of Assembly.

₡.16. 4*thly*, the Revenue raised by the Assembly, and granted to the College, is a Duty on all Skins and Furs exported: This Fund raises about an hundred pounds a year, and is paid by the Collectors, to the College Treasurer.

₡.17. 5*thly* and *lastly*, The Fund raised by Act of Parliament in *England* upon the Trade there, is a Duty of one Penny *per* pound, upon all Tobacco exported to the Plantations, and not carried directly to *England*. This Duty was laid by *Stat.* 25. *Car.* 2. *cap.* 7. and granted to the King and his Successors; and by their Gracious Majesties King *William* and Queen *Mary*, it was given to the College. This Duty do's not raise both in *Virginia* and *Maryland*, above two hundred pounds a year, and is accounted for, to the College Treasurer.

CHAP. V.

Of the Levies for payment of the Publick County, and Parish Debts.

¶.18. THey have but two Ways of raising Money Publickly in that Country, *viz.* by Duties upon Trade, and a Poll-Tax, which they call Levies. Of the Duties upon Trade, I have spoken sufficiently in the preceding Chapter: I come therefore now to speak of the Levies, which are a certain Rate, or Proportion of Tobacco, charged upon the head of every Tithable Person in the Country, upon all alike, without distinction.

They call all Negroes above sixteen years of Age Tithable, be they Male or Female; and all white Men of the same Age. But Children and white Women, are exempted from all manner of Duties.

That a true account of all these Tithable Persons may be had, they are annually listed in Crop-time, by the Justices of each County respectively; and the Masters of Families are obliged under great Penalties, then to deliver to those Justices, a true list of all the Tithable Persons in their Families.

Their Levies are of three sorts, *viz.* Publick, County, and Parish Levies.

¶.19. Publick Levies are such as are proportion'd, and laid equally by the General Assembly, upon every Tithable Person throughout the whole Colony. These serve to defray several expences appointed by Law, to be so defrayed; such as the executing of a Criminal Slave, who must be made good to his Owner. The taking up of Run-aways, and the paying of the Militia, when they

Anno 1703. Taken from the Lists of the preceding Year.

S. supplied. V. vacant.

Counties Names.	Acres of Land.	Numb. of Souls	Tithe-ables	Women & Chil.	N° of Militia	N° of l. Horse.	N° of Fo. & Drag.	N° and Names of Parishes in each County.
Henrico	148757	2413	915	1498	345	98	247	1 Henrico, S.
Prince George	161239	4045	1406	2639	625	203	422	1 Bristol, S. / Martin Brandon, S. / Wianoke, S. / Weftover, S.
Charles-City								1
Surry	111050	2230	880	1350	350	62	288	2 Southwark, V. Lyons Creek, S.
Isle of Wight	142796	2714	841	1873	514	140	374	2 Warwick Squeek, S. Newport, S.
Nanfamond	131172	2530	1018	1512	591	142	449	2 Upper, V. Lower Parish's, V. Chuckatuck, V.
Norfolk	112019	2279	717	1572	380	48	332	3 Elizabeth River, S.
Princess Anne	98305	2037	686	1351	284	69	215	1 Lynhaven, V.
James-City	108362	2990	1297	1693	401	123	278	4 Wallingford, V. Wilmington, S. James-City, S. Merchants-Hundred, V. / Bruton, S.
York	60767	2357	1208	1149	390	68	322	3 Hampton, V. York, S. Newpocoson, S.
Warwick	38444	1377	482	895	201	49	152	2 Denby, V. Mulberry Island, V.
Elizabeth-City	29000	1188	469	715	196	54	142	1 Elizabeth-City, S.
New Kent	173104	3374	1325	2049	420	120	300	2 Blifsland, S. Saint Peters, S.
King William	84324	1834	803	1031	698	189	509	1 Saint Johns, S.
King and Queen	131716	2842	1244	1598	594	121	473	2 Stratton Major, S. Saint Stephens, S.
Gloucester	142450	5834	2628	3206	199	56	143	4 Petfo, S. Abbington, S. Ware, S. Kingston, S.
Middlefex	49500	1632	776	856	438	139	299	1 Christ-Church, S.
Essex	140920	2400	1090	1310	504	122	382	2 South Farnham, S. Sittenburn, V. Saint Maries, S.
Richmond	. .	2622	1392	1230	345	84	261	2 North Farnham, S. Overworton, S.
Stafford	. .	2033	863	1170	1605	451	133	318	Saint Paul, V. Washington, S.
Westmorland	. .	2736	1131	1605	451	133	318	2 Copley, S. Washington, S.
Lancaster	. .	2155	941	1214	271	42	229	2 Christ-Church, S. Saint Maries White Chappel, S.
Northumberland	. .	2099	1168	931	522	103	392	2 Fairfield and Bowtracy, V. Wiccocomoco, S.
Accomack	200923	2804	1041	1763	456	101	355	1 Accomack, V.
Northampton	99384	2081	712	1369	347	70	277	1 Hungers, V.
25 Counties.	2164372 Besides the Nor.Neck.	60606	25023	35583	9522	2363	7159	49 Of which, 34 are Supplied, and 15 Vacant.

The French Refugees are not accounted within this List.

Census List

happen to be imployed upon Service. Out of these they likewise pay the several Officers of the Assembly, and some other Publick Officers. They further defray the charge of the Writs, for the meeting of the House of Burgesses, and such like.

The Authority for Levying this Rate, is given by a short Act of Assembly, constantly prepared for that purpose.

℣.20. The County Levies are such as are peculiar to each County, and laid by the Justices upon all Tithable Persons, for defraying the charge of their Counties; such as the building and repairing their Court-Houses, Prisons, Pillories, Stocks, &c. and the payment of all Services, render'd to the County in General.

℣.21. The Parish Levies are laid by the Vestry, for the pavment of all charges incident to the several Parishes, such as the building, furnishing, and adorning their Churches and Chappels; buying Glebes, and building upon them; paying their Ministers, Readers, Clerks, and Sextons.

CHAP. VI.

Of the Courts *of* Law *in* Virginia.

¶.22. I Have already in the Chronology of the Government, hinted what the Constitution of their Courts was in old time, and that Appeals lay from the General Court to the Assembly. That the General Court from the beginning, took cognizance of all Causes whatsoever, both Ecclesiastical and Civil, determining every thing by the Standard of Equity and good Conscience. They us'd to come to the merits of the cause, as soon as they could without Injustice, never admitting such impertinences of Form and Nicety, as were not absolutely necessary: and when the substance of the case was sufficiently debated, they us'd directly to bring the Suit to a Decision. By this Method all fair Actions were prosecuted with little Attendance, all just Debts were recover'd with the least expense of Money and Time; and all the tricking, and foppery of the Law happily avoided.

The Lord *Colepepper*, who was a Man of admirable Sense, and well Skilled in the Laws of *England*, admired the constitution of their Courts, and kept them close to this plain Method, retrenching some Innovations, that were then creeping into them, under the notion of Form; although, at the same time, he was the occasion, of taking away the liberty of Appeals to the Assembly.

But the Lord *Howard* who succeeded him, (tho' he was himself a Man absolutely unskill'd in the legal proceedings of *England*,) endeavour'd to introduce as many of the *English* Forms as he could, being directly opposite to the Lord *Colepepper* in that point.

After him Sir *Edmund Andros*, when he was Governor,

caused the Statutes of *England* to be allowed for Law there; even such Statutes, as were made of late time, since the grant of the last Charter.

And Lastly, Governor *Nicholson*, a Man unacquainted with all Law, except that of *Morocco*, where he learnt the way of governing by force, has endeavour'd to introduce all the quirks of the *English* Proceedings, by the help of some wretched Pettifoggers, who have had the direction both of his Conscience and his Understanding.

¶.23. They have two sorts of Courts, that differ only in Jurisdiction; namely, the General Court, and the County-Courts. I don't mention the Court of Admiralty, of which there is neither Judge, nor any Salary appointed for him; and indeed, upon these terms, no Man of any Rank or Abilities, wou'd care to undertake such a troublesom Office. Neither is there the least occasion of any such charge, because their County-Courts sitting so frequently, have hitherto supplied their place; and upon extraordinary occasion of dispatch in Maritime Affairs, the first Justice in Commission is authorised by Law, to call Courts out of course, to determine them.

¶.24. The General Court, is a Court held by the Governour and Council, who by Custom, are the Judges of it, in all civil Disputes: but in all criminal Cases, they are made Judges by the Charter.

This Court, as it did from the beginning, so it does still, takes cognizance of all Causes, Criminal, Penal, Ecclesiastical and Civil. From this Court there is no Appeal, except the thing in demand exceed the value of three hundred pounds Sterling; in which case, an Appeal is allowed to the Queen and Council in *England*, and there determin'd by a Committee of the Privy Council, call'd the Lords of Appeals; the like Custom being used for all the other Plantations. In Criminal cases I don't know that there's any Appeal from the Sentence of this

Court; but the Governor is authorised, to pardon Persons found guilty of any Crime whatsoever, except of Treason, and willful Murder; and even in those cases, he may reprieve the Criminal, if the Court represent him, to be an object of Mercy; which Reprieve stands good, and may be continued, until her Majesties pleasure be signified therein.

¶.25. This Court is held twice a year, beginning on the 15th of *April*, and on the 15th of *October*: Each time it continues eighteen Days, excluding Sundays, if the business hold them so long: And these are the only times of Goal-Delivery.

¶.26. The Officers attending this Court, are the Sheriff of the County, wherein it sits, and his Under-Officers. Their business is to call the Litigants, and the Evidences into Court, and to impannel Juries: But each Sheriff in his respective County, makes Arrests, and returns the Writs to this Court.

¶.27. The way of impanneling Juries to serve in this Court, is thus: The Sheriff and his Deputies every Morning that the Court sits, goes about the Town, summoning the best of the Gentlemen, who resort thither, from all parts of the Country. The Condition of this Summons is, that they attend the Court that day, to serve upon the Jury, (it not being known whether there will be occasion or no:) And if any cause happen to require a Jury, they are then sworn to try the issue, otherwise they are in the Evening of course, dismist from all further Attendance; though they be not formally discharged by the Court. By this means are procur'd the best Juries this Country can afford; for if they should be summon'd by Writ of *Venire*, from any particular County, that County cannot afford so many qualify'd Persons as are here to be found, because of the great resort of Gentlemen, from all parts of the Colony to these Courts as well to see Fashions, as to dispatch their particular Business. Nor is Visinage necessary there, to distinguish the several Customs of particular places, the whole Country being as one Neighbourhood, and having the same Tenures of Land, Usages and Customs.

The Grand-Juries are impanneled much after the same manner; but because they require a greater number of Men, and the Court is always desirous to have some, from all parts of the Country, they give their Sheriff order the Morning before, to provide his Pannel.

¶.28. In Criminal Matters this Method is a little altered; because a knowledge of the Life, and Conversation of the Party, may give light to the Jury in their Verdict. For this reason a Writ of *Venire* issues in such cases, to summon six of the nearest Neighbours to the Criminal, who must be of the same County wherein he liv'd; which Writ of *Venire* is return'd by the Sheriff of the respective County, to the Secretaries Office, and the Names are taken from thence, by the Sheriff attending the General Court, and put in the front of the Pannel, which is fill'd up with the Names of the other Gentlemen summon'd in the Town, to be of the Petty-Jury for the Tryal of that Criminal. If the Prisoner have a mind to challenge the Jurors, the same liberty is allowed him there as in *England;* and if the Pannel fall short, by reason of such challenge, it must then be made up of the By-standers.

¶.29. All Actions are in that Country brought to a Determination the third Court at farthest, unless some special extraordinary reason be shewn, why the Party can't make his Defence so soon. The course is thus; upon the Defendant's Non-appearance, order goes against the Bail, (for a *Capias* is always their first Process) on condition, that unless the Defendant appear, and plead at the next Court, Judgment shall then be awarded for the Plaintiff: When the Defendant comes to the next Court, he is held to plead; and if his Plea be Dilatory, and over-rul'd, he is held to plead over immediately; and if it can be, the Merits are tryed that Court; but the next it is ended without fail, except something happen to make it highly unreasonable. Thus a year and half ends a Cause in the General Court, and three Months in the County-Court. If any one Appeal from the Judgment of the County-Court, the Tryal always comes on, the succeeding General Court; so that all business begun in the County-Court, tho' it runs to the utmost of the Law, (without some extraordinary event) is finished in nine Months.

¶.30. Every one that pleases, may plead his own Cause, or else his Friends for him, there being no restraint in that case, nor any licensed Practitioners in the Law: If any one be dissatisfied with the Judgment of the County-Court, let it be for any Sum, little or great, he may have an Appeal to the next General Court, giving Security to answer, and abide the Judgment of that Court: but an Action cannot originally be brought in the General Court, under the value of ten pounds Sterling, or of two thousand pounds of Tobacco.

¶.31. The County-Courts are constituted by Commission from the Governor, with advice of Council. They consist of eight or more Gentlemen of the County, called Justices of the Peace, the Sheriff being only a Ministerial Officer. This Court is held Monthly, and has Jurisdiction of all Causes within the County, not touching Life or Member: But in the case of Hog-stealing, they may Sentence the Criminal to lose his Ears; which is allow'd by a particular Act for that purpose. In all things they proceed in the same manner as the General Court.

¶.32. Besides this Monthly Court, there is a day appointed, to be kept annually by the Justices of the said Court, for the care of all Orphans and of their Estates; and for the binding out, and well ordering of such fatherless Children, who are either without any Estate, or have very little.

At these Courts, they inquire into the keeping and management of the Orphan, as to his Sustenance and Education: They examine into his Estate, and the Securities thereof; If the Sureties continue to be Responsible, if his Lands and Plantations be kept improving, and in Repair, &c. If the poor Orphan be bound an Apprentice to any Trade, then their business is to inquire, how he is kept to his Schooling, and Trade; and if the Court find he is either misused, or untaught, they take him from that Master, and put him to another of the same Trade, or of any other Trade, which they judge best for the Child.

Another charitable Method in favour of the poor Orphans there, is this; That besides their Trade and Schooling, the Masters are generally obliged, to give them at their Freedom, Cattle, Tools, or other things, to the value of five, six, or ten pounds, according to the Age of the Child when bound, over and above the usual quantity of Corn, and Cloaths. The Boys are bound till one and twenty years of Age, and the Girls till eighteen: At which time, they who have taken any care to improve themselves, generally get well Married, and live in Plenty, tho they had not a farthing of paternal Estate.

Though these Courts be yearly appointed for that use, yet the Justices do not fail every County-Court, as occasion happens, to do every thing that can be for the benefit of Orphans; and this Annual Court seems to be only a review of their years Work, or a Retrospection into the observance of their former Orders.

CHAP. VII.

Of the Church and Church Affairs.

¶.33. THeir Parishes are accounted large or small, in proportion to the number of Tithables contain'd in them, and not according to the extent of Land. For the Particulars of these, and the number of the Parishes in each County, see the List* in the conclusion of this Book, which will answer the end of a Prolix Description.

¶.34. They have in each Parish a convenient Church, built either of Timber, Brick, or Stone, and decently adorn'd with every thing necessary for the celebration of Divine-Service.

If a Parish be of greater extent than ordinary, it hath generally a Chappel of Ease; and some of the Parishes have two such Chappels, besides the Church, for the greater convenience of the Parishioners. In these Chappels the Minister preaches alternately, always leaving a Reader, to read Prayers and a Homily, when he can't attend himself.

¶.35. The People are generally of the Church of *England*, which is the Religion establisht by Law in that Country, from which there are very few Dissenters. Yet liberty of Conscience is given to all other Congregations pretending to Christianity, on condition they submit to all Parish Duties. They have no more than five Conventicles amongst them, namely, three small Meetings of Quakers, and two of Presbyterians. 'Tis observ'd, that those Counties where the Presbyterian Meetings

*See statistical table, "Anno 1703," p. 253.

are, produce very mean Tobacco; and for that reason can't get an Orthodox Minister to stay amongst them; but whenever they cou'd, the People very orderly went to Church: As for the Quakers, 'tis observ'd by letting them alone, they decrease daily.

₡.36. The Maintenance for a Minister there, is appointed by Law at 16,000 pounds of Tobacco *per Annum*, (be the Parish great or small) as also a Dwelling-House and Glebe, together with certain Perquisites for Marriages, and Funeral Sermons. That which makes the difference in the Benefices of the Clergy, is the value of the Tobacco, according to the distinct Species of it, or according to the place of its Growth; Besides in large and rich Parishes, more Marriages will probably happen, and more Funeral Sermons.

The Fee by Law for a Funeral Sermon, is forty Shillings, or four hundred pounds of Tobacco; for a Marriage by Licence, twenty Shillings, or two hundred pounds of Tobacco, and where the Banes are proclaim'd, only 5 *s*. or 50 *l*. of Tobacco.

When these Salaries were granted, the Assembly valued Tobacco at 10 Shillings *per* Hundred; at which Rate, the 16,000 *l*. comes to fourscore pounds Sterling; but in all Parishes where the Sweet-sented grows, it has generally been sold of late, for near double that value, and never under.

In some Parishes likewise there are stocks of Cattle and Negros, on the Glebes, which are also allow'd to the Minister, for his Use and Incouragement; he only being accountable for the surrender of the same value, when he leaves the Parish.

₡.37. For the Well-governing of these, and all other Parochial Affairs, a Vestry is appointed in each Parish. These Vestries consist of twelve Gentlemen of the Parish, and were at first chosen by the Vote of the Parishoners;

but upon the Death of one, have been continued by the Survivor's electing another in his place. These are the Patrons of the Church, and in the Name of the Parish, have the Presentation of Ministers, as well as the sole power of all Parish Assessments. They are qualified for this Employment, by subscribing, to be conformable to the Doctrine and Discipline of the Church of *England*. If there be a Minister incumbent, he is always chief of the Vestry.

For the ease of the Vestry in General, and for discharging the Business of the Parish, they choose two from among themselves, to be Church-Wardens, which must be annually chang'd, that the burden may lie equally upon all. The business of these Church-Wardens, is to see the Orders, and Agreements of the Vestry perform'd; to collect all the Parish Tobacco's, and distribute them to the several Claimers; to make up the Accounts of the Parish, and to present all Profaneness and Immorality.

By these the Tobacco of the Minister is collected, and brought home to him in Hogsheads convenient for Shipping; so that he is at no further trouble, but to receive it in that Condition. This was ordain'd by the Law of the Country, for the ease of the Ministers, that so they being delivered, from the trouble of gathering in their Dues, may have the more time to apply themselves to the Exercises of their Holy Function, and live in a Decency suitable to their Order. It may here be observ'd, that the Labour of a dozen Negroes, does but answer this Salary, and seldom yields a greater Crop of Sweet-sented Tobacco, than is allow'd to each of their Ministers.

ℂ.38. Probates of Wills and Administrations, are according to their Law, grantable by the County Courts; but the Commission must be sign'd by the Governor without Fee. Marriage-Licenses are issued by the Clerks of those Courts, and sign'd by the first Justice in Commission, or by any other Person deputed by the Governor; for which a Fee of twenty Shillings must be paid to the Governor. The power of Induction upon Presentation of Ministers, is also by their Law lodged in the Governor's hands. All which Acts are contain'd in the first revisal of their Laws, since which her Majesty, and her Royal Predecessors, have always been pleased to give an instruction to their Governors to that purpose.

In the year 1642, when the Sectaries began to spread themselves so much in *England*, the Assembly made a Law against them, to prevent their Preaching, and propagating their Doctrines in that Colony. They admitted none to preach in their Churches, but Ministers ordain'd by some Reverend Bishop of the Church of *England*; and the Governor for the time being, as the most suitable publick Person among them, was left sole Judge of the Certificates of such Ordination, and so he has continued ever since.

€.39. The only thing I have heard the Clergy complain of there, is what they call Precariousness in their Livings; that is, they have not Inductions generally; and therefore are not intituled to a Free-hold: But are liable without Tryal or Crime alledged, to be put out by the Vestry: And though some have prevail'd with their Vestries, to present them for Induction; yet the greater number of the Ministers have no Induction: But are entertain'd from year to year, or for term of years, by agreement with their Vestries; yet are they very rarely turn'd out, without some great provocation; and then if they have not been abominably Scandalous, they immediately get other Parishes: For there is no Benefice whatsoever in that Country that remains without a Parson, if they can get one, and no qualified Minister ever yet return'd from that Country, for want of Preferment. They have now about a dozen vacant Parishes.

CHAP. VIII.

Concerning the College.

€.40.   THE College, as has been hinted, was founded by their late Majesties, King *William* and Queen *Mary* of happy Memory, in the Year 1692. Towards the founding of which, they gave 1985 *l.* 14 *s.* 10 *d.* They gave moreover towards the Indowment of it, 20,000 Acres of Land; the Revenue of 1 *d. per pound* on Tobacco, exported to the Plantations from *Virginia* and *Maryland;* and the Surveyor General's Place of that Colony then void, and appointed them also a Burgess to represent them in the Assemblies. The Land hitherto has yielded little or no Profit; the Duty of 1 *d. per* Pound, brings in about 200 pounds a year; and the Surveyor-General's Place, about 50 *l.* a year. To which the Assembly has added a Duty on Skins and Furs exported, worth about an hundred pounds a year.

€.41.   By the same Charter likewise, their Majesties granted a Power to certain Gentlemen, and the Survivors of them, as Trustees, to Build and Stablish the College by the Name of *William* and *Mary* College; to consist of a President, and six Masters, or Professors, and an hundred Scholars, more or less, Graduates, or Non-Graduates; enabling the said Trustees, as a Body Corporate, to enjoy Annuities Spiritual and Temporal, of the value of 2000 *l.* Sterling *per Annum,* with Proviso, to convert it to the building and adorning the College; and then to make over the remainder to the President and Masters, and their Successors: who are likewise to become a Corporation, and be enabled to Purchase, and hold to the value of 2000 *l.* a year, but no more.

¶.42.   The Persons nam'd in the Charter for Trustees, are made Governors and Visitors of the College, and to have a perpetual Succession, by the name of Governors and Visitors, with power to fill up their own Vacancies, happening by the Death or Removal of any of them. Their compleat number may be 18, but not to exceed 20, of which one is to be Rector, and annually chosen by themselves, on the first *Monday* after the 25*th* of *March*.

These have the nomination of the President and Masters of the College, and all other Officers belonging to it; and the power of making Statutes and Ordinances, for the better Rule and Government thereof.

¶.43.   The Building is to consist of a Quadrangle, two sides of which, are yet only carryed up. In this part are already finished all conveniences of Cooking, Brewing, Baking, *&c.* and convenient Rooms for the Reception of the President, and Masters, with many more Scholars than are as yet come to it; in this part are also the Hall, and School-Room.

¶.44.   When the last Governor was removed, which was before any room was finished in the College, and the Boys were taught by the College-Master, in a little School-House close by it; it had more Scholars than it has now. Which Misfortune has happen'd, by reason of the late confusion, occasion'd by the furious proceedings of the present Governor, so that many chose to send their Sons to *England*, and others to keep theirs at Home, rather than put them to the hazard of being harassed, and living in the Combustion which that Gentleman makes among them.

The Method of Teaching is likewise very much impair'd by the chief Masters minding his Country Affairs: For by this means he is obliged to live several Miles from the College, upon his own Plantation; so that he cannot give that Attendance and Application, which was design'd, by appointing so good a Salary, as 100 *l. per Annum* besides Perquisites.

The College Revenue is behind-hand, and the *Maryland* Duty of 1 *d. per* Pound, has not been paid in of late, so that several of the Established Salaries are in arrear.

CHAP. IX.

Of the Militia in Virginia.

¶.45. THE Militia are the only standing Forces in *Virginia*. They have no Fortress, nor so much as any Cannon fit for Service. Neither are any of these made use of, except six small Pieces, that formerly were mounted on the Fort at *James* Town; but these are now remov'd to *Williamsburg*, where they are of no use, but to fire upon some Joyful Occasions. They are happy in the enjoyment of an Everlasting Peace, which their Poverty and want of Towns secure to them. They have the *Indians* round about in Subjection, and have no sort of Apprehension from them: And for a Foreign Enemy, it can never be worth their while to carry Troops sufficient to conquer the Country; for the scattering Method of their Settlement, will not answer the charge of an Expedition to plunder them. So that they feel none but the distant effects of War, which, however keep 'em so poor, that they can boast of nothing but the security of their Persons, and Habitations. They fear no other Enemy, but only now and then, an insolent and oppressive Governor, who is pleas'd to abuse the Queen's Authority, by perverting it into Arbitrary Power, and to exasperate the People by their barbarous Treatment.

¶.46. The Governor is Lieutenant-General by his Commission, and in each County do's appoint the Colonel, Lieutenant-Colonel, and Major, who have under them Captains, and other Commission'd, and Subaltern Officers.

Every Freeman, (by which Denomination they call all, but indented, or bought Servants) from Sixteen, to Sixty years of Age, is listed in the Militia; which by a Law, is to be Mustered in a General Muster for each County, once a year; and in single Troops and Companies, three or four times more; and the most convenient Situation for each Troop and Company, is appointed for them to be Exercised in. The People there are very Skilful in the use of Fire-Arms, being all their Lives accustom'd to shoot in the Woods. This, together with a little exercizeing would soon make the Militia little inferior to Regular Troops.

℃.47. The number of the Militia is 2363 Light-Horse, and 7159, Foot and Dragoons: But as very few of the Planters are without Horses to ride on, so great part of them may easily be made into Dragoons, if occasion should require. The particular Proportion of each County, may be seen in the Table* at the end of this Book.

℃.48. Instead of the Soldiers they formerly kept constantly on Foot, under the name of Rangers, to scour the Frontiers clear of the *Indian* Enemy, they have lately appointed the Militia to March out upon such occasions, under the Command of the chief Officer of the County, where this shall be necessary. And if they upon such Expedition remain in Arms, three Days and upwards, they are then intituled to pay for the whole time; but if it prove a false Alarm, and they have no occasion to continue out so long, they can demand nothing.

℃.49. The number of Soldiers in each Troop of Light-Horse, and Dragoons, are from Thirty to Forty, as the

*See statistical table, "Anno 1703," p. 253.

convenience of the County will admit of the Division; and in a Company of Foot about Fifty. The present Governor has reduc'd 'em to this, whereas formerly a Troop of Horse consisted of fifty and upwards, and a Company of Foot of seventy effective Men. A Troop or Company may be got together in less than a days warning.

CHAP. X.

Of the Servants and Slaves in Virginia.

¶.50.　THeir Servants, they distinguish by the Names of Slaves for Life, and Servants for a time.

Slaves are the Negroes, and their Posterity, following the condition of the Mother, according to the Maxim, *partus sequitur ventrem.* They are call'd Slaves, in respect of the time of their Servitude, because it is for Life.

Servants, are those which serve only for a few years, according to the time of their Indenture, or the Custom of the Country. The Custom of the Country takes place upon such as have no Indentures. The Law in this case is, that if such Servants be under Nineteen years of Age, they must be brought into Court, to have their Age adjudged; and from the Age they are judg'd to be of, they must serve until they reach four and twenty: But if they be adjudged upwards of Nineteen, they are then only to be Servants for the term of five Years.

¶.51. The Male-Servants, and Slaves of both Sexes, are imployed together in Tilling and Manuring the Ground, in Sowing and Planting Tobacco, Corn, &c. Some Distinction indeed is made between them in their Cloaths, and Food; but the Work of both, is no other than what the Overseers, the Freemen, and the Planters themselves do.

Sufficient Distinction is also made between the Female-Servants, and Slaves; for a White Woman is rarely or never put to work in the Ground, if she be good for any thing else: And to Discourage all Planters from using any Women so, their Law imposes the heaviest

Taxes upon Female-Servants working in the Ground, while it suffers all other white Women to be absolutely exempted: Whereas on the other hand, it is a common thing to work a Woman Slave out of Doors; nor does the Law make any Distinction in her Taxes, whether her Work be Abroad, or at Home.

¶.52. Because I have heard how strangely cruel, and severe, the Service of this Country is represented in some parts of *England;* I can't forbear affirming, that the work of their Servants, and Slaves, is no other than what every common Freeman do's. Neither is any Servant requir'd to do more in a Day, than his Overseer. And I can assure you with a great deal of Truth, that generally their Slaves are not worked near so hard, nor so many Hours in a Day, as the Husbandmen, and Day-Labourers in *England.* An Overseer is a Man, that having served his time, has acquired the Skill and Character of an experienced Planter, and is therefore intrusted with the Direction of the Servants and Slaves.

But to compleat this account of Servants, I shall give you a short Relation of the care their Laws take, that they be used as tenderly as possible.

By the Laws of their Country.

1. All Servants whatsoever, have their Complaints heard without Fee, or Reward; but if the Master be found Faulty, the charge of the Complaint is cast upon him, otherwise the business is done *ex Officio.*

2. Any Justice of Peace may receive the Complaint of a Servant, and order every thing relating thereto, till the next County-Court, where it will be finally determin'd.

3. All Masters are under the Correction, and Censure of the County-Courts, to provide for their Servants, good and wholsome Diet, Clothing, and Lodging.

4. They are always to appear, upon the first Notice given of the Complaint of their Servants, otherwise to forfeit the Service of them, until they do appear.

5. All Servants Complaints are to be receiv'd at any time in Court, without Process, and shall not be delay'd for want of Form; but the Merits of the Complaint must be immediately inquir'd into by the Justices; and if the Master cause any delay therein, the Court may remove such Servants, if they see Cause, until the Master will come to Tryal.

6. If a Master shall at any time disobey an Order of Court, made upon any Complaint of a Servant; the Court is impower'd to remove such Servant forthwith to another Master, who will be kinder; Giving to the former Master the produce only, (after Fees deducted) of what such Servants shall be sold for by Publick Outcry.

7. If a Master should be so cruel, as to use his Servant ill, that is faln Sick, or Lame in his Service, and thereby render'd unfit for Labour, he must be remov'd by the Church-Wardens out of the way of such Cruelty, and boarded in some good Planters House, till the time of his Freedom, the charge of which must be laid before the next County-Court, which has power to levy the same from time to time, upon the Goods and Chattels of the Master; After which, the charge of such Boarding is to come upon the Parish in General.

8. All hired Servants are intituled to these Priviledges.

9. No Master of a Servant, can make a new Bargain for Service, or other Matter with his Servant, without the privity and consent of a Justice of Peace, to prevent the Master's Over-reaching, or scareing such Servant into an unreasonable Complyance.

10. The property of all Money and Goods sent over thither to Servants, or carry'd in with them; is reserv'd to themselves, and remain intirely at their disposal.

11. Each Servant at his Freedom, receives of his Master fifteen Bushels of Corn, (which is sufficient for a whole year) and two new Suits of Cloaths, both Linnen and Woollen; and then becomes as free in all respects, and as much entituled to the Liberties, and Priviledges of the Country, as any other of the Inhabitants or Natives are.

12. Each Servant has then also a Right to take up fifty Acres of Land, where he can find any unpatented: But that is no great Privilege, for any one may have as good a right for a piece of Eight.

This is what the Laws prescribe in favour of Servants, by which you may find, that the Cruelties and Severities imputed to that Country, are an unjust Reflection. For no People more abhor the thoughts of such Usage, than the *Virginians*, nor take more precaution to prevent it.

CHAP. XI.

Of the other Publick Charitable Works, and particularly, their Provision for the Poor.

€.53. THey live in so happy a Climate, and have so fertile a Soil, that no body is poor enough to beg, or want Food, though they have abundance of People that are lazy enough to deserve it. I remember the time, when five pound was left by a charitable Testator, to the Poor of the Parish he lived in; and it lay nine years, before the Executors could find one poor enough, to be intitul'd to any part of this Legacy; and at last it was all given to one old Woman. So that this may in truth, be term'd the best poor Man's Country in the World. But as they have no body that is poor to beggary, so they have few that are rich; because their Goods are so heavily burden'd with Duties in *England*, that they seldom can make any advantage of 'em.

€.54. When it happens, that by Accident or Sickness, any Person is disabled from Working, and so is forc't to depend upon the Alms of the Parish, he is then very well provided for; not at the common rate of some Countries, that give but just sufficient, to preserve the poor from perishing: But the unhappy Creature is receiv'd into some charitable Planter's House, where he is at the Publick Charge, boarded very plentifully.

Many when they are very Aged, or by long Sickness, become Poor, will sometimes ask to be free from Levies and Taxes; but very few do ever ask for the Parish-Alms, or indeed, so much as stand in need of them.

€.55. There are large tracts of Land, Houses, and other

things granted to Free-Schools, for the Education of Children, in many parts of the Country; and some of these are so large, that of themselves they are a handsom Maintenance to a Master: But the additional Allowance, which Gentlemen give with their Sons, render them a comfortable Subsistence. These Schools have been founded by the Legacies of well inclin'd Gentlemen, and the Management of them, hath commonly been left to the Direction of the County-Court, or to the Vestry of the respective Parishes, and I have never heard, that any of those Pious Uses have been Mis-apply'd. In all other Places, where such Indowments have not been already made, the People joyn, and build Schools for their Children, where they may learn upon very easie Terms.

CHAP. XII.

Of the Tenure by which they hold their Lands; and of their Grants.

§.56. THE Tenure of their Land there, is free and common Soccage, according to Custom of *East-Greenwich;* and is created by Letters Patents, issuing under the Seal of the Colony, and under the Test of the Governour in Chief for the time being; and I don't find, that the Name of any other Officer is necessary, to make the Patent valid; but it must be granted by consent of Council.

§.57. There are three ways of obtaining from her Majesty, a Title to Land there, *viz.* 1*st*, By Right and Survey. 2*d*, By Petition for Land Lapsed. 3*d*, By Petition for Land Escheated. The Conditions of the two former, are the Entry of Rights; the Condition of the third, a Composition of two pounds of Tobacco for every Acre.

§.58. A Right, is the Title any one hath by the Royal Charter, to fifty Acres of Land, in Consideration of his Personal Transportation into that Country, to settle and remain there; by this Rule also, a Man that removes his Family, is intituled to the same Number of Acres, for his Wife, and each of his Children.

§.59. A Patent for Land upon Survey, is acquired thus. First, the Man proves his Rights; that is, he makes Oath in Court, of the Importation of so many Persons, with a List of their Names. This List is then certified by the Clerk of that Court, to the Clerk of the Secretaries Office; who examines into the Validity of them, and files them in that Office, attesting them to be regular. When the Rights are thus certified, they are produced to the Surveyor of the County, and the Land is shewed to him; who thereupon is bound by his Oath to make the Survey, if the Land had been not Patented before. These Rights to Land, are as commonly sold by one Man to another, as the Land it self; so that any one, not having Rights by his own Importation, may have them by Purchase.

It is the business of the Surveyor also, to take care, that the Bounds of his Survey be plainly marked, either by natural Boundaries, or else by chopping Notches in the Trees, that happen in the lines of his Courses: But this is done at the charge of the Man that employs him.

This Survey being made, a Copy thereof is carried, with the Certificate of Rights to the Secretaries Office, and there (if there be no Objection) a Patent must of course be made out upon it, which is presented to the Governor and Council for them to pass; the Patentee having no more to do, but to send for it when it is perfected, and to pay the Fee, at the first Crop, to the Sheriff of the County, by whom annually the Fees are collected.

This Patent gives an Estate in Fee-simple, upon Condition, of paying a Quit-Rent of twelve pence for every fifty Acres, and of Planting or Seating thereon, within three years, according to their Law; that is, to clear, plant, and tend an Acre of Ground with Corn, or to build an House, and keep a stock of Cattle, for one whole year together upon the Land; after which 'tis presum'd they will continue the Settlement, and not let the Stock be lost, which after it has got a tast of those new Plantations, will never afterwards without Confinement, remain at an old one. I know that a certain grave Author[48] of much Learning, and little Knowledge of the Plantations, Ridicules this Law, in his Discourses on the Trade of *England*, Part 2. Pag. 236. But I believe if he had Land there, under the Conditions of that Law, he wou'd not, with all his Skill in shifting, be able either to avoid paying the Quit-rents, or to continue his Right, by erecting a Hutt of Bark, as he calls it. This Adventrous Gentleman, has several unjust Reflections upon that Country: But I impute them all to his Writing wholly in favour of the Propriety-Government, and upon other Peoples Information, who know as little of the Matter as himself.

¶.60. Lapsed Land, is when any one having obtain'd a Patent as before, doth not Seat or Plant thereon within three years, as the Condition of the Patent requires; but leaves it still altogether uninhabited, and uncultivated: In such case it is said to be Lapsed, and any Man is at liberty to obtain a new Patent of it in his own Name; the method of acquiring which Patent, is thus.

The Party must apply himself by Petition to the General Court, setting forth all the Circumstances of the Lapse. If this Petition be allow'd, the Court makes an Order, that a Patent be prepared for the Petitioner, upon the same Condition, of Seating or Planting within three years, as was in the former Patent. Thus Land may be lapsed or lost several times, by the negligence of the Patentees; who by such Omission, lose not only the Land, but all their Rights, and Charges into the bargain.

But if within the three years after the Date of the Patent, the Patentee shall Seat or Plant the said Land, as the Law directs: It cannot afterwards be forfeited, but by Attainder, or Escheat, in which case it returns to her Majesty again.

¶.61. When Land is supposed to Escheat, the Governor issues his Warrant to the Escheator, to make Inquest thereof: And when upon such Inquest, Office is found for the Queen, it must be recorded in the Secretaries Office, and there kept nine Months, to see if any Person will lay claim to it, or can traverse the Escheat. If any such appear, upon his Petition to the General Court, he is heard, before any Grant can be made. If no Person oppose the Inquest, the Land is given to the Man that shews the best equitable right thereto; and if there be none such, it is then granted to any one, that the Governor and Council shall think fit, the Grantee always paying two pounds of Tobacco *per* Acre into the Treasury of the Country, as a Fine of Composition with her Majesty for her Escheat; And thereupon a Patent issues reciting the Premises.

CHAP. XIII.

Of the Liberties and Naturalization of Aliens in Virginia.

§.62. CHristians of all Nations, have equal freedom there, and upon their Arrival, become *Ipso facto*, entituled to all the Liberties and Priviledges of the Country, provided they take the Oaths of Obedience to the Crown, and Government.

The Method of obtaining Naturalization is thus; the Party desiring it, goes before the Governor, and tenders his Oath of Allegiance, which the Governor thereupon Administers, and immediately makes Certificate of it under the Seal of the Colony. By this means, the Person Alien, is compleatly Naturalized to all Intents and Purposes.

§.63. All the *French* Refugees sent in thither by the Charitable Exhibition of his late Majesty King *William*, are Naturalized.

In the year 1699, there went over about three hundred of these, and the year following about two hundred more, and so on, till there arrived in all, between seven and eight hundred Men, Women, and Children, who had fled from *France* on account of their Religion.

Those who went over the first year, were advised to Seat on a piece of very rich Land, about twenty Miles above the Falls of *James* River, on the *South* side of the River; which Land was formerly the Seat of a Great and Warlike Nation of *Indians*, call'd the *Monacàns*, none of which are now left in those Parts; but the Land still retains their Name, and is call'd the *Monacàn* Town.

The Refugees that arrived the second year, went also

first to the *Monacàn* Town, but afterwards upon some Disagreement, several dispers'd themselves up and down the Country; and those that have arriv'd since, have follow'd their Example, except some few, that settl'd likewise at the *Mo[n]acàn* Town.

The Assembly was very bountiful to those who remain'd at this Town, bestowing on them large Donations, Money, and Provisions for their Support; they likewise freed them from every Publick Tax, for several years to come, and addrest the Governor, to grant them a Brief, to entitle them to the Charity of all well-dispos'd Persons throughout the Country, which together with the Kings Benevolence, supported them very comfortably, till they could sufficiently supply themselves with Necessaries, which now they do indifferently well, and begin to have Stocks of Cattle, which are said to give abundantly more Milk, than any other in the Country. I have heard that these People are upon a design, of getting into the breed of Buffaloes, to which end they lie in wait for their Calves, that they may tame, and raise a Stock of them: In which if they succeed, 'twill in all probability be greatly for their Advantage; for these are much larger than other Cattle, and have the benefit of being natural to the Climate.

They now make many of their own Cloaths, and are resolved, as soon as they have improv'd that Manufacture, to apply themselves to the making of Wine and Brandy, which they do not doubt to bring to Perfection.

The last year they began an Essay of Wine, which they made of the wild Grapes gather'd in the Woods; the effect of which, was Noble strong-bodied Claret, of a curious flavour. I heard a Gentleman, who tasted it, give it great Commendation. Now if such may be made of the wild Vine in the Woods, without Pruning, Weeding, or removing it out of the Shade, what may not be produc'd from a Vinyard skilfully Cultivated?

I must not here omit doing Justice to the Goodness

and Generosity of Colonel *Byrd*, towards these distressed *Hugonots*. Upon their first Arrival in that Country, he receiv'd them with all the tenderness of a Father; and ever since has constantly given them the utmost Assistance. He not only relieves them, but with a Charity very uncommon, is fond of doing it. He makes them the object of his particular care, employing all his Skill, and all his Friends, to advance their Interest, both publickly and privately. He spares no Expence, and what is more than that, he refuses no trouble for their Incouragement. What Liberties has he not all along allow'd them, upon his own Plantations, to furnish themselves from thence with Corn, and other Necessaries? His Mills have been at their Service, to grind their Corn Toll-free, and his People are order'd upon all occasions to assist them. How kind has he been in procuring them Contributions from other People? With what Zeal did he represent their Cause to the Assembly? And with what earnestness did he press all his Friends in their favour, who otherwise told him, they could not have believ'd their Case to be, as he related it? For even Poverty in all its Distress, cou'd not guard them from ill Reports, which wou'd have had a severe effect upon them, had they not been protected by the Interest, and Credit of this Honourable Gentleman. With what delight did he afterwards gather in the Benevolence, that was given? How frequently do's he continue still to visit their Families, and with what Importunity do's he press them, to make their wants known to him, that takes pleasure in relieving them? It is easie to imagin, how necessary to an Infant Settlement, are the Assistances of so generous a Friend. When several hundred Families of Men, Women, and Children are set ashoar Naked and Hungry, in a strange Land, they have not only necessity to struggle with, but likewise with the Envy of Ill-natur'd People, who fancy they come to eat the Bread out of their Mouths: All these Difficulties befell these poor

Refugees at their first Arrival there; but God Almighty rais'd up this Gentleman, not only to Succour them with his own Charity, but to solicit the Liberalities of other People. By these Helps they have hitherto Subsisted, and been put into some Condition to shift for themselves. However, they are not yet so far advanc'd, but that their Patron, may still have an opportunity, of shewing his Kindness towards them; which is to prevail with the Assembly, to bestow upon them a certain Title to the Land they now possess, to which as yet they have no other Right, but the bare sitting down upon unseated Land. This seems to be worthy of an early care, lest the Land which they have improv'd by their Industry from wild Woods, should hereafter unjustly be taken away from their Children.

CHAP. XIV.

Of the Currency and Valuation of Coins in Virginia.

C.64. THE Coin which chiefly they have among 'em, is either Gold, of the Stamp of *Arabia*, or Silver and Gold, of the Stamp of the *Spanish America*: But they have now very little Money there, and are still like to have rather less, than more, while matters remain in the ill Condition they are. For while they are forbid raising the Coin, and the Neighbouring Governments all around, are allow'd to enhance the rate of it with them, to above thirty *per Cent.* more than the Intrinsick Value; all their Money will be carry'd thither, which seems to be the greatest hardship in the World upon that Colony. It were much to be wish'd, that all the Colonies of the Continent under the Dominion of *England*, were oblig'd to have one and the same Standard for their Coin; that so one Government might not suffer by the unreasonable advances of another. The Inconveniences to *Virginia*, by the drawing away all the Specie, are inexpressible. For People want Money for traveling Expences; and for paying the small Jobbs of Labourers, and Artificers, who wou'd otherwise save abundance of time to themselves, which is now lost in looking after trivial Debts; besides the disadvantage of not being able to turn the Penny. By having no Ready-Money, many Law-suits commence, to demand those Debts, which by this means are contracted; besides the being forc'd to keep a thousand unnecessary Accounts.

Spanish Pistoles pass current there at 17 *s.* 6 *d.* *Arabian* Chequins at 10 *s.* Pieces of Eight, if they weigh 16 Penny Weight, (except of *Peru*,) at 5 *s.* *French* Crowns at 5 *s.* *Peru* pieces of Eight and *Dutch* Dollars, at 4 *s.* And all *English* Coin, as it go's in *England*.

PART II.

Of the Husbandry, and Improvements of Virginia.

CHAP. XV.

Of the People, Inhabitants of Virginia.

¶.65. I Can easily imagin with Sir *Josiah Child*,[49] that this, as well as all the rest of the Plantations, was for the most part at first peopled by Persons of low Circumstances, and by such as were willing to seek their Fortunes in a Foreign Country. Nor was it hardly possible it should be otherwise; for 'tis not likely that any Man of a plentiful Estate, should voluntarily abandon a happy Certainty, to roam after imaginary Advantages, in a New World. Besides which incertainty, he must have propos'd to himself, to encounter the infinite Difficulties and Dangers, that attend a New Settlement. These Discouragements were sufficient to terrifie any Man, that cou'd live easy in *England*, from going to provoke his Fortune in a strange Land.

¶.66. Those that went over to that Country first, were chiefly single Men, who had not the Incumbrance of Wives and Children in *England;* and if they had, they did not expose them to the fatigue and hazard of so long a Voyage, until they saw how it should fare with themselves. From hence it came to pass, that when they were setled there in a comfortable way of Subsisting a Family, they grew sensible of the Misfortune of wanting

Wives, and such as had left Wives in *England*, sent for them; but the single Men were put to their Shifts. They excepted against the *Indian* Women, on account of their being *Pagans*, and for fear they shou'd conspire with those of their own Nation, to destroy their Husbands. Under this Difficulty they had no hopes, but that the Plenty in which they liv'd, might invite Modest Women of small Fortunes, to go over thither from *England*. However, they wou'd not receive any, but such as cou'd carry sufficient Certificate of their Modesty, and good Behaviour. Those if they were but moderately qualified in all other Respects, might depend upon Marrying very well in those Days, without any Fortune. Nay, the first Planters were so far from expecting Money with a Woman, that 'twas a common thing for them to buy a deserving Wife, at the price of 100 Pound, and make themselves believe, they had a hopeful bargain.

¶.67. But this way of Peopling the Colony was only at first; for after the advantages of the Climate, and the fruitfulness of the Soil were well known, and all the dangers incident to Infant Settlements were over, People of better Condition retir'd thither with their Families, either to increase the Estates they had before, or else to avoid being persecuted for their Principles of Religion, or Government.

Thus in the time of the Rebellion in *England*, several good Cavalier Families went thither with their Effects, to escape the Tyranny of the Usurper. And so again, upon the Restoration, many People of the opposite Party took Refuge there, to shelter themselves from the King's Resentment. But they had not many of these last, because that Country was famous, for holding out the longest for the Royal Family, of any of the *English* Dominions; for which reason, the Roundheads went for the most part to *New-England*, as did most of those, that in the Reign of King *Charles* II. were molested on the account of their Religion, though some of these fell likewise to the share of *Virginia*. As for Malefactors condemn'd to Transportation, they have always receiv'd very few, and for many years last past, their Laws have been severe against them.

CHAP. XVI.
Of the Buildings in Virginia.

¶.68. THere are two fine Publick Buildings in this Country, which are the most Magnificent of any in *America:* One of which is the College before spoken of, and the other the Capitol or State-House, as it was formerly call'd: That is, the House for Convention of the General Assembly, for the Setting of the General Court, for the Meeting of the Council, and for keeping of their several Offices.

Not far from this, is also built the publick Prison of the Country, which is a large and convenient Structure, with Partitions for the different Sexes, and distinct Rooms for Petty-Offenders. To this is also annexed a convenient Yard to Air the Criminals in, for preservation of their Life and Health, till the time of their Trial.

These are all erected at Middle-Plantation, now nam'd *Williamsburgh*, where Land is laid out for a new Town. The College, and Capitol are both built of Brick, and cover'd with Shingle.

¶.69. The Private Buildings are of late very much improved; several Gentlemen there, having built themselves large Brick Houses of many Rooms on a Floor, and several Stories high, as also some Stone-Houses: but they don't covet to make them lofty, having extent enough of Ground to build upon; and now and then they are visited by high Winds, which wou'd incommode a towring Fabrick. They always contrive to have large Rooms, that they may be cool in Summer. Of late they have made their Stories much higher than formerly, and their Windows large, and sasht with Cristal Glass;

and within they adorn their Apartments with rich Furniture.

All their Drudgeries of Cookery, Washing, Daries, &c. are perform'd in Offices detacht from the Dwelling-Houses, which by this means are kept more cool and Sweet.

Their Tobacco-Houses are all built of Wood, as open and airy as is consistent with keeping out the Rain; which sort of Building, is most convenient for the curing of their Tobacco.

Their common covering for Dwelling-Houses is Shingle, which is an Oblong Square of Cypress or Pine-Wood; but they cover their Tobacco-Houses with thin Clapboard; and tho' they have Slate enough in some particular parts of the Country, and as strong Clay as can be desired for making of Tile, yet they have very few tiled Houses; neither has any one yet thought it worth his while, to dig up the Slate, which will hardly be made use of, till the Carriage there becomes cheaper, and more common.

CHAP. XVII.

Of the Edibles, Potables, *and* Fewel *in* Virginia.

¶.70. THE Families being altogether on Country-Seats, they have their Graziers, Seedsmen, Gardiners, Brewers, Bakers, Butchers, and Cooks within themselves: they have a great Plenty and Variety of Provisions for their Table; and as for Spicery, and other things that the Country don't produce, they have constant supplies of 'em from *England*. The Gentry pretend to have their Victuals drest, and serv'd up as Nicely, as at the best Tables in *London*.

¶.71. When I come to speak of their Cattle, I can't forbear charging my Country-men with exceeding Ill-Husbandry, in not providing sufficiently for them all Winter, by which means they starve their young Cattle, or at least stint their Growth; so that they seldom or never grow so large as they would do, if they were well manag'd; for the humour is there, if People can but save the lives of their Cattle, tho' they suffer them to be never so poor in the Winter, yet they will presently grow fat again in the Spring, which they esteem sufficient for their purpose. And this is the occasion, that their Beef, and Mutton are seldom or never so large, or so fat as in *England:* And yet with the least feeding imaginable, they are put into as good case, as can be desired.

But the Pork, Bacon, and Fowls of all sorts, both Dunghil-Fowl, and Water-Fowl, Tame and Wild, must be allowed to have very much the advantage in their several kinds, of those in *England*.

Their Fish is in vast plenty and variety, and extraordinary good in their kind. Beef and Pork are commonly sold there, from one Penny, to two Pence the Pound; their fattest and largest Poulets at Sixpence a piece; their Capons at eight-pence or nine-pence a piece; their Chickens at three or four Shillings the Dozen; their Ducks at Eight-pence, or Nine-pence a piece; their Geese at Ten pence or a Shilling; their Turkey-Hens at Fifteen or Eighteen pence; and their Turky-Cocks at two Shillings or half a Crown. But Oysters, and Wild-Fowl are not so dear, as the things I have reckon'd before, being in their Season the cheapest Victuals they have. Their Deer are commonly sold for eight, ten, or twelve Shillings a Head, according to the scarcity.

₡.72. The Bread in Gentlemen's Houses, is generally made of Wheat, but some rather choose the Pone, which is the Bread made of *Indian* Meal. Many of the poorer sort of People so little regard the *English* Grain, that though they might have it with the least trouble in the World, yet they don't mind to sow the Ground, because they won't be at the trouble of making a Fence particularly for it. And therefore their constant Bread is Pone, not so called from the Latine, *Panis*, but from the *Indian* Name *Oppone*.

₡.73. A Kitchin-Garden don't thrive better or faster in any part of the Universe, than there. They have all the Culinary Plants that grow in *England*, and in far greater perfection, than in *England:* Besides these, they have several Roots, Herbs, Vine-fruits, and Salate-Flowers peculiar to themselves, most of which will neither increase, nor grow to Perfection in *England*. These they dish up various ways, and find them very delicious Sauce to their Meats, both Roast and Boild, Fresh and Salt; such are the Red-Buds, Sassafras-Flowers, Cymnels, Melons, and Potatoes, whereof I have spoken at large in the 4*th* Chapter of the Second Book.

It is said of New-*England*, that several Plants will not grow there, which thrive well in *England*, such as Rue, Southernwood, Rosemary, Bays, and Lavender: And that others degenerate, and will not continue above a year or two at the most; such are July-Flowers, Fennel, Enula Campana, Clary, and Bloodwort: But I don't know any *English* Plant, Grain, or Fruit, that miscarries in *Virginia;* but most of them better their kinds very much, by being sowed or planted there. It was formerly said of the Red-top Turnip, that there in three or four years time, it degenerated into Rape; but that happen'd merely by an Error in saving the Seed; for now it appears, that if they cut off the top of such a Turnip, that has been kept out of the Ground all the Winter, and plant that top alone without the Body of the Root, it yields a Seed, which mends the Turnip in the next sowing.

₡.74. Their Small-drink is either Wine and Water, Beer, Milk and Water, or Water alone. Their richer sort generally brew their Small-Beer with Malt, which they have from *England*, though they have as good Barley of their own, as any in the World; but for want of the convenience of Malt-Houses, the Inhabitants take no care to sow it. The poorer sort brew their Beer with Mollasses and Bran; with *Indian* Corn Malted by drying in a Stove; with Persimmons dried in Cakes, and baked; with Potatoes; with the green stalks of *Indian* Corn cut small, and bruised; with Pompions; and with the *Batates Canadensis*, or *Jerusalem Artichoke*, which some People plant purposely for that use, but this is the least esteem'd, of all the sorts before mention'd.

Their Strong Drink is *Madera* Wine, which is a Noble strong Wine; and Punch, made either of Rum from the *Caribbee* Islands, or Brandy distilled from their Apples, and Peaches; besides *French-Brandy*, Wine, and strong Beer, which they have constantly from *England*.

€.75. Their Fewel is altogether Wood, which every Man burns at Pleasure, it being no other charge to him, than the cutting, and carrying it home. In all new Grounds it is such an Incumbrance, that they are forced to burn great heaps of it, to rid the Land. They have very good Pit-Coal (as is formerly mention'd) in several places of the Country, but no Man has yet thought it worth his while to make use of them, having Wood in Plenty, and lying more convenient for him.

CHAP. XVIII.

Of the Cloathing in Virginia.

§.76. THey have their Cloathing of all sorts from *England*, as Linnen, Woollen, Silk, Hats, and Leather. Yet Flax, and Hemp grow no where in the World, better than there; their Sheep yield a mighty Increase, and bear good Fleeces, but they shear them only to cool them. The Mulberry-Tree, whose Leaf is the proper Food of the Silk-Worm, grows there like a Weed, and Silk-Worms have been observ'd to thrive extreamly, and without any hazard. The very Furrs that their Hats are made of, perhaps go first from thence; and most of their Hides lie and rot, or are made use of, only for covering dry Goods, in a leaky House. Indeed some few Hides with much adoe are tann'd, and made into Servants Shoes; but at so careless a rate, that the Planters don't care to buy them, if they can get others; and sometimes perhaps a better manager than ordinary, will vouchsafe to make a pair of Breeches of a Deer-Skin. Nay, they are such abominable Ill-husbands, that tho' their Country be over-run with Wood, yet they have all their Wooden Ware from *England;* their Cabinets, Chairs, Tables, Stools, Chests, Boxes, Cart-Wheels, and all other things, even so much as their Bowls, and Birchen Brooms, to the Eternal Reproach of their Laziness.

CHAP. XIX.

Of the Temperature of the Climate, and the Inconveniencies attending it.

¶.77. THE Natural Temperature of the Inha[bit]ed part of the Country, is hot and moist: tho' this Moisture I take to be occasion'd by the abundance of low Grounds, Marshes, Creeks, and Rivers, which are every where among their lower Settlements; but more backward in the Woods, where they are now Seating, and making new Plantations, they have abundance of high and dry Land, where there are only Crystal Streams of Water, which flow gently from their Springs, and divide themselves into innumerable Branches, to moisten and enrich the adjacent Lands.

¶.78. The Country is in a very happy Situation, between the extreams of Heat and Cold, but inclining rather to the first. Certainly it must be a happy Climate, since it is very near of the same Latitude with the Land of Promise. Besides, As *Judæa* was full of Rivers, and Branches of Rivers; So is *Virginia:* As that was seated upon a great Bay and Sea, wherein were all the conveniences for Shipping and Trade; So is *Virginia*. Had that fertility of Soil? So has *Virginia*, equal to any Land in the known World. In fine, if any one impartially considers all the Advantages of this Country, as Nature made it; he must allow it to be as fine a Place, as any in the Universe; but I confess I am asham'd to say any thing of its Improvements, because I must at the same time reproach my Country-Men with a Laziness that is unpardonable. If there be any excuse for them in this Matter, 'tis the exceeding plenty of good things, with which Nature has blest them; for where God Almighty is so Merciful as to work for People, they never work for themselves.

All the Countries in the World, seated in or near the Latitude of *Virginia*, are esteem'd the Fruitfullest, and Pleasantest of all Clymates. As for Example, *Canaan*, *Syria*, *Persia*, great part of *India*, *China* and *Japan*, the *Morea*, *Spain*, *Portugal*, and the Coast of *Barbary*, none of which differ many Degrees of Latitude from *Virginia*. These are reckon'd the Gardens of the World, while *Virginia* is unjustly neglected by its own Inhabitants, and abus'd by other People.

¶.79. That which makes this Country most unfortunate, is, that it must submit to receive its Character from the Mouths not only of unfit, but very unequal Judges; For, all its Reproaches happen after this manner.

Many of the Merchants and others that go thither from *England*, make no distinction between a cold, and a hot Country: but wisely go sweltering about in their thick Cloaths all the Summer, because they used to do so in their *Northern* Climate; and then unfairly complain of the heat of the Country. They greedily Surfeit with their delicious Fruits, and are guilty of great Intemperance, through the exceeding Generosity of the Inhabitants; by which means they fall Sick, and then unjustly complain of the unhealthiness of the Country. In the next place, the Sailers for want of Towns there, are put to the hardship of rowling most of the Tobacco, a Mile or more, to the Water-side; this Splinters their Hands sometimes, and provokes 'em to curse the Country. Such Exercise, and a bright Sun, makes them hot, and then they imprudently fall to drinking cold Water, or perhaps New Cyder, which in its Season, they find at every Planter's House; Or else they greedily devour all the green Fruit, and unripe Trash they can meet with, and so fall into Fluxes, Fevers, and the Belly-Ach; and then, to spare their own Indiscretion, they in their Tarpawlin Language, cry, God D——— the Country. This is the true State of the case, as to the Complaints of its being Sickly; For, by the most impartial Observation I can make, if People will be perswaded to be Temperate, and take due care of themselves, I believe it is as healthy a Country, as any under Heaven: but the extraordinary pleasantness of the Weather, and the goodness of the Früit, lead People into many Temptations. The clearness and brightness of the Sky, add new vigour to their Spirits, and perfectly remove all Splenetick and sullen Thoughts. Here they enjoy all the benefits of a warm Sun, and by their shady Groves, are protected from its Inconvenience. Here all their Senses are entertain'd with an endless Succession of Native Pleasures. Their Eyes are ravished with the Beauties of naked Nature. Their Ears are Serenaded with the perpetual murmur of Brooks, and the thorow-base which the Wind plays, when it wantons through the Trees; the merry Birds too, join their pleasing Notes to this rural Consort, especially the Mock-birds, who love Society so well, that whenever they see Mankind, they will perch upon a Twigg very near them, and sing the sweetest wild Airs in the World: But what is most remarkable in these Melodious Animals, they will frequently fly at small distances before a Traveller, warbling out their Notes several Miles an end, and by their Musick, make a Man forget the Fatigues of his Journey. Their Taste is regaled with the most delicious Fruits, which without Art, they have in great Variety and Perfection. And then their smell is refreshed with an eternal fragrancy of Flowers and Sweets, with which Nature perfumes and adorns the Woods almost the whole year round.

 Have you pleasure in a Garden? All things thrive in it, most surpriseingly; you can't walk by a Bed of Flowers, but besides the entertainment of their Beauty, your Eyes will be saluted with the charming colours of the Humming Bird, which revels among the Flowers, and licks off the Dew and Honey from their tender Leaves, on which it only feeds. It's size is not half so large as an *English* Wren, and its colour is a glorious shining mixture of Scarlet, Green, and Gold. Colonel *Byrd*, in his Garden, which is the finest in that Country, has a Summer-House set round with the *Indian* Honey-Suckle, which all the Summer is continually full of sweet Flowers, in which these Birds delight exceedingly. Upon these Flowers, I have seen ten or a dozen of these Beautiful Creatures together, which sported about me so familiarly, that with their little Wings they often fann'd my Face.

¶.80. On the other side, all the Annoyances and Inconveniences of the Country, may fairly be summed up, under these three Heads, Thunder, Heat, and troublesom Vermin.

I confess, in the hottest part of Summer, they have sometimes very loud and surprizing Thunder, but rarely any Dammage happens by it. On the contrary, it is of such advantage to the cooling and refining of the Air, that it is oftner wished for, than fear'd. But they have no Earthquakes, which the *Caribbee* Islands are so much troubled with.

Their Heat is very seldom troublesome, and then only by the accident of a perfect Calm, which happens perhaps two or three times in a year, and lasts but a few Hours at a time; and even that Inconvenience is made easie by cool Shades, by open Airy rooms, Summer-Houses, Arbors, and Grottos: But the Spring and Fall, afford as pleasant Weather, as *Mahomet* promis'd in his Paradise.

All the troublesom Vermine, that ever I heard any Body complain of, are either Frogs, Snakes, Musketa's,

Chinches, Seedticks, or Red-worms, by some call'd Potato-lice. Of all which I shall give an account in their Order.

Some People have been so ill inform'd, as to say, that *Virginia* is full of Toads, though there never yet was seen one Toad in it. The Marshes, Fens, and Watry Grounds, are indeed full of harmless Frogs, which do no hurt, except by the noise of their croaking Notes: but in the upper parts of the Country, where the Land is high and dry, they are very scarce. In the Swamps and running Streams, they have Frogs of an incredible bigness, which are call'd Bull-frogs, from the roaring they make. Last year I found one of these near a Stream of fresh Water, of so prodigious a Magnitude, that when I extended its Leggs, I found the distance betwixt them, to be seventeen Inches and an half. I am confident, six *French-Men* might have made a comfortable Meal of its Carcase.

Some People in *England*, are startled at the very Name of the Rattle-Snake, and fancy every corner of that Province so much pester'd with them, that a Man goes in constant danger of his Life, that walks abroad in the Woods. But this is as gross a Mistake, as most of the other ill reports of this Country. For in the first place, this Snake is very rarely seen; and when that happens, it never do's the least Mischief, unless you offer to disturb it, and thereby provoke it to bite in its own defence. But it never fails to give you fair warning, by making a noise with its Rattle, which may be heard at a convenient distance. For my own part, I have travell'd the Country as much as any Man in it of my Age, by Night and by Day, above the Inhabitants, as well as among them; and yet I never see a Rattle-Snake alive, and at liberty, in all my Life. I have seen them indeed after they have been killed, or pent up in Boxes to be sent to *England*. The bite of this Viper, without some immediate Application, is certainly Death; but Remedies are so well known, that none of their Servants are ignorant of them. I never knew any that had been hurt by these, or any other of their Snakes, although I have a general knowledge all over the Country, and have been in every part of it. They have several other Snakes which are seen more frequently, and have very little or no hurt in them, *viz.* such as they call Black-Snakes, Water-Snakes, and Corn-Snakes. The black Viper-Snake, and the Copper-bellied Snake, are said to be as Venemous as the Rattle-Snake, but they also are as seldom seen; these three poisonous Snakes, bring forth their young alive, whereas the other three sorts lay Eggs, which are hatched afterwards; and that is the distinction they make, esteeming only those to be Venemous, which are Viviparous. They have likewise the Horn-Snake, so call'd from a sharp Horn it carries in its Tail, with which it assaults any thing that offends it, with that force, that it will strike its Tail into the But-end of a Musquet, from whence it is not able to dis-engage it self.

All sorts of Snakes will charm both Birds, and Squirrels, and the *Indians* pretend to charm them. Several Persons have seen Squirrels run down a Tree, directly into a Snakes mouth; they have likewise seen Birds fluttering up and down, and chattering at these Snakes, till at last they have dropt down just before them.

Some few years agoe, I was a Bear-Hunting in the Woods above the Inhabitants, and having straggled from my Companions, I was entertain'd at my return, with the Relation of a pleasant Rencounter, between a Dog and Rattle-Snake, about a Squirrel. The Snake had got the Head and Shoulders of the Squirrel into his Mouth, which being something too large for his Throat, it took him up some time to moisten the Furr of the Squirrel with his Spawl, to make it slip down. The Dog took this Advantage, seiz'd the hinder parts of the Squirrel, and tugg'd with all his Might. The Snake on the other side wou'd not let go his hold for a long time, till at last, fearing he might be bruised by the

Dog's running away with him, he gave up his Prey to the Enemy, which he eat, and we eat the Snake, which was dainty food.

Musketaes are a sort of Vermin, of less danger, but much more troublesom, because more frequent. They are a long tail'd Gnat, such as are in all Fens, and low Grounds in *England*, and I think, have no other difference from them than the Name. Neither are they troubled with 'em any where, but in their low Grounds, and Marshes. These Insects I believe are stronger, and continue longer there, by reason of the warm Sun, than in *England*. Whoever is persecuted with them in his House there, may get rid of them, by this easie Remedy. Let him but set open his Windows at Sun-set, and shut them again before the Twilight be quite shut in, and all the Musketaes in the Room, will go out at the Windows, and leave the Room clear.

Chinches are a sort of flat Bug, which lurks in the Beadsteads and Bedding, and disturbs People's Rest a-nights. Every neat House-Wife contrives there, by several Devices, to keep her Beds clear of them. But the best way I ever heard, effectually to destroy them, is by a narrow search among the Bedding early in the Spring, before these Vermin begin to Nitt, and run about; for they lie snug all the Winter, and are in the Spring large and full of the Winters Growth, having all their Seed within them; and so they become a fair Mark to find, and may with their whole Breed be destroy'd.

Seed-Ticks, and Red-Worms are small Insects, that annoy People by day, as Musketaes, and Chinches do by Night: but both these keep out of your way, if you will keep out of theirs: for Seed-Ticks are no where to be met with, but in the track of Cattle, upon which the great Ticks fasten, and fill their Skins so full of Blood, that they drop off, and where-ever they happen to fall, they produce a kind of Egg, which lies about a Fortnight, before the Seedlings are Hatcht. These Seedlings run in Swarms up the next blade of Grass, that lies in their way, and then the first thing that brushes that blade of Grass, gathers off most of these Vermine, which stick like burrs, upon any thing that touches them.

Red-Worms lie only in old dead Trees, and rotten Loggs; and without sitting down upon such, a Man never meets with them, nor at any other Season, but only in the midst of Summer. A little warm Water, immediately brings off both Seed-Ticks, and Red-Worms, tho' they lie never so thick upon any part of the Body: but without some such Remedy, they are so small, that nothing will lay hold of them, but the point of a Pen-Knife, Needle, or such like. And tho' nothing be done to remove them, yet the itching they occasion, goes away after two days.

¶.81. Their Winters are very short, and don't continue above three or four Months, of which they have seldom thirty days of unpleasant Weather, all the rest being blest with a clear Air, and a bright Sun. However, they have very hard Frost sometimes, but it rarely lasts above three or four days, that is, till the Wind change; for if it blow not between the *North-East*, and *North-West* Points, from the cold Appellatian Mountains, they have no Frost at all. But these Frosts are attended with a Serene Sky, and are otherwise made Delightful, by the tameness of the Wild-fowl and other Game, which by their incredible Number, afford the pleasantest Shooting in the World.

Their Rains, except in the depth of Winter, are extreamly agreeable and refreshing. All the Summer long they last but a few Hours at a time, and sometimes not above half an Hour, and then immediately succeeds clear Sun-shine again: but in that short time it rains so powerfully, that it quits the debt of a long Drought, and makes every thing green and gay.

I have heard that this Country is reproacht with

suddain, and dangerous changes of Weather; but that Imputation is unjust: For tho' it be true, that in the Winter, when the Wind comes over those vast Mountains to the *North-West*, which are supposed to retain mighty Magazines of Ice, and Snow, the Weather is then very rigorous; yet in Spring, Summer, and Autumn, such Winds are only cool and pleasant Breezes, which serve to refresh the Air, and correct those Excesses of Heat, which the Situation wou'd otherwise make that Country liable to.

CHAP. XX.

Of the Diseases incident to Virginia.

¶.82. WHile we are upon the Climate, and its Accidents, it will not be improper, to mention the Diseases incident to *Virginia*. Distempers come not there by choaking up the Spirits, with a foggy and thick Air, as in some *Northern* Climes; nor by a stifling Heat, that exhales the vigour of those, that dwell in a more *Southerly* Latitude: But by a wilful and foolish indulging themselves in those Pleasures, which in a warm and fruitful Country, Nature lavishes upon Mankind, for their Happiness, and not for their Destruction.

Thus I have seen Persons impatient of Heat, lie almost naked upon the cold Grass in the Shades, and there often forgetting themselves fall asleep. Nay, many are so imprudent, as to do this in an Evening, and perhaps lie so all Night; when between the Dew from Heaven, and the Damps from the Earth, such impressions are made upon the humours of their Body, as occasion fatal Distempers.

Thus also have I seen Persons put into a great heat by excessive Action, and in the midst of that Heat, strip off their Cloaths, and expose their open Pores to the Air. Nay, I have known some mad enough in this hot Condition, to take huge draughts of cold Water, or perhaps of Milk and Water, which they esteem much more cold in Operation, than Water alone.

And thus likewise have I seen several People, (especially New-Comers) so intemperate in devouring the pleasant Fruits, that they have fallen into dangerous Fluxes, and Surfeits. These, and such like Disorders, are the chief occasions of their Diseases.

¶.83. The first Sickness that any New-Comer happens to have there, he unfairly calls a Seasoning, be it Fever, Ague, or any thing else, that his own folly, or excesses bring upon him.

Their Intermitting Fevers, as well as their Agues, are very troublesome, if a fit Remedy be not apply'd; but of late the Doctors there, have made use of the *Cortex Peruviana* with Success, and find that it seldom or never fails to remove the Fits. The Planters too, have several Roots natural to the Country, which in this case they cry up as Infallible. They have the Happiness to have very few Doctors, and those such as make use only of simple Remedies, of which their Woods afford great Plenty. And indeed, their Distempers are not many, and their Cures are so generally known, that there is not Mystery enough, to make a Trade of Physick there, as the Learned do in other Countries, to the great oppression of Mankind.

¶.84. When these Damps, Colds, and Disorders, affect the Body more gently, and do not seize People violently at first; then for want of some timely Application, (the Planters abhorring all Physick, except in desperate cases,) these small Disorders are suffer'd to go on, until they grow into a *Cachexie*, by which the Body is overrun with obstinate scorbutick Humours. And this in a more fierce, and virulent Degree, I take to be the Yaws.

¶.85. The Gripes is the Distemper of the *Caribbee* Islands, not of that Country, and seldom gets footing there, and then only upon great Provocations; Namely, by the Intemperances before mentioned, together with an unreasonable use of filthy and unclean Drinks. Perhaps too it may come by new and unfine Cyder, Perry, or Peach-drink, which the People are impatient to Drink before they are ready; or by the excessive use of Lime-Juice, and foul Sugar in Punch and Flip; or else by the constant drinking of uncorrected Beer, made of such windy, unwholsom things, as some People make use of in Brewing.

Thus having fairly reckon'd up all the principal Inconveniences of the Climate, and the Distempers incident to the Country, I shall add a Chapter of the Recreations and Amusements used there, and then proceed to the natural Benefits they enjoy. After which, I shall conclude with some hints concerning their Trade, and Improvements.

CHAP. XXI.

Of the Recreations, and Pastimes used in Virginia.

¶.86. FOR their Recreation, the Plantations, Orchards, and Gardens constantly afford 'em fragrant and delightful Walks. In their Woods and Fields, they have an unknown variety of Vegetables, and other rarities of Nature to discover and observe. They have Hunting, Fishing, and Fowling, with which they entertain themselves an hundred ways. Here is the most Good-nature, and Hospitality practis'd in the World, both towards Friends and Strangers: but the worst of it is, this Generosity is attended now and then, with a little too much Intemperance. The Neighbourhood is at much the same distance, as in the Country in *England:* but with this Advantage, that all the better sort of People have been abroad, and seen the World, by which means they are free from that stiffness and formality, which discover more Civility, than Kindness: And besides, the goodness of the Roads, and the fairness of the Weather, bring People oftener together.

¶.87. The *Indians*, as I have already observ'd, had in their Hunting, a way of concealing themselves, and coming up to the Deer, under the blind of a Stalking-Head, in imitation of which, many People have taught their Horses to stalk it, that is, to walk gently by the Huntsman's side, to cover him from the sight of the Deer. Others cut down Trees for the Deer to browze upon, and lie in wait behind them. Others again set Stakes, at a certain distance within their Fences, where the Deer have been used to leap over into a Field of

Peas, which they love extreamly; these Stakes they so place, as to run into the Body of the Deer, when he Pitches, by which means they Impale him.

¶.88. They Hunt their Hares, (which are very numerous) a Foot, with Mungrils or swift Dogs, which either catch them quickly, or force them to hole in a hollow Tree, whither all their Hares generally tend, when they are closely pursued. As soon as they are thus holed, and have crawl'd up into the Body of the Tree, the business is to kindle a Fire, and smother them with Smoak, till they let go their hold, and fall to the bottom stifled; from whence they take them. If they have a mind to spare their Lives, upon turning them loose, they will be as fit as ever to hunt at another time; for the mischief done them by the Smoak, immediately wears off again.

¶.89. They have another sort of Hunting, which is very diverting, and that they call Vermine Hunting; It is perform'd a Foot, with small Dogs in the Night, by the Light of the Moon or Stars. Thus in Summer-time they find abundance of Raccoons, Opossums, and Foxes in the Corn-Fields, and about their Plantations: but at other times, they must go into the Woods for them. The Method is to go out with three or four Dogs, and as soon as they come to the place, they bid the Dogs seek out, and all the Company follow immediately. Where-ever a Dog barks, you may depend upon finding the Game; and this Alarm, draws both Men and Dogs that way. If this Sport be in the Woods, the Game by that time you come near it, is perhaps mounted to the top of an high Tree, and then they detach a nimble Fellow up after it, who must have a scuffle with the Beast, before he can throw it down to the Dogs; and then the Sport increases, to see the Vermine encounter those little Currs. In this sort of Hunting, they also carry their great Dogs out with them, because Wolves, Bears, Panthers, Wild-Cats, and all other Beasts of Prey, are abroad in the Night.

For Wolves they make Traps, and set Guns bated in the Woods, so that when he offers to seize the Bate, he pulls the Trigger, and the Gun discharges upon him. What *Elian* and *Pliny* write,[50] of the Horses being benummed in their Legs, if they tread in the Track of a Wolf, does not hold good here; for I my self, and many others, have rid full Speed after Wolves in the Woods, and have seen live ones taken out of a Trap, and drag'd at a Horse's Tail; and yet those that follow'd on Horseback, have not perceived any of their Horses to falter in their pace.

₡.90. They have many pretty devices besides the Gun, to take wild Turkeys; And among others, a Friend of mine invented a great Trap, wherein he at times caught many Turkeys, and particularly seventeen at one time, but he could not contrive it so, as to let others in after he had entrapped the first flock, until they were taken out.

₡.91. The *Indian* Invention of Weirs in Fishing, is mightily improved by the English besides which, they make use of Seins, Trolls, Casting-Netts, Setting-Netts, Hand-fishing, and Angling, and in each find abundance of Diversion. I have set in the shade, at the Heads of the Rivers Angling, and spent as much time in taking the Fish off the Hook, as in waiting for their taking it. Like those of the *Euxine* Sea, they also Fish with Spilyards, which is a long Line staked out in the River, and hung with a great many Hooks on short strings, fasten'd to the main Line, about three or four Foot asunder. The only difference is, our Line is supported by Stakes, and theirs is buoyed up with Gourds.

¶.92. Their Fowling is answerable to their Fishing for plenty of Game, in its proper Season, no Plantation being so ill stored, as to be without a great deal. They have a vast variety of it, several sorts of which, I have not yet mention'd, as Beaver, Otter, Squirrels, Partridges, Pigeons, and an infinite number of small Birds, *&c.*

¶.93. The admirable Oeconomy of the Beavers, deserves to be particularly remember'd. They cohabit in one House, are incorparated in a regular Form of Government, something like Monarchy, and have over them a Superintendent, which the *Indians* call *Pericu.* He leads them out to their several Imployments, which consist in Felling of Trees, biting off the Branches, and cutting them into certain lengths, suitable to the business they design them for, all which they perform with their Teeth. When this is done, the Governor orders several of his Subjects to joyn together, and take up one of those Logs, which they must carry to their House or Damm, as occasion requires. He walks in State by them all the while, and sees that every one bear his equal share of the burden; while he bites with his Teeth, and lashes with his Tail, those that lag behind, and do not lend all their Strength. They commonly build their Houses in Swamps, and then to raise the Water to a convenient height, they make a Damm with Logs, and a binding sort of Clay, so firm, that though the Water runs continually over, it cannot wash it away. Within these Damms, they'l inclose Water enough to make a Pool, like a Mill-pond; and if a Mill happen to be built upon the same Stream, below their Damm, the Miller in a dry Season, finds it worth his while to cut it, to supply his Mill with Water. Upon which Disaster, the Beavers are so expert at their Work, that in one or two Nights time, they will repair the breach, and make it perfectly whole again. Sometimes they build their

Houses in a broad Marsh, where the Tide ebbs and flows, and then they make no Damm at all. The Doors into their Houses are under Water. I have been at the Demolishing one of these Houses, that was found in a Marsh, and was surpriz'd to find it fortify'd with Logs, that were six Foot long, and ten Inches through, and had been carried at least one hundred and fifty yards. This House was three Stories high, and contain'd five Rooms, that is to say, two in the lower, and middle Stories, and but one at the top. These Creatures have a great deal of Policy, and know how to defeat all the Subtilty and Strategems of the Hunter, who seldom can meet with them, tho' they are in great numbers all over the Country.

¶.94. There is yet another kind of Sport, which the young People take great Delight in, and that is, the Hunting of wild Horses; which they pursue sometimes with Dogs, and sometimes without. You must know they have many Horses foaled in the Woods of the Uplands, that never were in hand, and are as shy as any Savage Creature. These having no mark upon them, belong to him, that first takes them. However, the Captor commonly purchases these Horses very dear, by spoiling better in the pursuit; in which case, he has little to make himself amends, besides the pleasure of the Chace. And very often this is all he has for it, for the wild Horses are so swift, that 'tis difficult to catch them; and when they are taken, tis odds but their Grease is melted, or else being old, they are so sullen, that they can't be tam'd.

¶.95. The Inhabitants are very Courteous to Travellers, who need no other Recommendation, but the being Human Creatures. A Stranger has no more to do, but to inquire upon the Road, where any Gentleman, or good House-keeper Lives, and there he may depend upon being received with Hospitality. This good Nature is so general among their People, that the Gentry when they go abroad, order their Principal Servant to entertain all Visitors, with every thing the Plantation affords. And the poor Planters, who have but one Bed, will very often sit up, or lie upon a Form or Couch all Night, to make room for a weary Traveller, to repose himself after his Journey.

If there happen to be a Churl, that either out of Covetousness, or Ill-nature, won't comply with this generous Custom, he has a mark of Infamy set upon him, and is abhorr'd by all. But I must confess, (and am heartily sorry for the occasion) that this good Neighbourhood has of late been much depraved by the present Governor, who practices, the detestable Politicks of governing by Parties; by which, Feuds and Heart-burnings have been kindled in the Minds of the People; and Friendship, Hospitality, and Good-Neighbourhood, have been extreamly discouraged.

CHAP. XXII.

Of the Natural Product of Virginia, *and the Advantages of their Husbandry.*

¶.96. THE extream fruitfulness of that Country, has been sufficiently shewn in the Second Book, and I think we may justly add, that in that particularly it is not exceeded by any other. No Seed is Sowed there, but it thrives, and most Plants are improved, by being Transplanted thither. And yet there's very little Improvement made among them, nor any thing us'd in Traffique, but Tobacco.

Besides all the natural Productions mention'd in the Second Book, you may take notice, that Apples from the Seed, never degenerate into Crabs, or Wildings there, but produce the same, or better Fruit than the Mother-Tree, (which is not so in *England*,) and are wonderfully improved by Grafting and Managing; yet there are very few Planters that graft at all, and much fewer that take any care to get choice Fruits.

The Fruit-Trees are wonderfully quick of growth, so that in six or seven years time from the Planting, a Man may bring an Orchard to bear in great plenty, from which he may make store of good Cyder, or distill great quantities of Brandy; for the Cyder is very strong, and yields abundance of in Spirit. Yet they have very few, that take any care at all for an Orchard; nay, many that have good Orchards, are so negligent of them, as to let them go to ruine, and expose the Trees to be torn, and barked by the Catle.

Peaches, Nectarines, and Apricocks, as well as Plums and Cherries, grow there upon Standard Trees. They commonly bear in three years from the Stone, and thrive so exceedingly, that they seem to have no need of Grafting or Inoculating, if any Body would be so good a Husband; and truly I never heard of any that did Graft either Plum, Nectarine, Peach or Apricock in that Country.

Peaches and Nectarines I believe to be Spontaneous some-where or other on that Continent; for the *Indians* have, and ever had greater variety, and finer sorts of them than the *English*. The best sort of these cling to the Stone, and will not come off clear, which they call Plum-Nectarines, and Plum-Peaches, or Cling-Stones. Some of these are 12 or 13 Inches in the Girt. These sorts of Fruits are raised so easily there, that some good Husbands plant great Orchards of them, purposely for their Hogs; and others make a Drink of them, which they call Mobby, and either drink it as Cyder, or Distil it off for Brandy. This makes the best Spirit next to Grapes.

Grape-Vines of the *English* Stock, as well as those of their own Production, bear most abundantly, if they are suffered to run near the Ground, and increase very kindly by Slipping; yet very few have them at all in their Gardens, much less indeavour to improve them by cutting or laying. Indeed my Curiosity the last year, caused me to lay some of the white Muscadine, which came of a Stock removed thither from *England*, and they increased by this method to Admiration: I likewise set several Slips of the cuttings of the same Vine, and the Major part of the Sets bore Grapes in perfection the first year, I remember I had seven full Bunches from one of them.

When a single Tree happens in clearing the Ground, to be left standing with a Vine upon it, open to the Sun and Air; that Vine generally produces as much as 4 or five others, that remain in the Woods. I have seen in this case, more Grapes upon one single Vine, than wou'd load a *London* Cart. And for all this, the People never remove any of them into their Gardens, but content themselves throughout the whole Country, with the Grapes they find thus wild; much less can they be expected to attempt the making of Wine or Brandy from the Grape.

The Almond, Pomgranate and Fig, ripen there very well, and yet there are not ten People in the Country, that have any of them in their Gardens, much less endeavour to preserve any of them for future spending, or to propagate them to make a Trade.

A Garden is no where sooner made than there, either for Fruits, or Flowers. Tulips from the Seed-flower the second year at farthest. All sorts of Herbs have there a perfection in their flavour, beyond what I ever tasted in a more *Northern* Climate. And yet they han't many Gardens in the Country, fit to bear that name.

ℭ.97. All sorts of *English* Grain thrive, and increase there, as well as in any other part of the World as for Example, Wheat, Barley, Oats, Rye, Peas, Rape, *&c.* And yet they don't make a Trade of any of them. Their Peas indeed, are troubled with Wivels, which eat a Hole in them: But this Hole does neither dammage the Seed, nor make the Peas unfit for Boiling. And such as are sow'd late, and gather'd after *August*, are clear of that Inconvenience.

It is thought too much for the same Man, to make the Wheat, and grind it, bolt it, and bake it himself. And it is too great a charge for every Planter, who is willing to sow Barley, to build a Malt-House, and Brew-House too, or else to have no benefit of his Barley; nor will it answer, if he wou'd be at the Charge. These things can never be expected from a single Family: But if they had cohabitations, it might be thought worth attempting. Neither as they are now settled, can they find any certain Market for their other Grain, which if they had Towns, would be quite otherwise.

Rice has been tried there, and is found to grow as

well, as in *Carolina*, or in any other part of the Earth: But it labours under the same inconvenience, the want of a Community, to husk and clean it; and after all, to take it off the Planters Hands.

¶.98. I have related at large in the first Book, how Flax, Hemp, Cotton, and the Silk-Worms have thriven there, in the several essays made upon them; how formerly there was Incouragement given for making of Linnen, Silk, *&c.* and how all Persons not performing several things towards produceing of them were put under a Fine: But now all Incouragement of such things is taken away, and People are not only suffer'd to neglect them, but such as do go about them, are discouraged by their Governor, according to the Maxim laid down in the Memorials before recited.

Silk-grass is there spontaneous in many places, and may be cut several times in a Year. I need not mention what Advantage may be made of so useful a Plant, whose Fibres are as fine as Flax, and much stronger than Hemp. Mr. *Purchas* tells us, in his *Fourth Pilgrim*, Page 1786, That in the first Discovery of this part of the World, they presented Q. *Elizabeth* with a Piece of Grogram that had been made of it. And yet to this Day they make no manner of use of this Plant, no, not so much as the *Indians* did, before the *English* came among them, who then made their Baskets, Fishing Nets, and Lines, of it.

¶.99. The Sheep increase well, and bear good Fleeces, but they generally are suffer'd to be torn off their Backs by Briers, and Bushes, instead of being shorn, or else are left rotting upon the Dunghil with their Skins.

Bees thrive there abundantly, and will very easily yield to the careful Huswife, two Crops of Honey in a Year, and besides lay up a Winter-store sufficient to preserve their Stocks.

The Beeves, when any Care is taken of them in the Winter, come to great Perfection. They have noble Marshes there, which, with the Charge of draining only, would make as fine Pastures as any in the World; and yet there is not an hundred Acres of Marsh drained throughout the whole Country.

Hogs swarm like Vermine upon the Earth, and are often accounted such, insomuch that when an Inventory of any considerable Man's Estate is taken by the Executors, the Hogs are left out, and not listed in the Appraisement. The Hogs run where they list, and find their own Support in the Woods, without any Care of the Owner; and in many Plantations it is well, if the Proprietor can find and catch the Pigs, or any part of a Farrow, when they are young, to mark them; for if there be any markt in a Gang of Hogs, they determine the Property of the rest, because they seldom miss their Gangs; but as they are bred in Company, so they continue to the End.

ℭ.100. The Woods produce great Variety of Incense and sweet Gums, which distil from several Trees; as also Trees bearing Honey, and Sugar, as before was mention'd: Yet there's no use made of any of them, either for Profit or Refreshment.

All sorts of Naval Stores may be produced there, as Pitch, Tar, Rosin, Turpentine, Plank, Timber, and all sorts of Masts, and Yards, besides Sails, Cordage, and Iron, and all these may be transported, by an easy Water-Carriage.

ℭ.101. These and a Thousand other Advantages that Country naturally affords, which its Inhabitants make no manner of use of. They can see their Naval Stores daily benefit other People, who send thither to build Ships; while they, instead of promoting such Undertakings among themselves, and easing such as are willing to go upon them, allow them no manner of Encouragement, but rather the contrary. They receive no Benefit nor Refreshment from the Sweets, and precious things they have growing amongst them, but make use of the Industry of *England* for all such things.

What Advantages do they see the Neighbouring Plantations make of their Grain and Provisions, while they, who can produce them infinitely better, not only neglect the making a Trade thereof, but even a necessary Provision against an accidental Scarcity, contenting themselves with a supply of Food from hand to mouth, so that if it should please God, to send them an unseasonable Year, there wou'd not be found in the Country, Provision sufficient to support the People for three Months extraordinary.

By reason of the unfortunate Method of the Settlement, and want of Cohabitation, they cannot make a beneficial use of their Flax, Hemp, Cotten, Silk, Silkgrass, and Wool, which might otherwise supply their Necessities, and leave the Produce of Tobacco to enrich them, when a gainful Market can be found for it.

Thus they depend altogether upon the Liberality of Nature, without endeavouring to improve its Gifts, by Art or Industry. They spunge upon the Blessings of a warm Sun, and a fruitful Soil, and almost grutch the Pains of gathering in the Bounties of the Earth. I should be asham'd to publish this slothful Indolence of my Countrymen, but that I hope it will rouse them out of their Lethargy, and excite them to make the most of all those happy Advantages which Nature has given them; and if it does this, I am sure they will have the Goodness to forgive me.

FINIS.

THE TABLE.

BOOK I.

CHAP. I.

An History of the first attempts to settle *Virginia*, before the discovery of *Chesapeak Bay*.

		Page
C. 1.	Sir *Walter Raleigh* obtains Letters Patent for making Discoveries in *America*.	15
2.	Two Ships set out on the Discovery, and arrive at *Pamtego*.	15
	Their account of the Country.	16
	Their account of the Natives.	16
3.	Queen *Elizabeth* names the Country of *Virginia*.	16
4.	Sir *Richard Greenvill*'s Voyage.	17
	He Plants the first Colony under command of Mr *Ralph Lane*.	18
5.	The Discoveries and Accidents of the first Colony.	18
6.	Their distress by want of Provisions.	19
	Sir *Francis Drake* visits them.	19
	He gives them a Ship and Necessaries.	19
	He takes them away with him.	20

		Page
7.	Sir *Walter Raleigh* and Sir *Richard Greenville* their Voyages.	20
	The second Settlement made.	21
8.	Mr *John White*'s Expedition.	21
	The first *Indian* made a Christian there.	21
	The first Child born there of Christian Parentage.	21
	The third Settlement, incorporated by the name of *The City of Raleigh in Virginia*.	22
	Mr *White* their Governour sent home to sollicit for Supplies.	22
9.	Mr *John White*'s second Voyage, the last attempts to carry them Recruits.	22
	His disappointment.	22
10.	Captain *Gosnol*'s Voyage to the Coast of *Cape Codd*.	23
11.	The *Bristol* Voyages.	24
12.	A *London* Voyage, which discovered *New York*.	24

CHAP. II.

THE Discovery of *Chesapeak Bay*, by the Corporation of *London* Adventurers. Their Colony at *James Town*, and proceedings during the Government by an Elective President and Council.

C.13.	The Companies of *London* and *Plymouth* obtain Charters.	26
14.	Captain *Smith* first discovers the Capes of *Virginia*.	27
15.	He plants his first Colony at *James Town*.	28
	An account of *James Town* Island.	28

		Page
16.	He sends the Ships home, retaining *108* Men, to keep possession.	28
17.	That Colonies mismanagement.	29
	Their misfortunes upon discovery of a supposed Gold Mine.	30
18.	Their first supplies after Settlement.	31
	Their Discoveries and Experiments in *English* Grain.	31
	An Attempt of some to desert the Colony.	31
19.	The first Christian Marriage in that Colony.	31
	They make three Plantations more.	31

CHAP. III.

THE History of the Colony after the Change of their Government, from an Elective President to a Commissionated Governour, until the dissolution of the Company.

C.20.	The Company get a new Grant, and the Nomination of the Governours in themselves.	33
	They send 3 Governours in equal degree.	33
	All 3 going in one Ship are Shipwrackt at *Bermudas*.	33
	They build there two small Cedar Vessels.	33
21.	Captain *Smith*'s return for *England*.	34
	Mismanagements ruine the Colony.	34
	The first Massacre and Starving time.	34
	The first occasion of the ill Character of *Virginia*.	35
	The *500* men left by Captain *Smith* reduced to *60* in *6* months time.	36

		Page
22.	The *3* Governours sail from *Bermudas*, and arrive at *Virginia*.	36
23.	They take off the Christians that remain'd there, and design by way of *Newfoundland* to return to *England*.	36
	The Lord *Delaware* arrives, and turns them back.	37
24.	Sir *Tho. Dale* arrives Governour with Supplies.	37
25.	Sir *Thomas Gates* arrives Governour.	37
	He plants out a new Plantation.	37
26.	*Pocahontas* made Prisoner, and Married to Mr *Rolf*.	37
	The *Indians* desire of Intermarriage with the *English*.	38
27.	Peace with the *Indians*.	39
28.	*Pocahontas* brought to *England* by Sir *Tho. Dale*.	39
29.	Captain *Smith*'s Petition to the Queen in her behalf.	40
30.	His Visit to *Pocahontas*.	43
	An *Indians* account of the People of *England*.	43
31.	*Pocahontas* reception at Court, and Death.	44
32.	Captain *Yardley*'s Government.	44
33.	Governour *Argall*'s good Administration.	45
34.	*Powhatan*'s Death and Successors.	45
	Peace renewed by the Successors.	45
35.	Capt. *Argall*'s Voyage from *Virginia* to *New England*.	45
36.	He disseats the *French* Northward of *New England*.	46
37.	An account of those *French*.	47
38.	He also dis-seats the *French* in *Arcadia*.	47

		Page
39.	His Return to *England*.	47
	Sir *George Yardley* Governour.	47
40.	He resettles the deserted Plantation, and held the first Assembly.	47
	The method of that Assembly.	48
41.	The first Negroes carried to *Virginia*.	48
42.	Land apportion'd to Adventurers.	48
43.	A Salt-Work and Iron-Work in *Virginia*.	49
44.	Sir *Francis Wyat* made Governour.	49
	King *James* his Instructions in care of Tobacco.	49
	Captain *Newport*'s Plantation.	50
45.	Inferiour Courts in each Plantation.	50
	Too much familiarity with the *Indians*.	50
46.	The Massacre by the *Indians*, Anno 1622.	51
47.	The discovery and prevention of it at *James Town*.	51
48.	The occasion of the Massacre.	52
49.	A Plot to destroy the *Indians*.	54
50.	The discouraging effects of the Massacre.	54
51.	The Corporation in *England* are the chief cause of misfortunes in *Virginia*.	55
52.	The Company dissolv'd, and the Colony taken into the Kings hands.	56

CHAP. IV.

THE History of the Government, from the dissolution of the Company to the year 1704.

C.53. King *Charles I.* establishes the Constitution of Government in the methods appointed by the first Assembly. 57

		Page
54.	The ground of the ill settlement of *Virginia*.	57
55.	Lord *Baltemore* in *Virginia*.	58
56.	Lord *Baltemore* Proprietor of *Maryland*.	58
	Maryland nam'd from the Queen:	59
57.	Young Lord *Baltemore* seats *Maryland*.	59
	Misfortune to *Virginia*, by making *Maryland* a distinct Government.	59
58.	Great Grants and Defalcations from *Virginia*.	59
59.	Governour *Harvey* sent Prisoner to *England*, and by the King remanded back Governour again.	60
60.	The last *Indian* Massacre.	60
61.	A Character and Account of *Oppechancanough* the *Indian* Emperor.	61
62.	Sir *William Berkeley* made Governour.	61
63.	He takes *Oppechancanough* Prisoner.	61
	Oppechancanough's Death.	62
64.	A new Peace with the *Indians*, but the Country disturb'd by the troubles in *England*.	63
65.	*Virginia* subdu'd by the Protector.	63
66.	*Oliver* binds the Plantations by an Act of Navigation.	64
67.	His Jealousie and change of Governours in *Virginia*.	64
68.	Upon the death of *Matthews* the Protectors Governour, Sir *William Berkeley* is chosen by the People.	64
69.	He Proclaims King *Charles II.* before he was Proclaim'd in *England*.	65
70.	K. *Charles II.* renews Sir *W. Berkeley*'s Commission.	65
71.	Sir *William Berkeley* makes Coll. *Morryson* Deputy Governour, and goes to *England*.	66

		Page
	The King renews the Act concerning the Plantations.	66
72.	The Laws revised.	66
	The Church of *England* Established by Law.	66
73.	The Clergy provided for by Law.	66
74.	The publick charge of the Government sustain'd by Law.	67
75.	Encouragement of particular Manufactures by Law.	67
76.	The Instruction for all Ships to enter at *James Town* excused by Law.	67
77.	*Indian* affairs settled by Law.	68
78.	*James Town* encouraged by Law.	68
79.	Restraints upon Sectaries in Religion.	68
80.	A Plot to subvert the Government.	68
81.	The defeat of the Plot.	69
82.	An Anniversary Feast upon that occasion.	69
83.	The King commands the building a Fort at *James* Town.	70
84.	A new restraint on the Plantations by Act of Parliament.	70
85.	Endeavours for a Stint in planting Tobacco.	70
86.	Another endeavour at a Stint defeated.	70
87.	The King sent Instructions to build Forts, and confine their Trade to certain Ports.	71
88.	The disappointment of those Ports.	72
89.	Encouragement of Manufactures enlarg'd.	72
90.	An Attempt to discover the Country backward.	72
	Captain *Batt*'s relation of that discovery.	73
91.	Sir *William Berkeley* intends to prosecute that discovery in person.	74

327

		Page
92.	The grounds of *Bacon*'s Rebellion.	74
	Four Ingredients thereto.	74
93.	1st, The low price of Tobacco.	75
	2dly, The splitting the Country into Proprieties.	75
	The Country send Agents to complain of the Propriety Grants.	75
94.	3dly, New Duties by Act in *England* on the Plantations.	76
95.	4thly, Disturbances on the Land Frontiers by the *Indians*,	76
	1st, By the *Indians* on the head of the Bay.	77
	2dly, By the *Indians* on their own Frontiers.	77
96.	The people rise against the *Indians*.	78
	They chuse *Nath. Bacon, Jun.* for their Leader.	78
97.	He heads them, and sends to the Governour for a Commission.	78
98.	He begins his march without a Commission.	79
	The Governour sends for him.	79
99.	*Bacon* goes down in a Sloop with *40* of his Men to the Governour.	79
100.	He goes away in a huff, and is pursued and brought back by the Governour.	79
101.	*Bacon* steals privately out of Town, and marches down to the Assembly with *600* of his Volunteers.	80
102.	The Governour by advice of the Assembly signs a Commission to Mr *Bacon* to be General.	80
103.	*Bacon* being march'd away with his Men is proclaim'd Rebel.	81
104.	*Bacon* returns with his Forces to *James* Town.	81

		Page
105.	The Governour flies to *Accomack*.	81
	The people there begin to make terms with him.	81
106.	*Bacon* holds a Convention of Gentlemen.	82
	They propose to take an Oath to him.	82
107.	The form of the Oath.	82
108.	The Governour makes head against him.	84
	General *Bacon*'s death.	84
109.	*Bacon*'s followers surrender upon Articles.	84
110.	The Agents compound with the Proprietors.	85
111.	Souldiers arrive from *England*.	85
112.	A new Charter to *Virginia*.	85
113.	The desolation by *Bacon*'s Rebellion.	85
114.	Commissioners arrive in *Virginia*, and Sir *William Berkeley* returns to *England*.	86
115.	*Herbert Jeffreys*, Esq; Governour, concludes Peace with the *Indians*.	86
116.	Sir *Henry Chicheley*, Deputy Governour, builds Forts against the *Indians*.	87
	The Assembly prohibited the importation of Tobacco.	87
117.	Lord *Culpepper*, Governour.	87
118.	Lord *Colpepper*'s first Assembly.	87
	He passes several obliging Acts to the Country.	88
	Penalty for reflecting on the Governour, &c.	88
119.	He doubles the Governour's Salary.	89
120.	He imposes the Perquisite of Ships Money.	89
121.	He by Proclamation raises the value of *Spanish* Coins, and lowers it again.	89
122.	He repeals Laws by Proclamation.	90
123.	The people disturb'd at these proceedings.	91

		Page
	The several other examples of this way of repealing Laws.	91
124.	Sir *Henry Chichely*, Deputy Governour.	92
	The Plant cutting.	92
125.	Lord *Calepepper*'s second Assembly.	92
	He takes away Appeals to the Assembly.	93
126.	His advantage thereby in the propriety of the Northern Neck.	93
127.	He retrenches the new methods of Court proceedings.	94
128.	He dismantl'd the Forts on the heads of Rivers, and appointed Rangers in their stead.	95
129.	Mr Secretary *Spencer*, President.	95
130.	Lord *Effingham*, Governour.	95
	Some of his extraordinary methods of getting Money.	96
	Complaints against him.	96
131.	Duty on Liquors first raised.	96
132.	Court of Chancery by Lord *Effingham*.	97
133.	*Coll. Bacon* President.	97
	The College design'd.	97
134.	Esquire *Nicholson*, Lieutenant Governour.	97
	He studies popularity.	98
	The College proposed to him.	98
	He refuses to call an Assembly.	98
135.	He grants a Brief to the College.	98
136.	The Assembly address King *William* and Queen *Mary* for a College Charter.	98
	The Education intended by this College.	98
	The Assembly present the Lieutenant Governour.	99
	His method of securing this present.	99

		Page
137.	Their Majesty's grant the Charter.	99
	They grant liberally towards the building and endowing of it.	99
138.	The Lieutenant Governour encourages Towns and Manufactures.	100
	Gentlemen of the Council complain of him, and are misus'd.	100
	He falls off from the encouragement of the Towns and Trade.	100
139.	Sir *Edmond Andros* Governour.	100
	The Town-Law suspended.	101
140.	The project of a Post-Office.	101
141.	Sir *Edmond Andros* disorders their Court proceedings.	101
142.	The College Charter arriv'd.	101
	The College further endow'd, and the Foundation laid.	102
143.	Sir *Edmond* encouraged Country Manufactures and regulated the Secretaries Office.	102
144.	A Child born in the old Age of the Parents.	103
145.	*Francis Nicholson* Governour.	103
	His and Collonell *Quarry*'s Memorials against the Plantations.	104
146.	His pretended Zeal for the Church and College.	104
147.	He removes the General Court from *James* Town.	105
148.	The vexatiousness of his Administration.	105
149.	His abuse of Judicial proceedings.	106
150.	His Arbitrary Inclinations after the method of *Morocco*.	107
151.	His Arbitrary proceedings in Council.	107

		Page
152.	His interrupting and breaking open Letters.	108
153.	His Evesdropping and Inquisition Courts.	109
154.	The taking of the Pyrate.	109
155.	The Sham Bills of *900 l.* for *New-York*.	111
	Collonel *Quarry*'s unjust Memorials.	112

BOOK II.

OF the Natural Productions and Conveniencies of *Virginia* in its improv'd state, before the *English* went thither.

CHAP. I.

Of the Bounds and Coast of *Virginia*

		Page
C.1.	Of the present Bounds of *Virginia*.	117
2.	Of *Chesapeak Bay*, and the Sea Coast of *Virginia*.	117
3.	What is meant by the Word *Virginia* in this Book.	118

CHAP. II.

Of the Waters.

C.4.	Of the conveniency of the Bay and Rivers.	120
5.	Of the Springs and Fountains descending to the Rivers.	121
6.	Of Damage by the Worm in the Salts.	121
	Of the Ways of avoiding that Damage.	121

332

CHAP. III.

Of the Earth and Soil.

		Page
¶.7.	Of the Soil in general.	123
	Of the Lands in the Lower ⎫	123
	In the Middle ⎬ parts of	124
	In the Upper ⎭ the Rivers	124
8.	Of the Earths and Clays.	125
	Of the Coal, Slate and Stone, and why not used.	125
9.	Of Minerals, and therein of the Iron Mine formerly wrought upon.	126
	Of the supposed Gold Mines lately discovered.	126
	That this Gold Mine was the Supreme Seat of the *Indian* Temples formerly.	126
	That their Chief Altar was there also.	127
	Mr *Whittaker*'s account of a Silver Mine.	127
10.	Of the Hills in *Virginia*.	127
	Of the Springs in the High Lands.	128

CHAP. IV.

Of the Wild Fruits.

¶.11.	Of the Spontaneous Fruits in general.	129
12.	Of the Stoned Fruits, *viz*. Cherries, Plumbs, and *Persimmons*.	129
13.	Of the Berries, *viz*. Mulberries, Currans, Hurts, Cranberries, Rasberries, and Stra[w]berries.	130
14.	Of the Nuts, *viz*. Chesnuts, Chincapins, Hasle-nuts, Hiccory nuts, Walnuts and Acorns.	131

		Page
15.	Of Grapes, six sorts.	133
	Some reasons why the Essays of Vineyards have been ineffectual.	134
	The Report of some *French* Vigneroons formerly sent in thither.	136
16.	Of the Honey and the Sugar Trees.	136
17.	Of the Myrtle Tree, and Myrtle Wax.	137
	Of the Wax made from Cedar Berries.	138
	Of the Hops growing wild.	138
18.	Of the great variety of Seeds, Plants, and Flowers.	138
	Of the two Snake-roots.	139
	Of the *James Town* Weed.	139
	Of some curious Flowers.	140
19.	Of the creeping Vines bearing Fruit, *viz.* Melons, Pompions, Macocks, Gourds, and Maracocks.	141
20.	Of the other Fruits, Roots, and Plants of the *Indians*.	143
	Of the several sorts of *Indian* Corn and Pulse.	143
	Of Potattoes.	144
	Of Tobacco, as it was order'd by the *Indians*.	145

CHAP. V.

Of the Fish.

C.21.	Of the great plenty and variety of Fish.	146
	Of the vast Shoals of Herrings, Shads, &c.	146
22.	Of the Continuality of the Fishery.	147
	The names of some of the best edible Fish.	147
	The names of some that are not eaten.	147

		Page
23.	Of the *Indian* Children's catching Fish.	148
	Of the several Inventions of the *Indians* to take Fish.	148
24.	Of the Fishing Hawks and Bald Eagles.	151
	Of the Fish dropt into the Orchard.	152

CHAP. VI.

Of the Wild Fowl and Hunted Game.

¶.25.	Of the Wild Water Fowl.	153
26.	Of the Game in the Marshes and Watry Grounds.	153
27.	Of the Game in the Highlands and Frontiers.	153
	Of the *Possum*.	154
28.	Of some *Indian* ways of Hunting.	154
	Of Fire Hunting.	155
	Of their Hunting Quarters.	156
29.	Conclusion.	156

BOOK III.

OF the *Indians,* their Religion, Laws, and Customs, in War and Peace.

CHAP. I.

Of the Persons of the *Indians*, and their Dress.

Page

¶.1. Of the Person of the *Indians*, their colour and shape. 159

		Page
2.	Of the cut of their Hair, and ornament of their Head.	159
3.	Of their Vesture.	162
4.	Of the Garb peculiar to their Priests and Conjurers.	164
5.	Of the Womens Dress.	166

CHAP. II.

Of the Matrimony of the *Indians*, and management of their Children.

¶.6.	Of the conditions of their Marriage.	170
7.	Of the Maidens, and the story of their Prostitution.	170
8.	Of the management of the young Children.	171

CHAP. III.

Of the Towns, Building, and Fortification of the *Indians*.

¶.9.	Of the Towns and Kingdoms of the *Indians*.	174
10.	Of the manner of their Building.	174
11.	Of their Fewel, or Fire-wood.	176
12.	Of their Seats and Lodging.	176
13.	Of their Fortifications.	177

CHAP. IV.

Of the Cookery and Food of the *Indians*.

¶.14.	Of their Cookery.	178
15.	Of their several sorts of Food.	179

		Page
16.	Of their times of Eating.	181
17.	Of their Drink.	182
18.	Their ways of Dining.	182

CHAP. V.

Of the Travelling, Reception and Entertainment of the *Indians*.

C.19.	Of the manner of their Travelling, and Provision they make for it.	185
	Their way of concealing their Course.	185
20.	The manner of their reception of Strangers.	186
	Of the Pipe of Peace.	187
21.	Of their Entertainment of Honourable Friends.	188

CHAP. VI.

Of the Learning and Languages of the *Indians*.

C.22.	That they are without Letters.	190
	Of their descriptions by Hieroglyphicks.	190
	Of the Heraldry and Arms of the *Indians*.	190
23.	That they have different Languages.	191
	Of their general Language.	191

CHAP. VII.

Of the War and Peace of the *Indians*.

C.24.	Of their Consultations and War Dances.	192
25.	Of their Barbarity upon a Victory.	192
26.	Of the descent of the Crown.	193

		Page
27.	Of their Triumphs for Victory.	193
28.	Of their Treaties of Peace, and Ceremonies upon conclusion of Peace.	194

CHAP. VIII.

Of the Religion, Worship and Superstitious Customs of the *Indians*.

C.29.	Of their *Quioccasan* and Idol of Worship.	195
30.	Of their notions of God and worshipping the evil Spirit.	198
31.	Of their *Pawwawing* or Conjurations.	201
32.	Of their *Huskanawing*.	205
33.	Of the reasons of this Custom.	208
34.	Of their Offerings and Sacrifice.	210
35.	Of their set Feasts.	210
36.	Of their account of Time.	211
37.	Of their Superstition and Zealotry.	211
38.	Of their regard to the Priests and Magicians.	212
39.	Of the Places of their Worship and Sacrifice.	213
	Of their *Pawcorances* or Altar-Stones.	213
40.	Of their care of the Bodies of their Princes after death.	214

CHAP. IX.

Of the Diseases and Cures of the *Indians*.

C.41.	Of their Diseases in general, and burning for Cure.	217
	Of their Sucking, Scarifying and Blistering.	217
	Of the Priests secrecy in the Virtues of Plants.	218

		Page
	Of the Words *Wysoccan*, *Wighsacan* and *Woghsacan*.	218
	Of their Physick and the method of it.	218
42.	Of their Bagnio's and Baths.	219
	Of their Oyling after Sweating.	220

CHAP. X.

Of the Sports and Pastimes of the *Indians*.

C.43.	Of their Sports and Pastimes in general.	221
	Of their Singing.	221
	Of their Dancing.	221
	A Mask used among them.	222
	Of their Musical Instruments.	224

CHAP. XI.

Of the Laws and Authorities of the *Indians* among one another.

C.44.	Of their Laws in general.	225
	Of their Severity on Ill Manners.	225
	Of their implacable resentments.	226
45.	Of their Honours, Preferments and Authorities.	226
	Of the Authority of the Priests and Conjurers.	226
	Of the Servants or Black Boys.	226

CHAP. XII.

Of the Treasure or Riches of the *Indians*.

C.46.	Of the *Indian* Money and Goods.	227

CHAP. XIII.

Of the Handicrafts of the *Indians*.

		Page
C.47.	Of their Lesser Crafts, as making Bows and Arrows.	229
48.	Of their making Canoas.	229
	Of their Clearing Woodland Ground.	230
49.	An Account of the Tributary *Indians*.	232
50.	Conclusion.	233

BOOK IV.

Of the present state of *Virginia*.

PART I.

Of the Politie and Government.

CHAP. I.

Of the Constitution of Government in *Virginia*.

		Page
C.1.	Of the Constitution of Government in general.	237
2.	Of the Governour, his Authority and Salary.	238
3.	Of the Council, and their Authority.	240
4.	Of the House of Burgesses.	241

CHAP. II.

Of the Sub-divisions of *Virginia*.

		Page
¶.5.	Of the Division of the Country into Counties and Parishes.	243
6.	Of the Division of the Country by Necks of Land.	243
7.	Of the Division of the Country by Districts for Trade by Navigation.	244

CHAP. III.

Of the Publick Offices in the Government.

¶.8.	Of such General Officers as are immediately Commissionated from the Throne.	245
	Of the Auditor.	245
	Of the Secretary.	245
	Of the Secretaries Office.	245
	Of the Salaries of those two Officers.	246
9.	Of the other general Officers.	246
	Of the Ecclesiastical Commissary.	246
	Of the Countrys Treasurer.	246
10.	Of the other publick Officers by Commission.	246
	Of the *Escheators*.	247
	Of the Naval Officers, and Collectors of the Customs.	247
	Of the Clerks of Courts, Sheriffs and Surveyors of Land.	247
	Of the Coroners.	248
11.	Of the other Officers without Commission, *viz.* Constables, Headboroughs and Surveyors of the Highways.	248

CHAP. IV.

Of the Standing Revenues, or Publick Funds.

		Page
C. 12.	Of the Publick Funds in general.	249
13.	Of the Quit-rent Fund.	249
14.	Of the Funds for Maintenance of the Government.	250
15.	Of the Funds for extraordinary occasions, under the disposition of the Assembly.	250
16.	Of the Revenue granted by the Act of Assembly to the College.	251
17.	Of the Revenue raised by Act of Parliament in *England* from the Trade there.	251

CHAP. V.

Of the Levies for the payment of the Publick, County, and Parish Debts.

C. 18.	Of the several ways of raising Money publickly.	252
	Of Titheables.	252
19.	Of the Publick Levy.	252
20.	Of the County Levy.	254
21.	Of the Parish Levy.	254

CHAP. VI.

Of the Courts of Laws in *Virginia*.

C. 22.	Of the Constitution of their Courts.	255
23.	Of the several sorts of Courts among them.	256

		Page
24.	Of the General Court in particular, and its Jurisdiction.	256
25.	Of the times of holding General Court.	257
26.	Of the Officers attending this Court.	257
27.	Of Tryals by Juries in this Court.	257
	Of Impannelling Grand Juries.	258
28.	Of the Tryal of Criminals.	258
29.	Of the time Suits there generally depend.	258
30.	Of the Lawyers and Pleadings.	259
31.	Of the County Courts.	259
32.	Of Orphans Courts.	260

CHAP. VII.

Of the Church and Church Affairs.

C.33.	Of the Parishes.	261
34.	Of the Churches and Chapels in each Parish.	261
35.	Of the Religion of the Country.	261
36.	Of the Benefices of the Clergy.	262
37.	Of the disposition of Parochial affairs.	262
38.	Of the Probates, Administrations, and Marriage Licences.	263
39.	Of the Induction of Ministers, and precariousness of their Livings.	264

CHAP. VIII.

Concerning the College.

C.40.	Of the College Endowments.	265
41.	The College a Corporation.	265

		Page
42.	Governours and Visitors of the College in perpetual Succession.	266
	These have the nomination of President and Masters, and a power of making Statutes, &c.	266
43.	Of College Buildings.	266
44.	Of the Boys and Schooling.	266

CHAP. IX.

Of the Military Strength in *Virginia*.

C.45.	Of the Forts and Fortifications.	268
46.	Of the Listed Militia.	268
47.	Of the number of the Militia.	269
48.	Of the Service of the Militia.	269
49.	Other particulars of the Troops and Companies.	269

CHAP. X.

Of the Servants and Slaves.

C.50.	Of the distinction between a Servant and a Slave.	271
51.	Of the work of their Servants and Slaves.	271
52.	Of the Laws in favour of Servants.	272

CHAP. XI.

Of Provision for the Poor, and other publick Charitable works.

C.53.	Of a Legacy to the Poor.	275

		Page
54.	Of the Parish methods in maintaining their Poor.	275
55.	Of Free Schools, and Schooling of Children.	275

CHAP. XII.

Of the tenure of Lands and methods of Grants in *Virginia*.

C.56.	Of the Tenure and Patents of their Lands.	277
57.	Of the several ways of acquiring Grants of Land.	277
58.	Of Rights to Land.	277
59.	Of Patents upon Survey.	277
60.	Of Grants of Lapsed Land.	279
61.	Of Grants of Escheat Land.	279

CHAP. XIII.

Of the Liberties and Naturalization of the Aliens in *Virginia*.

C.62.	Of Naturalizations.	281
63.	Of the *French* Refugees at the *Monacan Town*.	281

CHAP. XIV.

Of the Currency and Valuation of Coins in *Virginia*.

C.64.	What Coins are current among them, at what rates, and why carried from among them to the Neighbouring Plantations.	285

PART II.

Of the Husbandry and Improvements of *Virginia*.

CHAP. XV.

Of the People, Inhabitants of *Virginia*.

		Page
ℭ.65.	Of the first Peopling of *Virginia*.	286
66.	Of the first Accession of Wives to *Virginia*.	286
67.	Of the other Ways by which the Country was encreased in People.	287

CHAP. XVI.

Of the Buildings in *Virginia*.

ℭ.68.	Of the Publick Buildings.	289
69.	Of the Private Buildings.	289

CHAP. XVII.

Of the Edibles, Potables, and Fewel in *Virginia*.

ℭ.70.	Of their Cookery.	291
71.	Of their Flesh, and Fish.	291
72.	Of their Bread.	292
73.	Of their Kitchin Gardens.	292
74.	Of their Drinks.	293
75.	Of their Fewel.	294

CHAP. XVIII.

Of the Cloathing in *Virginia*.

		Page
¶.76.	Of their Supplies in Cloathing.	295
	Of their Slothfulness in Handicrafts.	295

CHAP. XIX.

Of the Temperature of the Climate, and the Inconveniencies attending it.

¶.77.	Of the Natural Temper and Mixture of the Air.	296
78.	Of the Climate, and happy Situation of the Country in respect of the Latitude.	296
79.	Of the Occasions of its general ill Character.	297
	Of the Rural Pleasures natural to the Place.	298
80.	Of all the naturul Annoyances, or Occasions of Uneasiness	299
	Of the loud Thunders.	299
	Of the Heat of Summer.	299
	Of the troublesome Insects, wherein of the Frogs, Snakes, Musketa's, Chinches, Seedticks, and Red-worms.	299
81.	Of the Winters.	303
	Of the sudden Changes of the Weather.	304

CHAP. XX.

Of the Diseases incident to the Country.

¶.82.	Of the Diseases in general.	305
83.	Of the Seasoning.	306
84.	Of the Cachexy and Yaws.	306
85.	Of the Gripes.	306

CHAP. XXI.

Of the Recreations and Pastimes in *Virginia*.

Page

❡.86.	Of the Diversions in general.	*308*
87.	Of Deer-Hunting.	*308*
88.	Of Hare-Hunting.	*309*
89.	Of Vermine-Hunting.	*309*
90.	Of taking wild Turkies.	*310*
91.	Of Fishing.	*310*
92.	Of the small Game.	*311*
93.	Of the Beaver.	*311*
94.	Of Horse-Hunting.	*312*
95.	Of the Hospitality.	*312*

CHAP. XXII.

Of the Natural Product of *Virginia*, and the Advantages of Husbandry.

❡.96.	Of the Fruits.	*314*
97.	Of the Grain.	*316*
98.	Of Line, Silk, and Cotton.	*317*
99.	Of Bees and Cattle.	*317*
100.	The Usefulness of the Woods.	*318*
101.	The Indolence of the Inhabitants.	*318*
	The *Schedule*.	*319*

Notes

INTRODUCTION

1. This Introduction utilizes in a large measure material from an essay published by the present editor in *The William and Mary Quarterly*, Third Series, I (1944), 49-64. Punctuation, capitalization, and spelling in quotations cited in this introduction have been normalized in accordance with modern usage.
2. Urian Oakes, *New England Pleaded with* (Cambridge, 1673), p. 23.
3. Louis B. Wright, *The First Gentlemen of Virginia* (San Marino, Calif., 1940), p. 183.
4. A bibliographical description of the editions of Beverley's *History* can be found in William Clayton Torrence, *A Trial Bibliography of Colonial Virginia* (Richmond, 1908), pp. 86-90, 92-95, 97-100.

    Mr. Lester Cappon has called the editor's attention to excerpts from the 1722 edition of Beverley's *History*, which appeared in *The General Magazine and Historical Chronicle* of Philadelphia, edited by Benjamin Franklin. Portions of Book IV, Chaps. 1-6 and 12 were printed in the issues for February, March, and April, 1741, pp. 83-88, 147-153, 217-228.
5. Wright, *First Gentlemen of Virginia*, pp. 286-311, for biographical material on Major Robert Beverley and his son, the historian. See also Fairfax Harrison, "Robert Beverley, the Historian of Virginia," *Virginia Magazine of History and Biography*, XXXVI (1928), 333-444.
6. Wright, *First Gentlemen of Virginia*, p. 294.
7. *An Essay Upon The Government Of The English Plantations On The Continent Of America* (London, 1701). Ed. by Louis B. Wright (San Marino, Calif., 1945), Introduction, pp. ix-xxiv.
8. John Oldmixon, *The British Empire in America* (London, 1708), I, 215, 217, 243, 244, 281-83, 291.

9. Internal evidence does not substantiate the statement made in *Virginia Magazine of History and Biography*, XXXVI (1928), 342, that Lombrail pirated Ribou's text. The reverse seems to have been the case.
10. *Histoire de la Virginie* (Amsterdam, 1707), pp. 404-405; *Histoire de la Virginie* (Orleans and Paris, 1707), pp. 390-91.
11. Richmond Croom Beatty and William J. Mulloy, *William Byrd's Natural History of Virginia* (Richmond, 1940).
12. *Notes on Virginia* in *The Writings of Thomas Jefferson*, Andrew A. Lipscomb and Albert E. Bergh, eds. (Washington, 1903-04), II, 244.
13. Edition of 1705, Bk. I, Section 26.
14. *Ibid.*, Bk. III, Sect. 7.
15. Edition of 1722, p. 31.
16. Edition of 1705, Bk. III, Sect. 29.
17. *Ibid.*, Sect. 30.
18. *Ibid.*, Sect. 33.
19. *Ibid.*, Bk. I, Sect. 117.
20. *Ibid.*, Sect. 118.
21. *Ibid.*, Sect. 123.
22. *Ibid.*, Sect. 130.
23. *Ibid.*, Sect. 146.
24. *Ibid.*, Bk. IV, Sect. 83.
25. *Ibid.*, Sect. 63.
26. *Ibid.*, Sect. 79.
27. *Ibid.*, Bk. III, Sect. 49.
28. *Ibid.*, Bk. IV, Sect. 78.
29. *Ibid.*, Sect. 80.
30. *Ibid.*, Sect. 79.
31. *Ibid.*, Sect. 96.
32. *Ibid.*, Sect. 101.
33. For further information about the illustrations, see Torrence, pp. 87, 89-90; Randolph G. Adams, *A Brief Account of Raleigh's Roanoke Colony of 1585*, (Clements Library, Ann Arbor, Michigan, 1935), pp. 7-10; and Laurence Binyon, "The Drawings of John White, Governor of Raleigh's Virginia Colony," *Walpole Society* XIII (1924-25), 19-24.

34. Simon Gribelin, *A Book of Ornaments . . . With an Introduction by Philip Hofer and Technical Comment by Rudolph Ruzicka* (Meriden, Conn., 1941).

TEXT

1. *Harley*—Robert Harley, created the first Earl of Oxford in 1711, was regarded at the time of Beverley's writing as a friend of the colonies. The fact that in 1700 he supported a bill to bring colonial governors to trial in England for offenses committed in the colonies would have been sufficient to endear him to Beverley. [See Lee Francis Stock, ed., *Proceedings and Debates of the British Parliaments Respecting North America* (Washington, 1927), II, 363, 369.] Harley's reputation as a patron of letters may also have induced Beverley to dedicate his book to him.
2. *Banister*—John Banister, an English botanist, settled in 1678 in Charles City County and for a time was minister in Bristol parish. He had a considerable reputation in his time as a scientist. He was accidentally shot in May, 1692. An account of him is to be found in the *Dictionary of American Biography*.
3. *First Settlements*—The most detailed and convenient text for checking the modern historian's appraisal of events mentioned by Beverley in Bk. I is Thomas J. Wertenbaker's *Virginia Under the Stuarts, 1607-1688* (Princeton, 1914). Supplementary details of value may be found in Mary Newton Stanard's *The Story of Virginia's First Century* (Philadelphia, 1928), Mathew Page Andrews', *Virginia, the Old Dominion* (New York, 1937), and various other histories of the colony. The most accurate discussion of the transition from a chartered to a royal colony is Wesley Frank Craven's *Dissolution of the Virginia Company* (New York, 1932).

   Beverley's references to individuals who had a part in early Virginia history are for the most part self-explanatory, and the present editor has felt that elaborate annotation would serve no useful purpose. To appraise all of Beverley's interpretations and statements of fact would be to rewrite Virginia's history, a task which would duplicate discussions already easily available.
4. *Capt. Gosnell*—Bartholomew Gosnold, one of Raleigh's captains,

who commanded the "Goodspeed" in the expedition to Jamestown in 1607.
5. See pp. 121-122.
6. *Capt. Argall*—Samuel Argall, lieutenant of Sir Thomas Dale, was designated "admiral of Virginia" and was later governor.
7. Beverley is in error. The Burgesses first convened in August, 1619.
8. The correct date is August, 1619.
9. *Col. Byrd*—William Byrd I, father of William Byrd of Westover.
10. The Company was dissolved by decree of the Court of the King's Bench, May 24, 1624. See Craven, *Dissolution of the Virginia Company*, ch. 10.
11. Harvey was forcibly sent to England in May, 1635, and returned to Virginia as governor in January, 1637. He was succeeded by Sir Francis Wyatt in November, 1638. Berkeley became governor in 1642.
12. *Capt. Dennis*—Robert Dennis, who was appointed one of four Parliamentary Commissioners to reduce Virginia to obedience to the Commonwealth government.
13. *Three governors*—Richard Bennett, 1652-55; Edward Digges, 1655-58; and Samuel Mathews, 1658-60.
14. *Captain Henry Batt*—Captain Thomas Batts led an expedition which set out in 1671 to discover the sources of the Virginia rivers and the great South Sea. Beverley attributes the leadership of the party to Henry Batts, brother of Thomas. [See Clarence Alvord and Lee Bidgood, *The First Explorations of the Trans-Allegheny Region by the Virginians, 1650-1674* (Cleveland, 1912), pp. 183-184.] Beverley again refers to the expedition in Bk. II, Par. 10.
15. *Bacon's Rebellion*—For both contemporary descriptions and recent scholarship dealing with Bacon's uprising against Sir William Berkeley, see the "Essay on Authorities" in Thomas J. Wertenbaker's *Torchbearer of the Revolution* (Princeton, 1940), pp. 215-225.
16. *Ludwell and Park*—Thomas Ludwell, secretary of state, 1661-1678, and Daniel Parke, secretary of state, 1678-1679.
17. *Middle-Plantation*—Early name for the site chosen for the town of Williamsburg.

18. *Bacon's death at Dr. Green's*—Bacon died at the house of Major Thomas Pate in Gloucester County.
19. *Ingram and Walklate*—Joseph Ingram, who succeeded Bacon when the latter died, and Gregory Wakelett, second in command to Ingram.
20. *Secretary Spencer*—Nicholas Spencer, secretary of state, 1679-1689.
21. *Mr. Neal's project*—Thomas Neale, an English promoter, received a royal patent in the last decade of the seventeenth century to establish a postal system in the colonies and appointed Andrew Hamilton of New Jersey as his deputy in America.
22. *Col. Quarrey*—Robert Quarry, a professional colonial official, was at this time surveyor general of customs.
23. *Mr. Fowler*—Bartholomew Fowler, attorney general in 1699.
24. *Purchas*—Samuel Purchas, *Purchas His Pilgrimage. Or Relations Of The World And The Religions Observed in All Ages And places discouered* (London, 1613), Bk. VIII, p. 639. Beverley was careless in citing authorities and missed the exact reference by four books.
25. *Whittaker*—Alexander Whitaker, *Good Newes From Virginia* (London, 1613), was published by the Virginia Company of London as a promotional tract.
26. *Authors cited*—Thomas Hariot, *A briefe and true report of the new found land of Virginia* (London, 1588); Captain John Smith, *The Generall Historie Of Virginia* (London, 1624); Samuel Purchas, *Purchas His Pilgrimes* (London, 1625). Beverley also cites Purchas' *Pilgrimage* (London, 1613), a sort of theological geography, with a section on Virginia. By "Du Lake," Beverley means Joannes de Laet, a popular Flemish geographer and philologist whose Latin work, *Novus Orbis* (Leyden, 1633), gave some attention to Virginia. Beverley probably read the French version, *L'Histoire du Nouveau Monde* (Leyden, 1640).
27. *Grape Culture*—The space which Beverley here devotes to the discussion of growing grapes illustrates a personal interest. He believed that Virginia had possibilities of becoming a great wine-producing country, and he himself made extensive experiments with vine-growing. [See Wright, *The First Gentlemen of Virginia*, p. 301.]

28. *Peter Martyr*—Pietro Martire d'Anghiera, an Italian geographer, whose principal work, *De orbe novo decades octo* (Complutum, 1530), appeared in numerous versions. Beverley probably read Michael Lok's translation, published in 1612.
29. *Malabaricus*—*Hortus Indicus Malabaricus*. In 12 parts (Amsterdam, 1678-1703), a botanical work of composite authorship.
30. *Verbiest*—Ferdinand Verbiest, Jesuit missionary to China, *Voyage de l'Empereur de la Chine dans la Tartarie* (Paris, 1695).
31. *Virginia Indians*—For modern studies of the Virginia Indians, see Maurice A. Mook, "The Anthropological Position of the Indian Tribes of Tidewater Virginia," *William and Mary College Quarterly*, Second Series, XXIII (January, 1943), 27-40. Mr. Mook states that he has in preparation a collation of the early accounts of the Indians, including Beverley's *History*. See also the same author's "The Aboriginal Population of Tidewater Virginia," *American Anthropologist*, XLVI (April-June, 1944), 193-208.
32. See pp. 162, 166, 227-228.
33. *Roanoke*, a kind of wampum made of white beads.
34. *Lahontan*—Louis A. de LaHontan, *New Voyages to North-America* (London, 1703).
35. See p. 227.
36. *Hennepin*—Louis Hennepin, *A New Discovery of A Vast Country in America* (London, 1696), p. 74.
37. See p. 220.
38. See p. 212.
39. See p. 226.
40. *DeBry*—Theodore DeBry, *Collectiones peregrinationum in Indiam Orientalem et Indiam Occidentalem* (25 parts; Frankfort on Main, 1590-1634).
41. *Parkinson*—John Parkinson, *Theatrum Botanicum: The Theater Of Plants* (London, 1640).
42. *Bellonius*—Pierre Belon, *Les Observations de plusieurs singularitez et choses memorables, trouvées en Grece, Asie, Indée, Egypte, Arabie, & autres pays estranges* (Paris, 1558).
43. *Olearius*—Adam Olearius, *The Voyages & Travels Of The Ambassa-*

dors *From the Duke of Holstein to the Great Duke of Muscovy, and the King of Persia.* Trans. by John Davies (London, 1662), p. 89. Beverley's page reference is incorrect.

44. *Piso*—Willem Piso, Dutch naturalist, . . . *Historiae rerum naturalium Brasiliae* (Leyden, 1648).
45. *Lord Bacon*—Francis Bacon, *Sylva Sylvarum: Or, A Naturall History* (London, 1658). There were earlier and later editions, but this seems a likely edition for Beverley to have used.
46. *Clusius*—Charles de L'Ecluse, French botanist, *C. Clusii Exoticorum libri decem* (Leyden, 1605).
47. Cf. Philip Alexander Bruce, *Institutional History of Virginia in the Seventeenth Century* (2 vols., New York, 1910); and his *Economic History of Virginia in the Seventeenth Century* (2 vols., New York, 1895).
48. *Certain grave author*—Beverley's criticism here is directed against Charles Davenant, author of *Discourses On The Publick Revenues, And On The Trade of England. In Two Parts* (London, 1698). In 1701 Richard Parker, the printer of Beverley's *History*, published an eloquent reply to Davenant's treatise under the title of *An Essay Upon The Government Of The English Plantations On The Continent Of America*, edited by Louis B. Wright (San Marino, Calif., 1945). Indications in the text of the essay suggest that Beverley may have written it, or have had a hand in its production.
49. *Child*—Sir Josiah Child, *A New Discourse Of Trade* (London, 1698), p. 183.
50. *Elian and Pliny*—Various Latin editions of Claudius Aelianus' *De Natura Animalium* were available to Beverley, but there was no English translation which he could use. Of Caius Plinius Secundus' natural history he probably used *The Historie of the World, commonly called the Naturall Historie*, translated by Philemon Holland (London, 1601).

Principal Changes in the Edition of 1722

WHEN Beverley revised his *History* for reprinting in 1722, he made the major alterations in Bks. I and IV. Throughout there are minor verbal changes. In 1722 he omitted the dedication to Robert Harley and supplied a new preface. A part of his revision consisted in changing chronological references and topical allusions which the passage of time had made out-of-date. Many of the alterations consist merely of the addition or omission of a modifying phrase. A great many slight revisions of this kind occur in Bk. IV. By referring to page numbers in the present edition, an indication is given below of places where the principal revisions occur.

pp. 38-39. Paragraph on intermarriage with the Indians omitted.

p. 44. Two sentences concerning Pocahontas revised.

p. 59. Sentence added on appointing agents to examine tobacco.

p. 60. Phrase "countenancing them . . . instructions," omitted.

p. 64. Sentence on Berkeley's loyalty adds "and he never took any post or office under the usurper."

p. 68. Phrase, "by a mistaken Zeal," omitted.

p. 68. Phrase, "and might otherwise . . . of that," omitted.

p. 70. Phrase, "to enter upon Manufactures," changed to read, "to enter upon manufacturing flax and hemp."

p. 74. Explanatory paragraph added to description of Batts' return.

p. 74. Clause added about Spotswood's crossing of great ridge of mountains.

pp. 81-82. Three phrases changed for stylistic reasons.

p. 82. Clause added in praise of Major Robert Beverley's loyalty to Berkeley.

p. 84. Phrase added attributing command of sloops to Major Beverley.

p. 85. Paragraph 111 omitted and new one substituted.
p. 85. Paragraph 112 omitted.
p. 86. Sentence about Nicholson's "wild Project" to move capital to Williamsburg modified.
p. 87. Sentence, "In these . . . getting them pass'd," omitted.
p. 88. Three paragraphs, "But he put a Sting . . . Country now groans under," omitted.
pp. 89-90. Three satirical phrases omitted.
pp. 90-91. Paragraphs 122 and 123 omitted.
p. 92. Two qualifying phrases added.
p. 93. Satirical phrases modified.
pp. 95-96. Statements concerning Culpeper modified.
pp. 97-98. Satirical and other phrases modified.
p. 99. Three sentences, "They appointed . . . will be considered," omitted.
pp. 99-102. Several sentences concerning the college omitted or revised.
p. 103. To the phrase ending "least burdensome to the People" is added "designing the greatest part at his own cost."
pp. 104-105. Numerous satirical and unfavorable expressions omitted or modified.
pp. 105-109. Beginning with "This imaginary City" to the end of Paragraph 153 all is omitted. Paragraphs 148-154 rewritten.
pp. 111-113. Several modifications of statements concerning Nicholson.
p. 117. Last sentence in Paragraph 1 rewritten.
p. 118. Phrase, "or now by the river Mississippi," added to statement of bounds of Virginia.
p. 131. Two sentences modified.
p. 132. Description of walnuts revised slightly.
p. 133. Minor alterations in description of grapes.
pp. 134-135. Four paragraphs beginning "But here I find . . ." and ending ". . . may be an Objection" omitted.
p. 138. Sentence about cedar berries omitted.
p. 138. Sentence about a blue berry added.
p. 139. "This operates by a violent Vomit and Sweat" omitted.
p. 139. Two sentences speculating about narcotic herb added.

p. 147. Sentence about specimen of dried fish owned by Governor Spotswood added.
p. 149. Phrase stating that prints in the book were drawn to the life omitted.
p. 159. Statement concerning beauty of Indian women modified.
p. 164. Statement that Indians in the pictures are exactly represented omitted.
p. 168. Sentence defining word *runtees* added.
p. 171. Two paragraphs concerning freedom and innocence of Indian women omitted.
p. 178. Sentence concerning Indian method of cooking fish added.
p. 181. Phrase about West Indian cassava added.
p. 209. A citation from Puffendorf added.
pp. 232-233. Statistics concerning the Indians modified.
pp. 237-261. Numerous small changes in the description of the government to bring the book up-to-date, particularly in the citation of statistics and names of officials.
pp. 238-239. Section added on the authority of the governor.
pp. 239-240. Passage unfavorable to Culpeper omitted.
pp. 240-241. Passage describing power of the Council modified and part omitted.
pp. 243-244. Four paragraphs listing counties and parishes added; other changes to bring details up-to-date.
pp. 244-247. Numerous phrases changed, omitted, or added.
pp. 247-248. Statements concerning the counties, and the fees and duties of county officials modified.
pp. 249-251. Statistics and facts dealing with the public funds much revised.
pp. 255-256. Statements concerning the governors omitted or modified.
pp. 256-257. Considerable revision of statements concerning the courts.
pp. 259-260. Many omissions and revisions in descriptions of the courts.
pp. 261-262. Statement about Presbyterians and Quakers modified.
pp. 262-264. Several changes concerning ecclesiastical regulations to bring the book up-to-date.

pp. 266-267. Paragraph 44 concerning the college rewritten and expanded.
p. 268. Two sentences concerning the poor equipment of the militia omitted.
pp. 268-269. Sarcastic remarks about an oppressive governor omitted; two other sentences about the militia modified.
pp. 269-270. Paragraph 47 rewritten; Paragraphs 48-49 revised.
p. 274. Details concerning benefits to freed servants revised.
p. 275. Satirical statement concerning English merchants added.
p. 277. Paragraphs 56, 57, and 58 slightly revised.
pp. 278-279. Paragraph 59 revised and section omitted.
pp. 282-284. Long section on Col. Byrd omitted.
p. 285. Long passage on the scarcity of money omitted and a brief statement substituted.
pp. 287-288. Statement concerning immigration of malefactors modified.
p. 289. Section on buildings much revised and two paragraphs added.
p. 299. Section on Col. Byrd omitted.
p. 300. Statement concerning frog sufficient for six Frenchmen altered.
p. 301. Long section on rattlesnakes added.
p. 302. Statement about eating snake altered and another long section on rattlesnakes added.
p. 306. Satirical statement about the fewness of doctors omitted.
p. 308. Statement about Virginians being well-travelled omitted.
p. 313. Sarcastic passage about the governor omitted.
p. 315. Statement about Beverley's own vine culture revised.
pp. 315-316. Statement about almonds, figs, and pomegranates omitted.
p. 317. Unfavorable allusion to the governor omitted.

INDEX

Abridgement of the Public Laws of Virginia, An, xvi
Accomack, 81
Aldred, John, 110
Algernoon Fort, 34
Amidas, Philip, 15
Andros, Edmund, 100–103, 255
Anne, Queen, 39–43
Arcadia, 47
Argall, Samuel, 37–38, 44–47
Arrahattuck, 37
Auditor of revenue, 245, 249

Bacon, Francis, 220
Bacon, Nathaniel, xxvii–xxviii, 34, 74, 78–85
Bacon's Rebellion, 34, 74, 78–85
Barlow, Arthur, 15
Batt, Henry, 73–74
Belon, Pierre, 219
Bennett, Richard, 64
Berkeley, William, xiv, xxvii, 65–66, 68, 72, 239, 249; subjection to Cromwell's government, 60–63; Bacon's rebellion, 78–85
Bernard, J. F., xx
Beverley, Major Robert, xiv
Beverley, Robert, xi; inheritance, xiv; schooling, xiv; political career, xiv, xv; marriage, xiv; antagonism toward royal governors, xiv, xv, xxvii–xxx, 6, 87 ff., 103–11; trip to England, xv, xvii; literary works of, xvi, xvii; scientific curiosity, xvi, 305–7; interest in agriculture, xvi, xxxiii, 143–45, 282–83, 315–16, 318–19; pride in Virginia, xvi, xxxiii, 296–304, 314–19; influence of Oldmixon on, xvii–xix;

championship of colony rights, xvi, xxi, 6–7, 64, 66, 70–71; royalism, xxi; attitude toward Indians, xxii, xxv, xxvii, 16, 29, 39, 192–93, 233
Biard, Father, 47
Biencourt, 47
Birkenhead, 69–70
Blair, James, xiii, 98–99
Blandfield, xiv
Brent, George, 94
Buildings, 289–90
Burgesses, House of, xiv–xv, 48, 237–42
Burrows, Anna, 31
Byrd, Ursula, xiv
Byrd, William, I, xi, xvi, xxx, 55, 126, 204, 211, 283–84
Byrd, William, II, xvii, xx

Calumet, 187–88
Calvert, Caecilius, Lord Baltimore, 58–59, 68
Campbell, Charles, xxiii
Canoes, Indian, 186, 230
Capitol, first burning of, 86; taxes for rebuilding of, 96; second burning of, 102–3; re-filing of state papers, 102–3; Nicholson's plans for, 105; edifice, 289
Caribbean route, 22–23, 27, 36
Carolina, 15, 70–71, 87, 134–35
Carter, Robert, 94
Cavaliers, 287
Charity, 275–76
Charles, Cape, 28
Charles I, 56, 59, 63
Charles II, 65, 70, 75, 239, 288
Chesapeake Bay settlement, 19–20
Chicheley, Henry, 92, 95, 239
Child, Josiah, 286

361

Chilton, Edward, xiii
Climate, 296-304
Cockarouse, 149, 207, 226
Cod, Cape, 23, 45
Cohonks, 211
College, assignment of land to, 48; establishment of, 97-99, 101, 105, 265; subjects to be taught in, 98, charter for, 98-99, 265-66; money for, 99-100; religious leanings of, 99-100; representation in House of Burgesses, 241; payment of officers, 265-67; administration, 265-67; edifice, 289
Constitution, 57, 237
Convention, 241-43
Corn, Indian, 31, 123, 143-44, 180, 185
Coroner, 248
Cotton, 102, 319
Council, 237-38, 240-41
Counties, 243
Court clerk, 247
Courts, 50, 255-60; county, 50, 256, 259; general, 256; jury, 257-58; sheriff, 257-58
Cromwell, Oliver, 63-64
Croshaw, Capt., 52
Culpeper, Thomas, xxviii, 85, 87-95, 238-39, 249, 255
Currency, 285

d'Anghiera, Pietro Martire, 137
Dare, Ananias, 21
Dare, Virginia, 21
Dassamonpeak, Lord of. *See* Manteo
De Bry, Theodore, 181, 218
Defenses, forts, harbors, building of, 72, 86
de Laet, Joannes, 130, 218
de La Hontan, Louis A., xxvi, 134, 182, 188, 190-91, 195, 198
Delaware, Lord, 37, 45
de L'Ecluse, Charles, 224
Deliverance, 34
Dennis, Robert, 63
Digges, Edward, 64
Drake, Francis, 19-21
Dutch, 48, 63, 77
Duty, tobacco, 67, 75, 240, 247, 250-53, 280; fort, 76, 240, 247; liquor, 96, 247, 250; exported furs, 102, 227, 247, 251; districts for levying, 244; servants and slaves, 247, 250, 252; college, 265, 267

Effingham, Governor. *See* Francis, Lord Howard
Elizabeth, Queen, 5-7, 16-17
Elizabeth's Isle, 23
Escheat, 279-80
Escheators, 247, 279
Essay upon the Government of the English Plantations on the Continent of America ... By an American, xvi-xvii

Falling Creek, 49, 54, 126
Fish, 146-53
Fitzhugh, William, xii, xx, 94
Flax, 72, 319
Forts. *See* Defenses
Fowl, 153-56, 298
Francis, Lord Howard of Effingham, xxviii, 91, 97, 255
French settlements, 36, 46-47; grape culture, 134-36, 281-84
Fruits, 123, 129-31, 137-38, 141-43, 314-16
Fuel, 294
Fur trade, 23, 77; duty on export, 102, 227, 247, 251

Game, 153-56
Gates, Thomas, 33, 36-37
General Assembly, 48, 57
Glass manufacture, 49, 54, 126
Gold, search for, 30-31
Gosnold, Bartholomew, 23-24
Government, evolution of, 22, 27, 33, 36-37, 47-48, 51, 56-57, 66-67, 85, 97, 237-43, 245-48
Governors, establishment of office, 33, 237-38; John White, 21-22; Lord Delaware, 37; Thomas Dale, 39; Samuel Argall, 44; John Harvey, 60; William Berkeley, xiv, xxvii, 60-68; Richard Bennett, 64; Edward Digges, 64; Samuel Mathews, 64; Herbert

362

Jeffreys, 86; Thomas Culpeper, xxviii, 85, 87 ff.; Francis, Lord Howard of Effingham, xxviii, 91, 97; Francis Nicholson, xv, xxix, 86, 97, 99, 100, 103-11; Edmund Andros, 100-103; duties and powers, salary, 237-40
Grain, English, 23-24, 316
Grenville, Richard, 17-18, 20
Gribelin, Simon, xxxv

Hakluyt, Richard, 27
Harbors. *See* Defenses
Hariot, Thomas, 130, 138, 218
Harley, Robert, 5-7
Hartwell, Henry, xiii
Harvey, John, 60
Hatteras, Cape, 20, 22, 25
Hemp, 72, 123, 319
Hennepin, Louis, xxvi, 187, 195, 198
Henrico, 37, 127
Henry, Cape, 28
Henry, Prince of Wales, 37
Herbs, 292-93
Historians (17th century) of Virginia, xii-xiii
History and Present State of Virginia, The, debt to John Smith, xxiii; literary qualities of, xiii; historical value, xxii; editions of, xiii, xx, xxiii-xxiv, xxvii-xxxi; weaknesses of, xxii; influence of Oldmixon on, xvii-xix; significance of, xxi; style of, xxi-xxii; sections of, xxii, 10-11; scientific observations, xvi; treatment of Indians, xxii, xxv-xxvii, xxxi; championship of colony rights, xvi, xxi, 6-7; pride in Virginia, xvi, xxxiii; agriculture, xvi, xxxiii; original printing of text, xxxiv; illustrations, xxxv; dedication, 5-7; preface, 8-11
History of the World, The, 15
Hortus Indicus Malabaricus, 137
Hospitality, 312-13
Huguenots, xx, xxx, 281-84
Husbandry, 291-92, 317-18
Huskanawing, xxvii, 206-9

Illnesses, 305-7

Indians, naïveté, 16; friendliness, 16; cause of discontent, 29, 39; massacres by, 34, 51-54, 59-61, 85, 135; intermarriage, 38; Chickahomony tribe, 39, 45; violence of, 77; trade agreements with, 86; vegetables of, 123, 143-45; pawcorance, 127, 205, 213-14; hunting and fishing, 148-49, 154-56, 310-11; cockarouse, 149, 207; agriculture, 156; physical characteristics, 159; women, 159, 166, 170-71, 188; dress, 159-60, 162-66, 194.
    Religion: altars, 127, 205, 213-14; priests' clothing, 164-65; house of worship, 195-98; idol, 197-98, 201; conjurers, 198, 201-5, 213; priests, 198, 201-5, 212, 217-18; okee, 198, 206; quioccos, 198; kiwasa, 198; religious beliefs, 200-201, 211; sacrifices, 202, 205-6, 210; method of conjuring, 202-5; burial of kings, 214, 216; powwow, 204, 212; piety of, 211-12; totems, 213.
    Marriage customs of, 170; treatment of children, 171-72; government, 174, 225-26; houses, 174-75; villages, 175, 232-33; fortifications, 177; cookery, 178-82; habits and ways of eating, 181-84; taste for liquor, 182; reception of visitors, 186-89; canoes, 186, 230; calumet, 187-88; writing, 190, 214; heraldry, 190; language, 191; Algonquin tribe, 191; Occaneeche tribe, 191; matchacomoco, 192; preparation for war, 192; timidity of, 192-93; kingly descent, 193; ceremonial dances, 193, 223; physicians, 198, 201-5, 212, 217-18; feast days, 210; time system, 211; cohonks, 211; cures, 217-20; wisoccan, 218; sports, 221-24; pastimes, 221-24; musical instruments, 224; mediums of exchange, 227-28; wampum, 227-28; weapons of, 229; tools of, 229; household utensils, 230; influence of Europeans upon, 233
Ingram, Joseph, 84
Insurrections, colonial, 34-35, 69-70, 78-85
Itopatin, 45

James I, 28
James II, 93
Jamestown, xxix, 28, 30, 36, 70, 86, 105
Jeffreys, Herbert, 86-87, 239
Johnson, Nathaniel, 135
Jordan, Claude, xx
Jury, 257-58

Kiquotan, 32, 34, 110
Kiwasa, 198. See also Okee and Quioccos

Lane, Ralph, 18
Lawrence, Richard, 86
Laydon, John, 31
Leather, 100
Lee, Richard, xii, 94
Lieutenant Governor, office of, 239
Linen, 100
Lombrail, Thomas, xx
London Company, 22, 26-27, 49, 56
Long Island, 24
Ludwell, Philip, xxix, 94, 96
Ludwell, Thomas, 75

Manteo, 16, 21
Manufactures, glass, 49, 54, 126; silk, 56, 67, 131, 295, 319; potash, 72; flax, 72, 319; leather, 100; linen, 100; cotton, 102, 319; hemp, 72, 123, 319; wool, 319
Maple sugar, 136-37
Martha's Vineyard, 23
Martin, Capt., 55
Maryland, 31, 58-59, 68-71, 87, 117-18
Matchacomoco, 192
Mathews, Samuel, 64
Middle Plantation. See Williamsburg
Militia, 265-67
Minerals, gold, 30-31, 126; iron, 49, 54-55, 126; salt, 49, 67; lead, 55, 126; crystal, 127; silver, 127
Monacan Town, 281-82
Morrison, Francis, 66

Nansamond, 31
Nantaquaus, 40
Naturalization, 88, 281
Naval divisions, 244
Naval officers, 243-44, 247

Navigation, Act of, 64, 66
Neale, Thomas, 101
Necks of land, 92-94, 243-44, 249
Negroes, 48, 204, 250, 252, 263, 271-74
Nemattanow, 52-53
Newfoundland, 36, 45
Newport, Captain, 33, 36, 55
New York, 77; Nicholson's plan to build and garrison fort at, 111-12; French wine experiments at, 134, 281-82
Nicholson, Francis, xv, xxix, 86, 97, 99-100, 103-11
North Carolina. See Carolina
Northern Neck, 92-94, 249

Okee, 198, 206, 208. See also Quioccos
Oldmixon, John, xvii-xix
Olearius, Adam, 219
Oppechancanough, 45, 49, 52, 54, 60-62
Orphans, 260

Parishes, 243
Park, Daniel, 75
Parker, Richard, xi, xvi
Parkinson, John, 218
Passenger, Captain, 110
Pastimes, 308-11
Patience, 34
Pawcorance, 127, 214
Peak. See Wampum
Penticost Harbor, 24
Piracy, 109-11
Piso, Willem, 220
Plants, 138-39, 141
Plymouth Company, 27
Pocahontas, xxv, 38-44, 222
Port Royal, 47
Post office, 101
Potash, 72
Powell, Nathaniel, 47
Powhatan, 38-40, 43, 45, 222
Powhatan settlement, 32
Powwow, 204, 212
Precincts, 243
President of Council, 237, 240
Prison, 289
Purchas, Samuel, 130, 147, 218
Puritans, 63

364

Quarry, Robert, xv, 112
Quioccos, 198, 216. *See also* Okee
Quioccosan, 195-98, 201
Quit rent, 56, 60, 91, 94, 99, 112, 249-50, 278-79

Raleigh, Walter, 15, 20, 23
Raleigh, City of, 22
R. B., xi, xiii-xxx. *See also* Beverley, Robert
Rebecka. *See* Pocahontas
Religion, payment of ministers, 66; churches and glebes provided, 66; parish officers instituted, 66; suppression of, 68; college as instrument for Church of England, 99-100; officers, 245-47, 263; parishes, 261; churches, 261; faiths, 261-62; ministers, 262, 264; vestry, 262, 264. *See also* Indians
Rice, 123
Roanoke. *See* Wampum
Roanoke, colony at, 15, 18, 20-23, 25
Rockahomonie. *See* Corn, Indian
Rolfe, John, xxv, 38-39
Rolfe, Thomas, 44
Roundheads, 287
Royal veto, 242
Runtees. *See* Wampum

Sandy Point, 80
Schools, 275-76
Secretary of State, 245-56
Servants, 271-74
Settlements, Roanoke, 15, 18, 20-23, 25; Chesapeake Bay, 19-20; Cape Cod, 23, 45; Jamestown, 28; Nansamond, 31; Powhatan, 32; Kiquotan, 32; Arrahattuck, 37; French settlements, 36, 46-47, 134-36, 281-84; on James and York Rivers, 48; Carolinas, 15, 70-71, 87, 134-35; Maryland, 31, 58-59, 68-71, 87, 117-18
Sheriff, 247-48, 257-58
Shoram, 110-11
Silk, 56, 67, 131, 295, 319
Slavery, 48, 204, 250, 252, 263, 271-74
Smith, John, xi, xxiii, 27, 31, 34-35, 39-43, 130, 147, 181, 193-94, 202-4, 218, 220, 222
South Carolina. *See* Carolina.
Spencer, Nicholas, 94-95
Spotswood, Alexander, xvi
Stafford County, xii, 103
Summers, George, 33, 36
Surveyor, 247-48

Taxes, 75; poll tax, 96, 250; authority for levying, 254; quit rent, 56, 60, 91, 94, 99, 112, 249-50, 278-79; duties, 67, 75-76, 102, 240, 244, 247, 250-53, 265, 267, 280
Tenure of land, 277, 279-80
Title of land, 277
Tobacco, 44, 49, 59, 65; duty on, 67, 75, 240, 247, 250-53, 280; low price of, 74-75; crop curtailment, 70-72, 92; restrictions on inter-plantation sale, 87; payment of quit rent in, 91; tax on inter-plantation sale, 99; Indian cultivation of, 145; use in Indian sacrifice, 210; payment of ministers in, 263; drying houses of, 290
Trade, suppression of colony, 64, 66, 70-71, 88, 104
Trees, 123-24, 136-37, 140, 318

Uttamaccomack, 43

Vegetables, 142-45
Verbiest, Ferdinand, 155
Vermin, 300-303
Vineyards, 56, 73, 133-36, 282-83, 315-16
Virginia, origin of name, 17; college, 48, 97-101, 105, 241, 265-67, 289; taxes, 56, 60, 66-67, 91, 94, 96, 99, 102, 112, 240, 244, 247, 249-53, 265, 267, 278-80; grants of Charles II, 75, 85; wild life, 73; boundaries, 117-18; shipping entrance, 117; coasts, 118; rivers, 120; springs, 121-22, 128; soil, fertility of, 123, 293, 314; trees, 123-24, 136-37, 140; clay, 125; contour, 124; minerals of, 30-31, 49, 54-55, 126-27; fruits, 123, 129-31, 137-38, 141-43; moun-

Virginia (*Continued*)
tains, 128; nuts, 131-33; vineyards, 56, 73, 133-36, 282-83, 315-16; plants, 138-39, 141; vegetables, 143-45; fish, 146-53; fowl, 153-56; game, 153-56; enactment of laws, 242; government, 237-43; divisions of, 243-44; public offices, 245-48; religion, 246-47, 261-64; courts, 255-67; militia, 268-70; schools, 275-76; currency, 285; scarcity of women, 286-87; buildings, 289, 290; husbandry, 291-92, 317-18; clothing, 295; climate, 296-304; illness, 305-7; pastimes, 308-11; title of land, 277; tenure of land, 277, 279-80

Virginia companies, London Company, 22, 26-27, 49; Plymouth Company, 27

Voyages to Virginia, Raleigh's expeditions, 15, 17, 20-21; Gosnold's, 23; Bristol merchants', 24; John Smith's, 27; of three joint governors, 33, 36; Lord Delaware's, 37; Dale's, 37; Gates's, 37; Argall's, 37

Wakelett, Gregory, 84
Wampum, 161, 227-28
Wanchese, 16
Werowance, 206, 225-26
Westover, xi, xxxi
Whaling, 76
White, John, 21-22
William and Mary, 98-100, 251, 265, 281. *See also* College.
Williamsburg, xxix, 82-83, 86, 105, 268, 289
Women, scarcity of, 286-87
Wool, 319
Wysoccan, 207

Yardley, George, 39, 44-45, 49